Sartre Explained

IDEAS EXPLAINED™

Daoism Explained, Hans-Georg Moeller

Frege Explained, Joan Weiner

Luhmann Explained, Hans-Georg Moeller

Heidegger Explained, Graham Harman

Atheism Explained, David Ramsay Steele

Sartre Explained, David Detmer

IN PREPARATION

Ockham Explained, Rondo Keele

Rawls Explained, Paul Voice

Phenomenology Explained, David Detmer

Deleuze and Guattari Explained, Rohit Dalvi

Sartre Explained

From Bad Faith to Authenticity

DAVID DETMER

OPEN COURT
Chicago and La Salle, Illinois

Volume 6 in the Ideas Explained™ Series

To order books from Open Court, call 1-800-815-2280 or visit www.opencourtbooks.com.

Open Court Publishing Company is a division of Carus Publishing Company.

First printing 2008
Second printing 2009

Printed and bound in the United States of America.

Library of Congress Cataloging-in-Publication Data

Detmer, David, 1958-
    Sartre explained : from bad faith to authenticity / David Detmer.
      p. cm. — (Ideas explained ; v. 6)
      Summary: "A guide to the work of Jean-Paul Sartre addressing his major theories and how the different strands of his thought are interrelated, and overviewing works from all of his literary genres including philosophical writings, novels, and plays"—Provided by publisher.
    Includes bibliographical references and index.
    ISBN-13: 978-0-8126-9631-8 (trade paper : alk. paper)
    1. Sartre, Jean-Paul, 1905-1980. I. Title.
  B2430.S34D46 2008
  1934—dc22

                                           2008012340

Contents

Acknowledgments   vii

Abbreviations   ix

Introduction   1
  Sartre's Reputation   4
  Why Read Sartre?   15

1. Phenomenology   17
  The Transcendence of the Ego   19
  Intentionality   29
  The Emotions   35
  Imagination and *The Imaginary*   46

2. *Nausea*   51
  Absurdity   55
  Life and Art   58
  Why Write?   60

3. *Being and Nothingness*   63
  Interrogation   65
  Destruction   66
  Absence   67
  Anguish   70
  Bad Faith   75
  Knowledge   89
  Others   92
  The Body   96
  Concrete Relations with Others   103
  Freedom   110
  Existential Psychoanalysis   122
  Ethics   134

4. *No Exit*   143

   A Philosophical Play   145
   Bad Faith Dramatized   147
   Hell Is Other People   149
   Death   153

5. *The Devil and the Good Lord*   159

   Atheism   162
   Conversion   163
   Good and Evil   165
   Violence   169

6. *Saint Genet*   173

   Existential Psychoanalysis Illustrated   174
   Inventing the Homosexual Subject   178
   Freedom and Facticity   178
   Understanding that Overcomes Difference   181

7. *Critique of Dialectical Reason*   187

   Marxism   188
   Dialectic   189
   Practico-Inert and Counter-Finality   191
   The Progressive-Regressive Method   193
   Criticisms of Marxism   194
   Two Kinds of Freedom   196
   Scarcity and Violence   198
   Totalization   200
   Series and Group   201
   The Ethics of Violence   203
   Inauthenticity   211
   Propaganda   212
   Priorities   213

Suggestions for Further Reading   217

   By Sartre   217
   About Sartre   224

Index   229

Acknowledgments

I would like to thank my colleagues in the North American Sartre Society and at *Sartre Studies International* for all the friendly (as opposed to merely collegial) help they have offered me during the period of my researching and writing this book. I should mention, especially, Steve Hendley, Ken Anderson, Connie Mui, Adrian van den Hoven, Bruce Baugh, and Hazel Barnes. Many other Sartre scholars have inspired and/or instructed me over the years, either through their writings, their presentations at the biennial conferences of the North American Sartre Society, or through personal communications, and I hope they will forgive me for my failure to name them here.

Robert Bernasconi and Tom Flynn graciously agreed to read and to comment on portions of a draft of this book, for which I thank them. Needless to say, they cannot be held responsible for the defects in my presentation.

Also deserving of thanks are my colleagues in the Department of English and Philosophy at Purdue University Calumet for many years of stimulating philosophical discussions, both informally and through our regular colloquia. In this connection, I would like to express my gratitude (with due apologies for the inevitable accidental omissions) to John Rowan, Eugene Schlossberger, Neil Florek, Phyllis Bergiel, David Turpin, Robin Turpin, John Wachala, Connie Sowa-Wachala, and Carolyn Jones. Special thanks are due to Sam and Susan Zinaich, and also to Michael Dobberstein, for hosting our regular "philosophy parties," at which I have had the opportunity to develop and to discuss some of the ideas that I am now presenting here.

I would also like to acknowledge the Purdue University Calumet Office of Research and Professional Development for awarding me a Purdue University Calumet Faculty Research Time Release

Award for Spring 2007, which aided me in the research and writing of this book.

Finally, my biggest thanks go to Kerri and Arlo, for their love, support, kind encouragement, and helpful suggestions.

Abbreviations

The following abbreviations have been used when referring to Sartre's works. The date in square brackets at the conclusion of each entry is the date of the original French publication.

ASJ   *Anti-Semite and Jew*, trans. George J. Becker (New York: Schocken Books, 1965) [1946].

BEM   *Between Existentialism and Marxism*, trans. John Mathews (New York: William Morrow, 1974) [1971].

BN   *Being and Nothingness*, trans. Hazel E. Barnes (New York: Washington Square Press, 1992) [1943].

BO   "Black Orpheus," trans. John MacCombie, in *"What Is Literature?" and Other Essays* (Cambridge, MA: Harvard University Press, 1988) [1948].

CDR   *Critique of Dialectical Reason*, trans. Alan Sheridan-Smith (London: Verso, 1982) [1960].

CN   *Colonialism and Neocolonialism*, trans. by Azzedine Haddour, Steve Brewer, and Terry McWilliams (New York: Routledge, 2001) [1964].

DGL   *The Devil and the Good Lord*, trans. Kitty Black, in *The Devil and the Good Lord and Two Other Plays* (New York: Vintage, 1960) [1951].

DH   *Dirty Hands*, trans. L. Abel, in *No Exit and Three Other Plays* (New York: Vintage, 1955) [1948].

E   *The Emotions: Outline of a Theory*, trans. Bernard Frechtman (New York: The Wisdom Library, 1948) [1939].

EH   "Existentialism Is a Humanism," translated as *Existentialism & Humanism*, trans. Philip Mairet (London: Methuen, 1973) [1946].

HN   *Hope Now* (with Benny Lévy), trans. Adrian van den Hoven (Chicago: University of Chicago Press, 1996) [1980].

In   *Imagination: A Psychological Critique*, trans. Forrest Williams (Ann Arbor: University of Michigan Press, 1972) [1936].

Iy   *The Imaginary: A Phenomenological Psychology of the Imagination*, trans. Jonathan Webber (New York: Routledge, 2004) [1940].

ILTM   "Introducing *Les Temps modernes*," trans. Jeffrey Mehlman, in *"What is Literature?" and Other Essays* (Cambridge, MA: Harvard University Press, 1988) [1945].

INT   "Intentionality: A Fundamental Idea of Husserl's Phenomenology," trans. Joseph P. Fell, *Journal of the British Society for Phenomenology* 1, no. 2 (May 1970) [1939].

LBSM   "A Long, Bitter, Sweet Madness," Interview with Jacqueline Piatier, trans, Anthony Hartley, *Encounter* 22, no. 6 (June 1964) [1964].

L/S   *Life/Situations: Essays Written and Spoken*, trans. Paul Auster and Lydia Davis (New York: Pantheon, 1977) [1971–1975].

MR   "Materialism and Revolution," in *Literary and Philosophical Essays*, trans. Annette Michelson (New York: Collier Books, 1962) [1946].

N   *Nausea*, trans. Robert Baldick (Harmondsworth, Middlesex, England: Penguin, 1965) [1938].

NE   *No Exit*, trans. Stuart Gilbert, in *No Exit and Three Other Plays* (New York: Vintage, 1955) [1944].

NFE   *Notebooks for an Ethics*, trans. David Pellauer (Chicago: University of Chicago Press, 1992) [1983].

SBH   *Sartre by Himself*, trans. Richard Seaver (New York: Outback Press, 1978) [1976]. (Note: This volume is the transcript of a documentary film on Sartre.)

SFM   *Search for a Method*, trans. Hazel E. Barnes (New York: Vintage, 1968) [1957].

SG   *Saint Genet*, trans. Bernard Frechtman (New York: Mentor, 1964) [1952].

SOT   *Sartre on Theater*, ed. Michel Contat and Michel Rybalka, trans. Frank Jellinek (New York: Pantheon, 1976) [1973].

TAE   *Truth and Existence*, trans. Adrian van den Hoven, ed. Ronald Aronson (Chicago: University of Chicago Press, 1992) [1989].

TE   *The Transcendence of the Ego*, trans. Forrest Williams and Robert Kirkpatrick (New York: Noonday Press, 1957) [1937].

WD   *The War Diaries of Jean-Paul Sartre*, trans. Quintin Hoare (New York: Pantheon, 1984) [1983].

WIL   "What Is Literature?", trans. Bernard Frechtman, in *"What Is Literature?" and Other Essays* (Cambridge, MA: Harvard University Press, 1988) [1947].

WL   "The Writer and his Language," in *Politics and Literature*, trans. J.A. Underwood and John Calder (London: Calder & Boyars, 1973) [1965].

Introduction

The French philosopher Jean-Paul Sartre (1905–1980) was an extraordinarily versatile and prolific writer and thinker. His gigantic corpus includes two long, dense, complicated, systematic works of philosophy (*Being and Nothingness* and *Critique of Dialectical Reason*) in addition to many shorter philosophical contributions; several novels, plays, and screenplays; a book of short stories; essays on literary and art criticism; scores of political and journalistic writings; an autobiography (covering only his childhood); and a handful of distinctive, lengthy, and highly original biographies of other writers.

What is more amazing is the level of success he achieved in each of these genres:

- He was by far the most famous philosopher, worldwide, of the post–World War Two era. Indeed, no other philosopher in his or her lifetime has reached as large an audience, or attained as high a level of fame, as has he. (Fifty thousand people attended his funeral.) His philosophical works have sold millions of copies, and continue to reach a worldwide readership.

- He was the major representative of the philosophical movement called "existentialism," which dominated European intellectual life in the 1940s and 1950s, and later enjoyed significant popularity in other countries as Sartre's works came to be translated into other languages.

- College courses in existentialism continue to be popular, despite the fact that Sartre's thought is long past its height of intellectual fashion. Sartre has never ceased to be widely read (and widely appreciated) by undergraduate students.

- He won the Nobel Prize for Literature in 1964, but declined the award. (He refused awards often. He turned down the Legion of Honor, which the French government offered him in 1945 in recognition of his wartime resistance activities; refused election in 1949 to the Académie Française, an elite group of just forty; and declined induction into the prestigious Collège de France.)

- Many, though by no means all, of his literary works have achieved both popular success and enduring critical acclaim. Several of his plays were box office hits, and a few of them continue to be performed. (All of them continue to be read and studied). *Nausea* ranks as one of the great novels of the twentieth century. "The Wall" and "Childhood of a Leader" have achieved a similar status in the genre of short stories. His massive studies of the lives of Jean Genet and of Gustave Flaubert count among the most controversial and important biographies of the twentieth century. And his many critical essays together constitute an essential guide to the literary, dramatic, and visual arts of his time.

- He co-founded and edited a journal, *Les Temps modernes* (*Modern Times*), which continues to play a substantial role in the intellectual life of contemporary France.

- He is the most written-about writer of the twentieth century.

- He was a significant participant, by means of both his writing and his activism, in the political issues of his times. For example, he opposed the wars in Vietnam and Algeria, and was one of the first philosophers to devote considerable attention to the issue of race (in such essays as *Anti-Semite and Jew* and "Black Orpheus," in the play *The Respectful Prostitute*, and in the appendix on black Americans in the posthumously published *Notebooks for an Ethics*, among other writings).

- His consistent advocacy for the victims of economic, political, and racial oppression won him perhaps a wider readership and degree of influence among black and Third World intellectuals than any other white European writer has ever received, before or since. (To give just one famous example,

Frantz Fanon praised Sartre's account of anti-Semitism in *Anti-Semite and Jew* as containing the finest pages he had ever read, and explicitly cited it as inspiring his own analysis of anti-black racism.)

Central to all of Sartre's activities was his attempt to describe the salient features of human existence: freedom, responsibility, the emotions, relations with others, work, embodiment, perception, imagination, death, and so forth. In this way he attempted to bring clarity and rigor to the murky realm of the subjective, limiting his focus neither to the purely intellectual side of life (the world of reasoning, or, more broadly, of thinking), nor to those objective features of human life that permit of study from the "outside." Instead, he broadened his focus so as to include the meaning of all facets of human existence. Thus, his work addressed, in a fundamental way, and primarily from the "inside" (where Sartre's skills as a novelist and dramatist served him well) the question of how an individual is related to everything that comprises his or her situation: the physical world, other individuals, complex social collectives, and the cultural world of artifacts and institutions.

He engaged critically with leading currents of thought of his time, most notably Marxism and Freudianism, and revised each in such a way as to give more emphasis to human freedom and responsibility, central concerns of all of his work. In politics he opposed colonialism, fascism, and racism, all for the same reason—they are attempts to suppress the freedom of others. He advocated both socialism and individual liberty, and tried to find the right balance between collectivism and individualism.

Sartre's political concerns led him to side consistently with those who are despised, oppressed, and impoverished, and to take stands seemingly in opposition to the interests of his own nation and class. Thus, while most European intellectuals of Sartre's time, including those regarded as politically "progressive" in their thinking, tended to take for granted the colonial exploitation of the Third World by wealthy Western nations, Sartre made a point of championing the interests of the Third World, and of publishing the writings of Third World authors in his journal, *Les Temps modernes*. By repeatedly making the point that the luxurious lifestyle to which he and his colleagues in the wealthy countries had become accustomed was built on the suffering of others, Sartre won the respect of the exploited around the world, and the resentment of those many in the privileged classes who would have preferred not to be confronted with ethical questions concerning their cheerful acquiescence in the status quo. Little wonder, then, that when Sartre died, the tone of the obituaries and articles that appeared varied considerably from one part of the world to another. While the European and American press debated Sartre's pros and cons (generally his literary and philosophical work was celebrated, while his political activities were criticized), the African, Latin American, and Caribbean media mourned the loss of a true friend.

There is no one remotely like him today, and it is difficult to think of any other historical figure who has achieved so much in so many different literary genres and in philosophy, in addition to engaging so extensively with the political, intellectual, and cultural life of his or her time. While a very few individuals have succeeded in combining important contributions to a technical discipline with sustained and courageous political engagement—the philosophers John Dewey and Bertrand Russell, the chemist Linus Pauling, and the linguist Noam Chomsky all come to mind—only Sartre, to my knowledge, combined the writing of important novels and plays with these two achievements. This allowed him to reach different audiences, and to make his points in different ways, than would have been the case had he confined his efforts to his formal discipline. Indeed, the prominent American philosopher Richard Rorty claims that "no other philosopher has had such success in using stories, plays, novels, critical essays, and philosophical treatises to complement and reinforce each other."[1]

Sartre's Reputation

Despite these achievements, Sartre has always been a controversial figure, and his present reputation is difficult to determine. While he is clearly one of the most widely read and studied writers and philosophers of the twentieth century, the acclaim he has won has always been matched with a considerable amount of harsh criticism. Indeed, few writers have ever been subjected to more vilification. His work has been widely banned and censored. In 1946

---

[1] Richard Rorty, "Feeling His Way," *The New Republic* 192, no. 15 (April 15, 1985): 32–34.

the British censor banned his play *No Exit*. In 1948 Pope Pius XII put all of Sartre's works on the "Index" of works Catholics are forbidden to read. His play *Dirty Hands* was forbidden, as "hostile propaganda against the USSR," in the Soviet Union and throughout the Eastern Bloc for decades. Stalin's cultural commissar, Alexander Fadayev, called Sartre "a Jackal with a typewriter, a hyena with a fountain pen." Henri Lefebvre attacked Sartre on behalf of the French communists, calling him "the manufacturer of the war machine against Marxism." And the French Christian philosopher, Gabriel Marcel (who was himself often called an existentialist, though he rejected the label), referred to Sartre as "a patented corrupter of youth," a "systematic blasphemist," and "the grave-digger of the West." And these were among the more gentle and polite of the expressions of disapproval! In October 1960, in response to Sartre's activities in opposition to the French war in Algeria, 10,000 French army veterans staged a demonstration in which they marched in the streets of Paris chanting "Shoot Sartre!" Sartre's home, where he lived with his mother, was subsequently twice bombed by right-wing terrorists. The offices of his journal, *Les Temps modernes*, were also bombed.

Now that Sartre is dead, the denunciations of his work and character have, of course, become less frequent and less severe. Moreover, there are several indications that Sartre has established himself as a writer and thinker of major, and permanent, importance. Books, articles, and dissertations devoted to his work continue to appear regularly. Several scholarly societies devoted to the study of his writings have been established, and most of them organize regular conferences for that purpose. Significantly, these societies are located not only in France and elsewhere on the European continent, but also in the United Kingdom, in North America, and in Africa. Having been an active member of the North American Sartre Society since 1990, I have noticed that its biennial conferences keep getting bigger, with most of the new recruits coming from the ranks of the young. This evidence, though admittedly anecdotal, undermines the assumption that Sartre's ideas have been superseded by newer intellectual currents and rendered irrelevant for contemporary times, retaining appeal only for older scholars, nostalgic for times of their youth when existentialism was "hot." (It is perhaps also worth mentioning, in this regard, that the North American Sartre Society meetings attract a more diverse group of scholars—more women, and more scholars of African and Asian descent—than I find to be the case at other philosophy conferences I attend.) Moreover, at least one scholarly journal, *Sartre Studies International*, is concerned exclusively with Sartre scholarship. Finally, while assessments of Sartre's contribution as a whole vary widely, nearly everyone recognizes that he had tremendous range, writing with insight on dozens of topics, and that he had a great talent for addressing issues that were highly relevant to his times, even when he took them up at a high level of generality and philosophical abstraction.

But on the other hand, many philosophers seem to hold Sartre in a rather low regard, and it must be acknowledged that some of the common criticisms have merit. For example, even Sartre's most fervent admirers must admit that his work often suffered from his lack of interest in the physical sciences, that he was given to exaggeration, hyperbole, and one-sidedness, that some of his political judgments were foolish, and that, like everybody else, he simply got some things wrong.

Still, I think that the abuse and neglect that he suffers in some quarters is excessive, and is not, for the most part, based on a judicious assessment of the strengths and weaknesses of his many contributions. In short, I think Sartre is underrated. Several factors probably contribute to this:

(1) First, most English-speaking philosophers have little training in or knowledge of twentieth century continental European philosophy. This, coupled with the complexity and conceptual intricacy of Sartre's thought and the (sometimes unnecessary) difficulty of his writing in his two major philosophical works, stands as a formidable obstacle to the appreciation of his contribution. Such philosophers typically recognize the stylistic merit of Sartre's writing (excluding his two main philosophical works), from a literary standpoint, but find it lacking in the precision and logical rigor that philosophy, as they understand it, demands.

(2) From the standpoint of continental philosophy, on the other hand, there is something of the sense that Sartre is old hat, or even a fad that has now passed. Newer movements and figures have come along, placing Sartre in the awkward position of having been too recent to count as an established classic, but not new enough to seem cutting edge.

(3) Turning more specifically to the French intellectual scene, Sartre's immediate successors, the structuralists and post-structuralists, have largely ignored him. One would have thought, given Sartre's long-standing domination of French intellectual life, that the first order of business for this next generation would have been to subject his work to a careful and detailed critique. Instead, the new French philosophers have, with rare exceptions, simply turned their heads in new directions, perhaps in an attempt to escape his dominating presence. Such criticisms as they have directed at him have, for the most part, been brief and dismissive, rather than substantive. Indeed, often they have consisted of little more than the charge that Sartre is out of date, as in philosopher Michel Foucault's famous quip that Sartre's *Critique of Dialectical Reason* is "the magnificent and pathetic effort of a man of the nineteenth century to understand the twentieth century." But after a little time goes by, such dismissals themselves have a way of going out of date. Those who have just recently become old hat tend to get reexamined; and when this happens, there is a chance that some will see what all the excitement was about in the first place. In any case, as Sartre's immediate successors leave the scene, it seems likely that his work will get a fresh look from newer philosophers who have not had to find a way to emerge from his shadow.

(4) Another factor is that the worst piece Sartre ever wrote, in my judgment, is probably the one that has been most read by philosophers. I refer to his famous lecture, "Existentialism Is a Humanism," one of the very few attempts he made to popularize his philosophy. (I have noticed that many, perhaps most, of the harshly critical pieces on Sartre's philosophy written in English during the period of the 1950s and 1960s, when existentialism was hot and trendy among the general public and college students [as opposed to philosophy faculty] in the English-speaking world, rely almost exclusively on "Existentialism Is a Humanism." Why wade through the dense, technical, interminable jungle of *Being and Nothingness* when this short and snappy summary, offered by the master himself, is available?) Approached critically, and in conjunction with Sartre's other works, there is much of value to be found in this lecture. (For example, it provides answers to some questions that Sartre posed at the end of *Being and Nothingness*, and these answers aid us greatly in our effort to understand that book.) But taken by itself, as a guide to his thought, as many have done (and

quite reasonably so, it would seem, as it is by Sartre himself, and offered by him as a brief introduction to, and defense of, his philosophy), it is an unmitigated disaster, and for two reasons. First, it was presented at a time when Sartre's thought was undergoing a rapid transformation. He was starting to revise or reject some of his earlier notions, but had not yet formulated others that would become central to his thought. Moreover, at this time he held positions that do not appear in any of his other works, either earlier or later. Thus, the lecture utterly fails to be representative of his thinking as a whole, or of any sustained period of his thinking. But secondly, and far worse, the lecture is carelessly presented and poorly reasoned. (Sartre apparently had no written text when he delivered it—not even notes or an outline—but rather spoke extemporaneously.)

Let's consider just one example, which illustrates both of these defects. While Sartre's atheism remained constant throughout his philosophical career, it is only in "Existentialism Is a Humanism" that he presents his atheism as central to his thought. And he doesn't just say this once or twice in the lecture, but repeatedly, in many different formulations, and in different sections of the lecture. For example, he declares Dostoyevsky's dictum that "if God did not exist, everything would be permitted" to be the very "starting point" of existentialism (EH, 33), and defines "existentialism" as "nothing else but an attempt to draw the full conclusions from a consistently atheistic position" (EH, 56). Thus, readers familiar only with "Existentialism Is a Humanism" are invited to arrive at the mistaken belief that Sartre agrees with Dostoyevsky (or, more accurately, Dostoyevsky's character), and the equally erroneous understanding that Sartre's work is ultimately about atheism. On the other hand, those who read the lecture carefully and critically are likely merely to be confused on this issue, since Sartre also says there, right at the end (EH, 56): "[Existentialism] declares . . . that even if God existed that would make no difference from its point of view." Sartre offers no explanation as to how this startling sentence is to be reconciled with the others quoted above. Indeed, he shows no evidence of noticing the contradiction, in spite of the fact that he had ridiculed, on page 33, "a certain type of secular moralism which seeks to suppress God at the least possible expense," and which claims that "nothing will be changed if God does not exist." In any case, it is clear from Sartre's remarks, both before and after "Existentialism Is a Humanism," that his stable position is that God's nonexistence poses no threat to morality. In the *War Diaries*, written in 1939–1940 [prior to "Existentialism Is a Humanism"], but published posthumously, Sartre calls Dostoyevsky's statement a "great error," adding that "whether God exists or does not exist, morality is an affair 'between men' and God has no right to poke his nose in. On the contrary, the existence of morality, far from proving God, keeps him at a distance" (WD, 108). With regard to his post–"Existentialism Is a Humanism" position, in a 1951 interview Sartre affirms that the problem of morality "is the same whether God exists or not." Or again, in a 1974 conversation, Sartre, after first noting that Dostoevsky's dictum is "abstractly" true, immediately adds that "in another [way] I clearly see that killing a man is wrong. Is directly, absolutely wrong. . . ."[2] It is understandable, then, that philosophers who have read only "Existentialism Is a Humanism" would conclude, much too hastily but otherwise quite reasonably, that he is an incompetent philosopher. (Sartre himself subsequently pointed out that the lecture was "only a transitional work,"[3] and called its publication "a serious error," adding that its strong worldwide sales "bothered me, I have to admit," since "a lot of people . . . thought they understood what I meant by reading only [it]"[4] [SBH, 74–75].)

(5) An additional factor negatively affecting Sartre's reputation is the widespread sense that truly great philosophers are the ones who revolutionize philosophy. For Sartre, while a strikingly original thinker in terms of his arguments and theses, was indeed much less original methodologically and in his conception of philosophy. And just as painters in the modern period have come to be recognized above all for the radical newness of their styles—for conceiv-

---

[2] Jean-Paul Sartre, interviewed by Simone de Beauvoir in her "Conversations with Jean-Paul Sartre," in her *Adieux: A Farewell to Sartre*, trans. Patrick O'Brian (New York: Pantheon, 1984), 439. He goes on to state his "absolute" agreement with Beauvoir's claim that "a morality without God is more demanding, since if you believe in God you can always be forgiven for your sins . . . , whereas if you don't believe in God a wrong done to man is absolutely irreparable" (439–40).

[3] Sartre, as quoted in *Sartre and the Problem of Morality*, Francis Jeanson, trans. Robert V. Stone (Bloomington: Indiana University Press, 1980), 22, n. 4.

[4] "Existentialism Is a Humanism" sold 500,000 copies within one month of its publication, and today stands as the most widely read lecture of all time.

ing of an entirely new way of painting (think of Pablo Picasso's cubism, Henri Matisse's fauvism, Marcel Duchamp's dadaism, Jackson Pollock's drip style, and so on)—so have philosophers of the last hundred years or so been recognized for arguing that the entire history of philosophy has been based on some sort of mistake that they alone are prepared now to rectify (prominent examples include Edmund Husserl, Martin Heidegger, Ludwig Wittgenstein, and the logical positivists). Sartre, by contrast, for all of his substantive innovation, does almost all of his work in fields that have already been plowed to some degree by Husserl, Heidegger, Hegel, Marx, Kierkegaard, or Nietzsche, among others.

(6) It is easy to understand why social conservatives would tend to dislike Sartre. He was an atheist. He lived a bohemian lifestyle. He never married, and engaged in an unconventional relationship with Simone de Beauvoir (they chose not to live together, and each took many other lovers, though they remained devoted to each other, in their own fashion, for their entire adult lives).

(7) His belief that it is the duty of intellectuals to defend the powerless and expose the lies and the brutality of the powerful does not sit well with the powerful, or with those intellectuals who lack Sartre's courage (his example perhaps disturbs their consciences). He was condemned as "anti-French" for publicly supporting Algerian independence. (No one, it seems, can take the position that his or her own country is morally in the wrong in a war without being subjected to brutal personal attacks.) He opposed imperialism, colonialism, racism, fascism, and other forms of oppression. His main point in politics was that the world can be changed, that we are free to change it, and that we are responsible for doing so, given how intolerable current conditions are (hunger, poverty, war, racism, the threat of ecological disaster, and so forth). Note, also, that these conditions cannot reasonably be attributed to the evils of totalitarian communism. Rather, all of them continue to thrive under the dominant system of corporate capitalism. Thus, Sartre stood in opposition to those conservatives, or "realists," who hold that the status quo is somehow natural, inevitable, and unchangeable, and that the effort to change things deserves to be condemned as "utopian." He also opposes the stance of irony, skepticism, and passivity that characterizes so many of the "postmodernists" who succeeded him. British and American philosophers, perhaps because their countries have not been occupied

within living memory, tend not to be sympathetic to Sartre's call for engaged or committed writing. Having never had the experience of having to take sides, to make difficult choices, on a daily basis, with the stakes very high, they tend to find Sartre's account of the responsibilities of writers and intellectuals to be overly dramatic and unconvincing. Intellectuals in those countries, such as Bertrand Russell in England and Noam Chomsky in the United States who, despite their other differences with Sartre, have shared his commitment to radical political engagement, have been received with similar incredulity and contempt. Intellectuals who attack official enemies are lionized. Those who, like Sartre, Russell, and Chomsky, point out the crimes of their own nations are looked upon as traitors. Thus, whatever one might think of Sartre's political commitments, his courage cannot be doubted. By the mid- to late 1940s he was a famous, highly acclaimed, writer and an international celebrity. Had he chosen to, he could have spent the rest of his life quietly writing novels and plays, with the assurance that he would have readers, a more than adequate income, and the respect and admiration of the world-wide literary public. Instead he consistently championed unpopular political causes, defending the citizens of the Third World, "the wretched of the earth," against the economic and political interests of his own nation and class. In so doing he took huge risks with regard not only to his reputation, but to his life as well.

For example, he risked a prison sentence by signing an illegal petition condemning actions of the French military in Algeria. The petition called for independence for Algeria and advocated that French soldiers should refuse to fight the Algerians (and that they should receive amnesty for this insubordination). But French president Charles de Gaulle ordered that no action be taken against Sartre, quipping, "one does not imprison Voltaire." Similarly, Sartre wrote a letter, which was introduced at a trial of Francis Jeanson, Sartre's *Les Temps modernes* editorial colleague, in which he declared: "If Jeanson had asked me to carry a suitcase or to give sanctuary to Algerian militants and I could have done it without putting them in danger, I would have done it without hesitation." This caused something of a public scandal, and Sartre's actions were widely denounced as treasonous. Similarly, Sartre's journal documented atrocities carried out by the French against the Algerians that the mainstream French press had declined to cover.

It may well be that his actions, in putting the French conduct toward the Algerians under a critical spotlight, prevented thousands of Algerians from being tortured. He did everything he possibly could have done for the Algerian cause—wrote and published articles in support of the Algerian revolution, signed petitions, testified at trials, spoke at demonstrations, drew up manifestoes, and so forth. (These actions probably constituted the provocation for the "Shoot Sartre!" demonstration and the three bombing incidents mentioned earlier.)

Sartre took further heat for his opposition to the American attack on Vietnam. In 1965 he cancelled a scheduled lecturing trip to the United States in protest over the Vietnam War. When he was criticized for not coming to the United States for dialogue, to argue about and debate the merits of the war, Sartre replied:

> Discussion is possible only with those who are ready to put in question the whole American imperialist policy—not only in Vietnam but in South America, in Korea, and in all the countries constituting a "third world"; moreover, discussion is possible only with those Americans who will concede that American policy cannot be changed short of a complete turnover of American society. Now very few, even on the American Left, are ready to go that far.[5]

He later served as president of a war crimes tribunal organized by Bertrand Russell, a giant figure from the British analytical philosophy tradition, which found the U.S. and its allies guilty of war crimes in Vietnam.

In 1970 he took another courageous and unpopular political stand. A French Maoist newspaper, *La Cause du peuple*, had repeatedly been seized, and its editors arrested, by the French government, because of the ideas it advocated. Though Sartre was not a Maoist, he strongly supported freedom of the press, and consequently agreed to become the paper's editor-in-chief, so that his fame might shield the paper from further harassment. Sartre's actions ultimately had this effect, but not immediately. Sartre and Simone de Beauvoir distributed the paper on the street and, though they were not arrested, others who did so in another area

---

[5] Sartre, "Why I Will Not Go to the United States," *The Nation*, April 19, 1965.

were. Later, when Sartre and Beauvoir were arrested, along with sixteen others, the two celebrities were the only ones to be released immediately at the police station. When these other distributors of the paper were being tried, Sartre publicly denounced the prosecutor's double standard, pointing out that "if they are guilty, I am even more so." With that, he and Beauvoir resumed their activity of risking prison by distributing the newspaper, which advocated ideas that they largely did not endorse. They were not arrested, and the paper was never confiscated again.

Such actions made up a major part of the last decade of Sartre's life. During that period he increasingly involved himself in political action, championing the cause of workers, immigrants, victims of racism and colonialism, and victims of police brutality, among many others.

(8) But the nastiest, and most frequently leveled, political criticism of Sartre (and one that is often put forth even by those who acknowledge Sartre's intellectual brilliance and talent as a writer and who are not in principle horrified by leftist political activism) is that Sartre was a defender of Stalin's murderous regime in the Soviet Union. And indeed, while Sartre was for most of his life an independent, non-Stalinist, leftist, it is true that he took many indefensible stands in support of authoritarian Eastern Bloc regimes, especially during the 1952–1956 period. But at least three points can be made in his defense.

First, Sartre's support for Stalin during the period in question was grudging, and was based on his conclusion that historical circumstances presented him with few options, and no good ones. His attitude toward Stalinism was clearly expressed in the following comment from 1951: "To the extent that I am inspired by a rather broad Marxism, I am an enemy for Stalinist Communists." But Sartre temporarily supported the USSR because the Cold War eliminated any space for neutrality or independence. One had to choose sides. The U.S., in addition to enforcing racist segregationist policies in its southern states and in its military, was supporting every repressive regime on the planet that enhanced American economic and military interests. The USSR, for all its faults, at least showed some interest in economic rights and practical freedom (that is, the freedom to obtain what one needs to lead a decent life, as opposed to the more minimal freedom of simply being left alone and not harassed.) Sartre could not abide the

idea that it was acceptable for children to be born into poverty and
to be condemned to lives of misery. He apparently thought it more
likely that oppression in the communist bloc would eventually
lessen, perhaps when Cold War tensions diminished, than that the
capitalists would ever abandon their ruthless prioritizing of profits
over people. Similarly, his brief flirtation with the French
Communist Party, which he clearly loathed, was based on his conviction that the workers had at that time no other effective advo-
cates in France.

Secondly, Sartre's journal did, contrary to popular myth, publi-
cize and condemn the existence of Soviet labor camps, devoting an
entire issue to this one topic in 1950. Sartre himself announced that
"there is no Socialism when one in twenty citizens is in a camp."

Finally, from 1956 through the end of his life he demonstrated
a repeated willingness to condemn misdeeds undertaken by osten-
sibly socialist or leftist governments. For example, Sartre's reaction
to the Soviet attack on Hungary in 1956 was uncompromising: "I
condemn the Russian aggression completely and unreservedly."
When the French Communist Party defended the Soviet invasion,
Sartre declared that "it is not possible, and never will be possible,
to renew relations with the men who are in charge of the PCF at
the moment. Every sentence, every gesture, is the culmination of
thirty years of lies and sclerosis." Similarly, he responded to the
Soviet invasion of Czechoslovakia in 1968 by calling the Soviets
"war criminals." And in 1972 he condemned political repression in
Cuba, in spite of the fact that he had gone on record as an enthu-
siastic supporter of the Castro revolution in its early years.

(9) The last factor I will mention is the widespread belief that
Sartre's thought is passé, not just in the sense, discussed above,
that it is no longer new, and that we have gotten bored with it and
have turned our attention to newer figures, but rather in the sense
that his ideas are specifically geared to the circumstances in which
they were formulated, and have little relevance to our contemporary situation. Many consider Sartre's philosophy to be simply a
product of World War II, and in particular of the tense atmosphere
of Nazi-occupied France. Sartre's reply, I think, would be that this
extreme situation forced him (and other French citizens) to confront their freedom and responsibilities in a radical way, a way that
softer times would allow a person to avoid. But our freedom and
responsibility is, in a sense, even greater in calmer times (because

we then have much more opportunity to get things done, and to change things), making our tendency to try to hide it from ourselves even more deplorable. Our own times are certainly not free of war, violence, and oppression. We can use our freedom to oppose it, or we can make other choices.

Why Read Sartre?

Thus, I would argue that Sartre's work rewards study and thought, and indeed that the time is ripe for a return to it. For one thing, much of his work is addressed to matters of contemporary interest. Few philosophers have written more on, for example, racism, torture, and political violence and terrorism. And perhaps even fewer have spoken more powerfully on behalf of the idea that the contemporary world's horrific injustices are not inevitable, but rather are the result of human choices, and that we have the freedom, power, and responsibility to change things for the better. Moreover, it seems likely that much of value in his writings may remain to be discovered, having been obscured first by the excessive enthusiasm and violent denunciations which greet any "hot" cultural phenomenon, and then by the neglect which yesterday's news always receives. Sartre's gigantic and varied corpus, remarkable as almost anyone must concede that it is, thus stands before us an underutilized resource. When we return to that resource, I suggest that we will find (a) that Sartre is sometimes right, and (b) that when he is wrong, the problem is usually that he offers a one-sided and/or exaggerated account, as opposed to a wholly wrong-headed or uninteresting one. Thus, his work opens up possibilities for his readers, and encourages them to do their own creative, critical, and constructive thinking. We can make progress by incorporating into our own thinking Sartre's unique and original insights, provided that we correct his exaggerations and supplement his vision with relevant truths lying in his blind spots.

So let us begin. But immediately we confront a problem: how are we to consider all of the material comprising Sartre's massive oeuvre in the compass of one short book? Obviously we cannot. We will have to select. In doing so, I suggest that we be guided by this statement of Sartre's, offered in response to a question as to how he would like to be remembered: "I would like them to remember *Nausea*, one or two plays, *No Exit* and *The Devil and the Good Lord*, and then my two philosophical works, more particularly the second one, *Critique of Dialectical Reason* [presumably the first one is *Being and Nothingness*]. Then my essay on Genet, *Saint Genet.* . . . If these are remembered, that would be quite an achievement, and I don't ask for more."[6] I agree with Sartre that these works rank among his finest and most important. Moreover, taken together, they provide a good overview of his major concerns, arguments, and conclusions. Accordingly, I will devote most of my attention to these six works. I will also discuss, on a smaller scale, many of Sartre's other writings, as these either shed further light on the issues raised by the six featured books or else contain important ideas not found in them. My aim will not be to provide a substitute for Sartre's own texts, or to offer the last word on how to interpret him, but rather simply to give such help as a newcomer to Sartre's writings might need in order to profit from reading his works directly.

I will begin with a chapter on Sartre's early "phenomenological" (the term will be explained shortly) writings. There is something to be said for starting at the beginning. The early phenomenological writings are his first significant ones, and they lay the foundation for what follows. Phenomenology (specifically the work of Edmund Husserl) was Sartre's first great philosophical enthusiasm, and he never entirely abandoned it. Indeed, I think that it provides one of the keys to understanding his entire output. Sartre himself apparently thought so, too. In an interview conducted within five years of his death, he stated that he had "never" left phenomenology, and declared: "I continue to think in those terms."[7] And, in response to the question, "was the real discovery, in terms of importance to you, Husserl?" Sartre replied, "Yes . . . you're quite right, it was Husserl" (SBH, 25–26). Thus, to understand Sartre we must understand his engagement with Husserlian phenomenology. To that topic we now turn.

---

[6] Sartre, quoted in *The Existentialists and Jean-Paul Sartre*, Max Charlesworth (London: George Prior, 1976), 154. Note also that in "Self-Portrait at Seventy," in L/S, 24, when asked which of his works he hopes the next generation will read, he responds with a list of five books: *Saint Genet, Critique of Dialectical Reason, The Devil and the Good Lord, Nausea,* and *Situations.*

[7] Sartre, in "An Interview with Jean-Paul Sartre," conducted and translated by Michel Rybalka, Oreste F. Pucciani, and Susan Gruenheck, in *The Philosophy of Jean-Paul Sartre*, ed. Paul Arthur Schilpp (La Salle, IL: Open Court, 1981), 24.

1

Phenomenology

Simone de Beauvoir tells the story of Sartre's first introduction to phenomenology. Sartre's friend, Raymond Aron (who would go on to become a significant intellectual figure in his own right, and who would clash with Sartre on politics), told him about it one night while he, Sartre, and Beauvoir were having apricot cocktails at a café. Aron pointed to his glass and said, "You see my dear fellow, if you are a phenomenologist, you can talk about this cocktail and make philosophy out of it!" Beauvoir reports that "Sartre turned pale with emotion at this. Here was just the thing he had been longing to achieve for years—to describe objects just as he saw and touched them, and extract philosophy from the process."[1] Indeed, Sartre's excitement was such as to lead him to stop at a bookstore on the way home to purchase a book on Husserl, which he proceeded immediately to read on the street as he walked along. His next step was to make arrangements to travel to Germany for a year to study phenomenology firsthand.

Phenomenology is the descriptive study of the objects of experience, that is, of phenomena. It is a kind of "empiricism," the doctrine that all knowledge ultimately comes from experience. But whereas other kinds of empiricism typically claim that all knowledge derives exclusively from *sense* experience, phenomenology removes this qualification. It focuses, additionally, on objects for consciousness which cannot be straightforwardly observed with any of the

---

[1] Simone de Beauvoir, *The Prime of Life*, trans. Peter Green (New York: Lancer Books, 1966), 162.

five senses but which are, nonetheless, accessible to us through experience. Aesthetic, ethical, logical, and mathematical phenomena, for example, are part of the subject matter of phenomenology. The aim of phenomenology is to describe these objects of experience—these phenomena—just as they appear to consciousness, and also to describe the acts of consciousness (such as thinking, perceiving, imagining, doubting, questioning, loving, hating, and so on) by and through which these objects are disclosed.

One of the distinctive features of phenomenology is that it scrupulously refrains from considering anything else. It sets aside, or "brackets," all things that are outside of the realm of experience, broadly conceived, even if they are accepted by many people on some other basis (for example, that of faith, or tradition, or because they are useful explanatory concepts). Sartre's strategy, throughout his intellectual career, has been to attempt to show that phenomenology undercuts the rationale for such positing. If we investigate the phenomena with sufficient care and patience, he suggests, we will find that they are usually adequate to meet our explanatory needs, leaving us with no legitimate reason for extravagant extra-experiential posits.

Sartre's approach is in this respect similar to that of the ancient Greek physician, Hippocrates, who authored the first book ever written on epilepsy. In Hippocrates' time, epilepsy was explained as resulting from divine curses or demonic possession. Hippocrates argued that no progress can be made from leaping to such supernatural explanations, for if we do so whenever something initially strikes us as mysterious, we will prematurely cut off inquiry. It is far better, Hippocrates reasoned, to seek a naturalistic explanation first, and to hold the supernatural explanations in reserve, to be used only (if at all) in the event that an exhaustive search for a naturalistic explanation fails. Similarly, Sartre says, in effect, "let's go as far as we can simply describing phenomena and abstaining from positing any objects that we do not experience, such as God, the transcendental ego, the Kantian thing-in-itself, the Freudian unconscious, and the idea of universal, deterministic causation. Perhaps we'll find that we don't need any of these any more than scientists need gods or demons."

Sartre began putting this strategy into practice at the very beginning of his career, in the several articles and short books on phenomenological topics that he wrote during, and immediately following, his period of intensive study of phenomenology; and he carried it through to the end. Moreover, it is in these early phenomenological writings that he first introduced many of the central concepts and doctrines that would later be given more famous expression in his philosophical magnum opus, *Being and Nothingness*.

The Transcendence of the Ego

The first of these phenomenological works, *The Transcendence of the Ego*, was written in 1934 (though not published until three years later) while Sartre was studying phenomenology in Berlin. The target of this essay—the extra-experiential posit that he urges us to abandon—is the "transcendental ego" that allegedly stands behind, initiates, and directs all conscious acts.

To see what is at stake here, let's consider an example. Suppose that I mow my lawn this afternoon. At first, I focus on the task at hand. I walk around my lawn, looking for twigs, branches, and other obstacles to remove before starting the mower. Then I concentrate on the mower itself, and on the path of my cutting, as I try to keep the lines straight. Later my attention wanders (not advisable while operating dangerous machinery!) as I think about my upcoming vacation, and freely imagine scenes I might witness and things I might do. Still later, my focus drifts to a conversation I recall having with a colleague about some proposed changes at my university. I question whether those changes really will come to pass, and, as I continue to think it over, I come to doubt that they will. Finally my attention returns to the job I'm performing and I finish mowing my lawn. Now, when we take up the task of giving a phenomenological account of this sequence of events, that is, of describing what is given in this stream of experience, we will have no trouble identifying several objects of experience (branches and other obstacles to be removed, the grass to be cut, the lawn mower to be started and operated, the imagined beach, tennis courts, museums, and restaurants of my forthcoming vacation, the recalled conversation with my colleague, the dubious promises of change at my university) together with the acts of consciousness (seeing, imagining, remembering, questioning, doubting) that are directed toward those objects and which disclose them. But in addition, according to Sartre, "most philosophers" (including his new hero, Husserl)[2] uphold the seemingly commonsense opinion that there is something else also to be found here: an "ego" (or "I" or "self") that resides "in" or "behind" my consciousness, operating (or controlling or directing) the flow of my conscious acts (TE, 31). According to this standard view, my ego accounts for the unity of my conscious acts; it is what makes them all "mine" and part of a coherent pattern, as opposed to a random, disparate, unconnected collection.

But Sartre denies all of this. On his view, the ego is not "in" or "behind" consciousness, but rather "outside, in the world, like the ego of another" (TE, 31). It is not an independently real entity that directs the flow of my conscious acts, but rather is an ideal object that emerges only well after this flow is underway. And it does not bring about the unity and coherence of the stream of my conscious experiences, but rather is itself brought about when consciousness, in one of the actions comprising its stream, recollects several of its past moments and synthesizes them with its present one.

Sartre offers several arguments against the existence of the transcendental ego (and in favor of his own alternative, nonegological, conception of consciousness), but I think these are best understood as elaborations on his generic argument, described above, against extra-experiential posits. Quite simply, he claims (1) that we do not encounter a transcendental ego in our experience, and (2) that we need not assume its existence in order to explain what we do find in experience.

Sartre's claim that the ego is not a datum of experience may seem paradoxical. After all, whenever I reflect upon my own experiences, I always find them to be connected to an experiencing "I." That is why I describe my experiences by saying that "*I* have been mowing my lawn," "*I* have been thinking about my upcoming vacation," "*I* doubt that my university will change its policy," and

---

[2] Sartre's interpretation of Husserl on this point is controversial, and may well be erroneous. But since my purpose in this book is to clarify Sartre's own views, rather than to assess his interpretations of the views of others, I will not pursue this point here. Clearly, many people, including several philosophers of the first rank, have held views similar to those that Sartre attacks. Thus, to the extent that Sartre's critique of those views is cogent, and his alternative conceptions of consciousness and of the ego sound, his discussion remains of interest irrespective of the question of the accuracy of his reading of Husserl.

so forth. Indeed, the presence of an I is so clearly and distinctly given when I reflect on any of my experiences that René Descartes, widely regarded as "the father of modern philosophy," argued that the one absolutely indubitable truth (and thus the one truth fit to serve as the starting point for all other knowledge) is that an "I," as a thinking substance, exists whenever there is a thought. (This is the famous "I think, therefore I am" argument.)

Sartre replies by pointing out that the I appears only in reflection, a mode of consciousness that is both temporally and logically posterior to "unreflected" or "prereflective" consciousness (what Sartre calls, for good reason, "consciousness in the first degree") (TE, 41). For in the prereflective mode, consciousness does not focus on itself. Instead, it is directed, so to speak, "outward." Thus, when I mow my lawn, my consciousness takes for its object, and is exhaustively concerned with, the branches to be removed, the lawn mower to be started and operated, the grass to be cut, and the like. The I does not seem to be part of the content of these experiences. It is only when my consciousness shifts to the reflective mode, in which it takes its own activities for its objects, that the I appears. This happens when my attention shifts from the grass to be cut to such thoughts as, "I've been out here mowing the lawn for more than an hour; I'm getting hot and thirsty; maybe I should take a break." Thus, we never encounter in experience the I as a subject or substance directing our conscious acts. In most of our conscious life, that is, when we are in the original, prereflective, mode, the I fails to appear at all. And when we are in the reflective mode, a derivative mode that depends upon a temporally prior stream of prereflective experience for its subject matter, the I appears only as an object. We never catch it "in the act" of directing our conscious acts. Rather, it appears only after our consciousness, which has been doing, or focusing on, something else, abandons or suspends those activities so as instead to take for its object its own earlier activities. This observation gives rise to the suspicion, which Sartre goes on to endorse and to defend at length, that the I is not *discovered* in reflection, but rather is *constituted* in reflective acts of consciousness.

In any case, we are now in a position to understand Sartre's reply to Descartes. Whereas Descartes had identified consciousness with reflection, Sartre counters that reflection is a secondary mode of consciousness, depending for its existence on the prior existence of a prereflective consciousness, which provides it with its subject matter. Indeed, Descartes' position conflates these two modes of consciousness, allowing Sartre to quip that "the consciousness which says *I Think* is precisely not the consciousness which thinks" (TE, 45). (In other words, the reflective consciousness that says, for example, "I am thinking about a chair," is distinct from the prereflective consciousness that actually was thinking about the chair. The reflective consciousness is not thinking about the chair, but rather about an earlier act of consciousness that *was* thinking about a chair.)

But even if Sartre is right in his contention that we never directly encounter an ego inhabiting or underlying consciousness, it hardly follows that there is no such ego, or even that we cannot know that there is one. For even if we do not *find* a transcendental ego, it may be that there *must* be one, given the other things that we do find. Thus, in order to complete his demonstration, Sartre must show that he can adequately account, on his nonegological theory of consciousness, for everything that the standard view employs the transcendental ego to explain.

For example, Sartre needs to explain how it is that we generally are able to report accurately on what we've just been doing or perceiving, even when we have not been focusing on ourselves while we were doing or perceiving it, but rather were directing our attention outward. If I am absorbed in the act of counting, for example, I am not focusing on, or thinking about, myself. Rather, the content of my thought is more accurately rendered as "12, 13, 14, 15," and so on. But if someone suddenly bursts into the room and asks me what I am doing, I am at no loss for an accurate reply. I am able to report that I am counting (or, more accurately, that I was counting prior to this interruption!). Since my consciousness encounters no I in its prereflective activity of counting, but rather concerns itself exclusively with numbers, and since, on Sartre's hypothesis, there is no substantival I standing behind and unifying my past action of counting and my present action of recalling that I've just been counting, how is it that I am aware that I've just been counting?

Sartre's answer turns on his distinction between "positional" (or "thetic") awareness, on the one hand, and "nonpositional" (or "nonthetic") awareness, on the other. To be aware of something positionally is to focus on it directly; to be aware of something nonpositionally is to be implicitly aware of it without focusing on it directly, or, to put it another way, without making it the object of one's attention. Now, on Sartre's view, one is always aware of much more than that on which one directly focuses. For example, if I am focusing on an apple, I am also aware, without focusing on it or making it explicit, that the apple is not the table on which it rests, and (more to the point) that it is not my consciousness of it. Thus, Sartre claims that my prereflective positional consciousness of, say, an apple, is always accompanied by a nonpositional awareness of its own apple-perceiving activities. So consciousness is always self-*aware*, even though it is only intermittently self-*reflective*. It is this self-awareness, then, that explains the easy transition from the prereflective mode of consciousness, in which I am not thinking about what I am doing (because I am, instead, simply doing it), to the reflective mode, in which I am able effortlessly to report accurately on what I've just been doing.

(Incidentally, reflective consciousness exhibits the same double structure [positional and nonpositional] as does prereflective consciousness. Thus, just as prereflective consciousness is positionally aware of, say, a chair, and nonpositionally aware of its own activity of being positionally aware of the chair [and of not itself being the chair], so is reflective consciousness positionally aware of this prior conscious action of having been positionally aware of the chair, and nonpositionally aware of its own current activity of being positionally aware of this prior consciousness [and of not itself being that consciousness]. In this way, consciousness introduces all sorts of negations into being that being itself does not introduce—a major theme of his subsequent book, *Being and Nothingness*.)

Sartre's idea that consciousness is nonpositionally self-aware also undergirds his explanation of the existence of the empirical ego (that is, the ego-as-object, which we encounter in experience, as opposed to the alleged ego-as-subject, or transcendental ego, which, Sartre contends, we do not experience). He claims that in reflection one's nonpositional self-awareness is objectified, and that the self or ego is constructed out of a synthesis of indefinitely many of these objectifications. I find that certain states, and actions, and dispositions have characterized my past history. My ego is constituted through reflective acts of consciousness that apprehend these consistencies and regularities, thereby constructing a self. The ego is an ideal synthesis of these discrete states, actions, and dispositions. Thus, to put it another way, by recalling (selectively) its own past acts, and by synthesizing them (again, selectively) with its present ones and with its projected and planned future ones, my consciousness constructs an ego or sense of self. This "I" is something I find in the world, through reflection, to have certain properties that are more or less stable, just as is the case other kinds of objects in the world. Moreover, in constructing an ego I construct a value system and self-image, and these guide my actions, so that the construction of an ego typically leads to a kind of inertia. (True, the properties of the "I" can change, through free actions; but then, other objects in the world, though unfree, have their own ways of changing as well.)

In this way Sartre also attempts to explain how his non-egological conception of consciousness can account for the many phenomena that the transcendental ego is traditionally invoked to explain, most notably the unity, individuation, and coherence of one's conscious experience. On Sartre's view, to the extent that our conscious experience is unified and coherent (and everyone must concede that much of it is not—there is undeniably a haphazard, disconnected, quality to some of our conscious life), this is due to a confluence of several factors.

One, as I have already mentioned, is that consciousness selectively reflects on its prior acts, fabricates out of this selected material the idea of a self or ego, and then chooses to regulate its subsequent conduct (to some degree) by reference to this concept of its self or ego. Similarly (though this point is developed much more fully in subsequent works than in *The Transcendence of the Ego*), Sartre makes the point that we typically give coherence to our conscious actions by relating them to one another instrumentally within a hierarchy of projects. (I set the alarm clock because I want to get up early; which I want to do so that I can get to work on time; which I want to do so that I might remain on the job, not be fired, and continue to draw a paycheck; which, in turn, I want to do so that I might be able to afford to go to college; which, finally, I want to do so that I can realize my life's dream of becoming an astronomer.) But an additional factor is simply the coherence of the objects with which our conscious acts are concerned. They tend to persist over time, and to remain the focus of our attention over time, thus unifying several temporally distinct moments of our conscious life and contributing to our experience of coherence and temporal continuity. Then there is the fact that consciousness acts, together with their objects, have, in common with so many complexes of objects and processes, their own lawlike ways of coming together and uniting (removing any need for an external organizing principle). Similarly, Sartre suggests that since each consciousness is embodied, and essentially tied to one body, consciousnesses are already individuated, and no external cause for their individuation is required. And the unity, durability, and continuity of the body also contribute to the unity, durability, and continuity of conscious experience. Finally (though the point is not clearly made until *Being and Nothingness*), my sense of self as a stable entity comes about largely through interactions with others. When other people look at me, and when they judge and categorize me, they tend to "freeze" me, to make an object of me, to give me an essence ("he's a coward," "he's an effete intellectual," "he's a slob," and so forth). This is perhaps the major source of my sense of self. The other gives me my (relatively stable and coherent) "me."

Sartre clarifies the nature of this self (and further explains the unity of conscious experience) through his analogy of the self and a melody. A melody is not an entity that exists independently of its notes, which it somehow directs or otherwise supports. Rather, the melody just is the unity produced by grasping the relations among the individual notes so as to hear them as a unity. Similarly, Sartre argues that the ego or self is not a preexistent substance that directs and unifies a sequence of thoughts, feelings, and acts; rather, the self is this sequence grasped and comprehended as a unity. The self is a "synthetic totality" of acts of consciousness, just as a melody is a synthetic totality of musical notes. Neither the self, nor the melody is something over and above (or behind) the individual elements that comprise it.

Sartre's comparison of the ego to a melody also clarifies his strange-sounding claim that my ego is out in the world, like the ego of another. If my ego were a substance lurking behind each of my conscious acts, then others would not have direct access to it, just as they lack such access to my consciousness itself. But my ego is not my consciousness. It is a construct based on an appraisal of the entire series of my conscious acts and other psychic qualities, such as my qualities and dispositions, in the same way that a melody is a construct based on an appraisal of a series of musical notes. Thus, just as my friend and I both have access to the same melody when we listen to it, so do we both have access to each other's egos. When my friend and I speak of my hatred or my love, we are talking about the same thing—a constituted unity that is distinct from the individual conscious acts that manifest it. To be sure, my friend and I will have to approach this object from different standpoints, and through the use of different methods, but these different methods might be equally adequate for the achievement of knowledge of my love or hatred. Indeed, in many cases the other's knowledge of my ego may well exceed my own.

One of the merits of Sartre's insistence that the ego is an object in the world (in concert with his distinctions between consciousness and ego, between the prereflective and reflective modes of consciousness, and between positional and nonpositional awareness) is that it explains how I can be ignorant of, or have false beliefs about, my ego. And it does so without having to postulate any exotic entities that are inaccessible to experience, such as the transcendental ego or the Freudian unconscious.

In the first place, though I perform most of my actions prereflectively, surely it would be foolish to say that I perform them unconsciously. My attention is usually directed outward, toward the objects which concern me, and not at all toward my consciousness, of which I have only a nonpositional awareness. Such awareness falls well short of knowledge, according to Sartre, for one can "know" (in his precise, technical sense) an object of experience only by focusing on it. Prereflectively, then, I can only be "aware" of my conscious act, without knowing it. Later, by reflecting on it, I can come to know that of which I had previously merely been aware. In this way, Sartre attempts to explain much of that which psychoanalysts explain by invoking the unconscious.

But knowledge of my consciousness is not knowledge of my ego. While my reflection yields reliable knowledge about my consciousness, Sartre's distinction between consciousness and the ego, and his claim that the latter is an object in the world, explains why it is that reflection yields conclusions about my ego that are quite fallible and open to doubt. While I can "see" one of my conscious acts in its entirety simply by reflecting on it (for it is "immanent," or given all at once), my ego, like a melody, is complex and many-sided, so that it cannot be wholly grasped in a single reflective act. Rather, like other "transcendent" objects in the world, it is given to me only in profile; I do not see all sides, or all aspects, of it at once. Thus, while I am unlikely to err in reflectively judging that I felt repulsed by the presence of a certain person just now, my judgment that "I hate him," in the sense that this feeling of repulsion stems from a stable disposition of mine, could easily be mistaken. Perhaps it flows instead from a fleeting anger, irritation, or feeling of jealousy on my part. In this way Sartre can account for my ignorance of, and false beliefs about, my ego, without having to postulate a Freudian unconscious.

I can be ignorant of my ego because my present consciousness stands apart from, and *is not*, my ego, just as it is not any one of its past actions. And this separation from, and noncoincidence of, my present consciousness and my ego also serves as the foundation for Sartre's analysis of freedom. I *am not*—cannot be identified with, am not trapped by—my liking or hating of someone, or my bigotry, or my tendency to sleep late on Sundays, and so forth, because I can reflect on these prior actions, states, and dispositions, taking them as objects. In this way I can go beyond them, becoming separate from and "unstuck" from them. The experience of not *being*, because I am at a distance from, my objects and myself (understood either as the ego or, more minimally, as one or a set of my states, traits, or dispositions), is the fundamental basis of my experience of freedom. My traits and dispositions do not determine me, because I *am not* them; rather, *they are objects for me*. I can objectify them, modify them, or negate them. The separation between consciousness and the ego (and its aspects) is thus fundamental to Sartre's phenomenology of freedom.

But it is also fundamental to his account of anguish, and of bad faith (to be understood, for now, and somewhat crudely, as self-deception). To explain this, Sartre tells the story of a patient of the psychologist Pierre-Marie Janet:

A young bride was in terror, when her husband left her alone, of sitting at the window and summoning the passers-by like a prostitute. Nothing in her education, in her past, nor in her character could serve as an explanation of such a fear. It seems to us simply that a negligible circumstance (reading, conversation, etc.) had determined in her what one might call a "vertigo of possibility." She found herself monstrously free, and this vertiginous freedom appeared to her *at the opportunity* for this action which she was afraid of doing. (TE, 100)

Sartre's claim is that all of us experience this sense of radical freedom from time to time, and we tend to be as frightened of it as
was Janet's patient. Sartre calls this fear of freedom "anguish,"
and suggests that our (false) belief in a transcendental ego may
be motivated by our desire to escape this anguish by taking refuge
in the comforting belief that we have a stable "self" that precludes us from doing dangerous or despicable things. As Sartre
puts it,

> Perhaps, in reality, the essential function of the ego is not so much
> theoretical as practical. . . . [P]erhaps the essential role of the ego is
> to mask from consciousness its very spontaneity. . . . Everything hap-
> pens . . . as if consciousness constituted the ego as a false representa-
> tion of itself, as if consciousness hypnotized itself before this ego
> which it has constituted, absorbing itself in the ego as if to make the
> ego its guardian and its law . . . (TE, 100–101)

Thus, whenever I comfort myself by saying, "no, I can't do that,
for I am good (or kind, or honest)," I am covering up the fact that
I make my ego (or, more accurately, my ego is a construct of my
consciousness); my ego does not make me. I am only as constrained by my ego as I choose to be. My lucid awareness of this is
obscured, and therefore my self-deception facilitated, by the fact
that my consciousness remains primarily in the prereflective mode.
Since my conscious choices are thus shielded from the critical
resources of reflection, the inertia of my ongoing projects leads to
actions that typically are regular and predictable.

The belief in the sort of transcendental ego that would strongly
circumscribe my freedom, diminish my responsibility, and eliminate my anguish is so tempting, according to Sartre, that I usually
attempt to uphold it even in reflection. My consciousness tries to
convince itself that it contains an ego—a thinglike substance with
a fixed essence. It does this to attempt to escape its anguished freedom, like that of Janet's patient. Sartre calls this kind of reflection
"impure." (He also calls it, borrowing a term from Husserl, "the
natural attitude.") But this kind of reflection cannot be sustained,
and it therefore cannot fully succeed in implanting the desired illusion, since consciousness is nonpositionally aware of itself as ego-
less and as free. Moreover, there is nothing to stop consciousness
from focusing on this awareness explicitly in an act of reflection,

and thereby coming to assess itself accurately, in an act of what Sartre calls "pure" reflection. This distinction between impure and pure reflection (and more specifically, the idea that it is possible, and, from an ethical standpoint, desirable, to shift from the former to the latter) is crucial to the interpretation of *Being and Nothingness* and other later writings, especially in connection with Sartre's discussions of anguish, bad faith, "radical conversion," and ethics.

Indeed, Sartre ends *The Transcendence of the Ego* with a brief, programmatic statement about the ethical and political implications of his argument in that work. His first point is that phenomenology brings a welcome return to realism. He claims that "for centuries we have not felt in philosophy so realistic a current," and explains that, whereas other prevailing philosophies tend to "drown reality in the stream of ideas," phenomenology "plunges man back into the world," and "gives full measure to man's agonies and sufferings, and also to his rebellions" (TE, 104–5). But this is not true if phenomenology retains the transcendental ego: "As long as the *I* remains a structure of absolute consciousness, one will still be able to reproach phenomenology for being an escapist doctrine, for again pulling a part of man out of the world and, in that way, turning our attention from the real problems." But Sartre rejects the transcendental ego, and thus places me, not in some inaccessible realm, underlying and directing consciousness, but rather out in the world, with other things, so that my "existence has the same essential characteristics as the world" (TE, 105). And this "is sufficient for the *me* to appear as 'endangered' before the World, for the *me* . . . to draw the whole of its content from the World." Sartre concludes that "no more is needed in the way of a philosophical foundation for an ethics and a politics which are absolutely positive" (TE, 106).

Intentionality

In an important 1939 article, entitled "Intentionality: A Fundamental Idea of Husserl's Phenomenology," Sartre further clarifies what he takes to be the realistic implications of phenomenology. This extremely brief (it runs just two pages) essay is wholly devoted to one important phenomenological principle, that of intentionality. This principle, which Sartre learned from Husserl (who in turn had learned it from his predecessor, Franz Brentano), simply states that every act of consciousness takes an object. To *see*, for example, is to see *something*. Moreover, in order to take an object, in any manner, consciousness must be active. To see is to see something, and to see something is to *focus*, to concentrate one's attention selectively on a portion of one's visual field, relegating other features to an undifferentiated background. In other words, consciousness (think, simply, of awareness), in all of its actions, "aims at" or is "directed toward" its object. The same goes for all intentional objects and for all acts of consciousness—hearing, loving, interrogating, imagining, or what have you.

Sartre argues that the discovery of consciousness's essentially intentional character entails realism because it refutes the popular conception of the mind as a kind of container of ideas. According to this widely held view, to be conscious of something is to be aware of a representation of it "in" one's mind. One does not come into contact with objects directly, but rather with "ideas," which stand for, or represent, the objects themselves. Thus, knowledge is a process whereby consciousness assimilates objects and makes them part of its own contents. In Sartre's metaphorical description of this view, the mind is a spider, which "trap[s] things in its web, cover[s] them with a white spit and slowly swallows them, reducing them to its own substance" (INT, 4). Such a conception undermines realism, since it implies that we can only make contact with ideas in our minds, and are cut off from knowing what things are "really" like outside of the world of mental constructs in which we live.

How does phenomenology refute this picture? Recall that phenomenology is concerned to describe accurately the objects of experience, just as they are given in experience, and the acts of consciousness by which the objects of experience are disclosed, just as those acts of consciousness appear in reflection. Sartre's point is that both kinds of data speak against the popular, assimilationist or representationalist, view, and in favor of direct realism—the position that through acts of consciousness we come into direct contact with external objects.

Consider, first, what we find when we attend carefully to the objects of experience. In support of his judgment that "one cannot dissolve things in consciousness," Sartre offers this description: "You see this tree, to be sure. But you see it just where it is: at the side of the road, in the midst of the dust, alone and writhing in the heat, eight miles from the Mediterranean coast" (INT, 4). In other words, the tree does not present itself as existing in your mind; rather, it is given as standing out there in the world.

And when we turn our attention to consciousness, we are forced to conclude, even more strongly, that the tree not only does not enter into consciousness, but "could not" do so, "for it is not of the same nature as consciousness" (INT, 4). For it is the nature of consciousness to intend objects, that is, to point away from itself and out toward the things with which it is concerned. Consciousness is revealed in reflection to be an activity, rather than a thing. It is a directedness toward objects, a bursting toward them, a revealing of them, a focusing on them. It is a *relation* to things, not a place, or a container of them. It is not the case that intentionality is one aspect or feature of consciousness. Rather, consciousness *is* intentionality. (Sartre sometimes uses the terms "consciousness" and "intentionality" interchangeably.) So consciousness does not reflect the world, or represent it, or take it inside of itself. Indeed, since it is an activity, rather than a thing, it has no inside. Its sole necessity is "to exist as consciousness of something other than itself" (INT, 5).

To support these claims, Sartre, in keeping with his phenomenological method, refers his readers to the data of their own experience: "Do you recognize in this description your own circumstances and your own impressions? You certainly knew that the tree was not you, that you could not make it enter your dark stomach and that knowledge could not, without dishonesty, be compared to possession" (INT, 4).

In Sartre's own description of consciousness, his preference (and talent) for exciting, dramatic language is put in full view. He tells us that consciousness "tear[s] [it]self" away from itself and "burst[s] toward" the world (INT, 4). One gets the impression, not only that consciousness is an activity of going out toward objects (as opposed to a thing that contains them), but also that this activity is violent, shattering, and explosive. Consciousness, he tells us,

> is clear as a strong wind. There is nothing in it but a movement of fleeing itself, a sliding beyond itself. If, impossible though it be, you could enter "into" a consciousness you would be seized by a whirlwind and

thrown back outside, in the thick of the dust, near the tree, for consciousness has no "inside." It is just this being beyond itself, this
absolute flight, this refusal to be a substance which makes it a consciousness." (INT, 4–5)

The strength of Sartre's position can perhaps best be appreciated by considering the ways in which it enables him to avoid the
many thorny problems that arise when one conceives of consciousness as a kind of thing, or substance. Consider, for example,
the intractable difficulties in which the towering figure in modern
French philosophy, René Descartes, embroiled himself when he
defined consciousnesses as thinking substances to be distinguished
from material bodies (or extended substances). First, there is the
puzzle as to how such radically different kinds of entities could
enter into any kind of relations with one another. Secondly, it is
difficult to imagine what such relations could be like. Where, for
example (since on Descartes' view bodies are spatial and consciousnesses are not), would these transactions take place? How
could bodies "enter into" the mind, so as to become objects of
knowledge? How could the mind be free when it is a thing thrust
into the deterministic world of things? And how, if we are closed
off from direct contact with external objects, but are instead limited to dealing with representations of them in the form of ideas
"in" the mind, can we possibly ward off skepticism? (That is, how
can we achieve genuine knowledge concerning what things are
really like if we cannot examine them directly, and thus cannot
evaluate whether or to what extent our "ideas" of them accurately
represent them?)

Sartre's thesis that consciousness is not a thing at all, and that
no substantival entity stands in or behind it, is proposed as a solution to all of these problems. For example, since consciousness is
not a thing, but rather an activity of bursting out toward objects
and confronting them directly, it is not constrained to being aware
only of its own states and of its representations of objective reality.
This eliminates the skeptical worry that the internal contents of
our minds might fail to match up with real external things.
Similarly, since the concepts of causality and determinism apply
only to our understanding of interactions among objects, they do
not apply to our understanding of consciousness, which is not a
thing. Finally, what Descartes attempts to describe with the cate-

gories "thinking substance" and "extended substance," Sartre tries to redescribe with the categories "intentionality" and "intentional object." Thus, when Sartre describes relations among conscious acts and their objects, he does not conceive of these relations as occurring among different kinds of things. Rather, he regards them as relations among beings, on the one hand, and a kind of nonthing (that is, consciousness, which is an activity, rather than a thing, and thus a no-thing), on the other. He thus avoids puzzles about how one kind of substance can get into the other one of a radically different nature, or about where this event would take place. Consciousness does not take things into itself; it shoots itself out to things, carving them up and articulating them by focusing on them and questioning them. (Most of Sartre's massive *Being and Nothingness* is devoted to detailed phenomenological descriptions of these, and the many other kinds of, interrelations among consciousness and its intentional objects).[3]

Sartre's main conclusions in this essay—that consciousness is the nonsubstantival activity of intending objects, and that in its intending activities it is directed toward external things, as opposed to mere subjective representations of them—is crucial to all his thought. Indeed, in a late interview ("The Itinerary of a Thought") he comments, "[what] I have tried to do all my life [is] to provide a philosophical foundation for realism" (BEM, 36–37); and in another he recalls that in 1924, during his student days, he had

---

[3] One brief passage from the "Intentionality" essay anticipates *Being and Nothingness* in a particularly interesting and surprising way. In the latter work Sartre suggests that human beings are haunted by a desire to achieve the solidity and stability of things, which simply "are what they are." To put it another way, he claims that we want to escape the fate of all conscious beings, which is constantly to put themselves at a distance from themselves, by reflecting on their past actions, projecting their not-yet-existing future ones, and, in general, taking themselves as objects for (and thus showing themselves to be different from), their current conscious acts. But this desire is in vain, and the project of acting on it ends in failure. It is the nature of consciousness to introduce all sorts of gaps and skips into being, and, in particular, always to remain at a distance from itself. While this aspect of Sartre's philosophy is often thought to be a product of his experiences and preoccupations of the 1940s, we find it already present in the "Intentionality" essay, where it is apparently derived solely from his investigations into the nature of consciousness: "When consciousness tries to recoup itself, to coincide with itself once and for all, closeted off all warm and cosy, it destroys itself" (INT, 5).

"had only one idea—that any theory which did not state that consciousness perceived exterior objects as they were was doomed to
failure."[4]

To avoid confusion, I should offer two clarifications regarding
Sartre's claim that intentionality entails realism. First, it is far from
clear that Sartre interprets Husserl correctly here. Husserl's thought,
while sufficiently complex as to permit of a range of interpretations, is often understood to be closer to idealism (the doctrine
that the essential nature of reality lies in consciousness) than to
realism. In any case, Sartre's position is interesting in its own right,
irrespective of the question of its accuracy as an interpretation of
Husserl. (And Sartre elsewhere criticizes Husserl for allegedly laps-
ing into a kind of idealism.) Secondly, my claim that Sartre defends
realism in his essay on intentionality may seem odd, since he explicitly condemns "realism" in that work. But the "realism" that he
criticizes there is representational realism, as opposed to the direct
realism that he endorses. He also criticizes the "realism" that he
rejects for reducing consciousness to the status of a natural object,
no different in kind than any other object, and for falsely claiming
that the world is objectively meaningful in itself, without needing
to be illuminated and articulated through human conscious activities. In short, while Sartre interprets phenomenology as a kind of
realism, he embraces it in part precisely because it represents a
viable alternative to the two dominant traditions in early twentieth-century French philosophy, idealism and (nonphenomenolog-
ical) realism, both of which he finds indefensible.

The extent of Sartre's commitment to realism can be fairly
gauged by considering his discussion of emotionally charged ways
of intending objects. For, as Sartre points out, "knowledge . . . is
only one of the possible forms of consciousness 'of' this tree; I can
also love it, fear it, [or] hate it . . ." (INT, 5). Now, many people
interpret such intending subjectively. Their idea is that value-qual-
ities do not really exist in things. Because of this ontological commitment—this theory about what does and does not really
exist—they assume that our acts of loving or fearing objects do not

---

[4] Jean-Paul Sartre, interviewed by Simone de Beauvoir in her "Conversations
with Jean-Paul Sartre," in her *Adieux: A Farewell to Sartre*, trans. Patrick O'Brian
(New York: Pantheon, 1984), 157.

disclose any information to us about the true qualities of those objects. But phenomenology asks us to suspend these ontological judgments and to inquire, instead, into the content of our experience. When we do so, we find nothing to suggest that we "project" our subjective reactions onto the neutral screen of the true being of external objects. Rather,

> it is things which abruptly unveil themselves to us as hateful, sympathetic, horrible, lovable. Being dreadful is a *property* of this Japanese mask, an inexhaustible and irreducible property which constitutes its very nature—and not the sum of our subjective reactions to a piece of sculptured wood.
>
> Husserl has restored to things their horror and their charm. He has restored to us the world of artists and prophets: frightening, hostile, dangerous, with its havens of mercy and love. He has cleared the way for a new treatise on the passions which would be inspired by this simple truth, so utterly ignored by the refined among us: if we love a woman, it is because she is lovable. (INT, 5)

The Emotions

Sartre's own "new treatise on the passions," his short book of 1939, *The Emotions: Outline of a Theory,* is "an *experiment* in phenomenological psychology." Accordingly, in this work Sartre investigates emotion "as a *phenomenon*" (E, 21). His principal finding is that the popular conception of emotions as something we *have,* or passively endure, is incorrect. It is more accurate to say that emotions are modes of awareness of the world.

This conclusion is suggested, first of all, by a consideration of intentionality. Since all emotion is a consciousness, and every consciousness is a consciousness *of* something, it follows that all emotions are directed toward objects. Sartre contends that the major flaw in all prephenomenological theories of emotion is that they fail to take notice of this intentional character of emotional consciousness. For them,

> flight in a state of fear is described as if the object were not, before anything else, a flight *from* a certain object, as if the object fled did not remain constantly present in the flight itself, as its theme, its reason for being, *that from which one flees.* And how can one talk about anger, in which one strikes, injures, and threatens, without mention-

ing the person who represents the objective unity of these insults, threats, and blows? In short, the affected subject and the affective object are bound in an indissoluble synthesis. Emotion is a certain way of apprehending the world. (E, 51–52)

To illustrate some of the ways in which one can go wrong by failing to recognize the intentional character of emotional consciousness—its directedness toward a frightening object—Sartre offers the example of William James's influential theory of the emotions. According to James, an emotion is simply a consciousness of certain physiological manifestations. For example, anger is the "projection in consciousness" of one's faster breathing, clenched muscles, "arterial tension," and the like (E, 22–23). Sartre objects, on phenomenological grounds, that emotion "has a meaning; it signifies something" (E, 24). That is, our emotional response to a situation depends upon our *understanding* or *interpretation* of that situation as, for example, threatening. In this way an emotion differs from pain, which one first experiences and only subsequently evaluates. Emotions, then, are not involuntary, reflex, reactions to external stimuli, but rather intentional conscious acts. One reason why philosophers have traditionally thought otherwise is that they have accepted the Cartesian dualism of (voluntary, purposeful) mind and (inert, unconscious) body. Sartre, here and elsewhere, rejects this dualism, conceiving of consciousness as embodied (or, if you prefer, of the body as conscious and purposeful).

Another important finding, evident in these examples of fear and anger, is that emotional consciousness is not reflective, but rather is directed out toward an object in the world. For example, so long as I am afraid, I do not reflect on my fear, for my attention is riveted to the object of my fear. Later, when the threat has passed, I may indeed reflect that I had been afraid. Originally, however, my emotional consciousness is not a consciousness of being afraid; rather, it is a consciousness of some frightening object. Fear, then, like other emotions, is a prereflective directedness toward an object. Reflection on my fear, by contrast, puts me at some distance from that fear. A consciousness that reflects on its own fear takes that fear, rather than, say, the snarling dog, for its object. When fear is the object for my consciousness, it is no longer a quality of my consciousness in its prereflective directedness toward a frightening object. To reflect on fear, then, is to be no longer really afraid.[5]

But if emotion, according to Sartre, is a prereflective intentional conscious act—a way of apprehending the world—we need to know how this emotional way of apprehending the world is to be distinguished from other, nonemotional, modes of apprehension. Sartre's answer is that emotional apprehension is of a magical world, whereas nonemotional apprehension is of an instrumental one. In Sartre's view, unproblematic situations do not typically call for emotion. We simply try to size up the situation; and then, on that basis, we seek to take the appropriate steps, and to use the best instruments, so as to bring about our desired result. But sometimes we find ourselves in situations in which no means for the achievement of our ends are available to us. In such situations, we find the real world—the world of instrumental reason, and of an order of causes and effects—intolerably frustrating. We turn away from this world, and instead embrace the irrational, "magical," world of emotions. As Sartre explains,

> when the paths traced out become too difficult, or when we see no path, we can no longer live in so urgent and difficult a world. All the ways are barred. However, we must act. So we try to change the world, that is, to live as if the connection between things and their potentialities were not ruled by deterministic processes, but by magic. (58–59)

Thus, emotion can be defined as a magical transformation of the world.

As a concrete illustration of this, consider the example of passive fear:

> I see a wild animal coming toward me. My legs give way, my heart beats more feebly, I turn pale, I fall and faint. Nothing seems less

---

[5] Sartre apparently changed his mind on this point later, for in *Being and Nothingness* he claims that anguish and shame are experienced reflectively. On the other hand, since he does make it clear that not all modes of affectivity are to be understood as emotions, perhaps he can be rescued from inconsistency on this point by interpreting anguish and shame as something other than emotions. Unfortunately, however, Sartre does not make it very clear just how these different modes of affectivity—emotions, moods, feelings, sentiments, and so forth—differ from one another.

adapted than this behavior which hands me over defenseless to the danger. And yet it is a behavior of *escape*. Here the fainting is a refuge. Let it not be thought that this is a refuge *for me*, that I am trying to save *myself* in order not to *see* the wild animal *any more*. I did not leave the unreflective level, but, lacking power to avoid the danger by the normal methods and the deterministic links, I denied it. I wanted to annihilate it. The urgency of the danger served as motive for an annihilating intention which demanded magical behavior. And, by virtue of this fact, I did annihilate it as far as was in my power. These are the limits of my magical action upon the world; I can eliminate it as an object of consciousness, but I can do so only by eliminating consciousness itself. . . . It is the same way that novices in boxing shut their eyes and throw themselves at their opponent. They want to eliminate the existence of his fists; they refuse to perceive them and by so doing symbolically eliminate their efficacity. Thus, the true meaning of fear is apparent; it is a consciousness which, through magical behavior aims at denying an object of the external world, and which will go so far as to annihilate itself in order to annihilate the object with it (62–64).

Another of Sartre's examples is that of active sadness. Suppose I wish to be excused from performing a difficult task. Let us say, for example, that it is my duty to give unpleasant or embarrassing testimony in court, and I desperately want to get out of it. Unfortunately, despite my best efforts, I cannot think of a way to extricate myself from this odious situation. So I resign myself to going through with it. But when the horrible moment when I must speak finally arrives, I suddenly find that I am overcome with sadness. I begin to weep uncontrollably, rendering my testimony impossible. Lacking any calm, rational way of dealing satisfactorily with my situation, I radically transform it, by means of altering myself, through the "magic" of emotion.

At other times it is the world, rather than myself, that I transform through the magic of emotion. Such is the case, for example, with passive sadness. Suppose I have just suffered a financial collapse. My old network of means for accomplishing my ends has collapsed with it. For instance, I no longer have a private automobile to use as a means of transportation. I could begin the project of radically reconstructing and reorganizing the means-end structure of my world (picking up a bus schedule, getting some good, cheap walking shoes, trying to find employment within walking distance of my residence, and so forth), but I have no desire to undertake such a task. Instead, I simply become sad, and wallow in my gloomy mood. Such passive sadness

> aims at eliminating the obligation to seek new ways, to transform the structure of the world by a totally undifferentiated structure. In short, it is a question of making the world an affectively neutral reality, a system in total affective equilibrium, of discharging the strong affective charge from objects, of reducing them all to affective zero, and, by the same token, of apprehending them as perfectly equivalent and interchangeable. In other words, lacking the power and will to accomplish the acts which we had been planning, we behave in such a way that the universe no longer requires anything of us. (E, 65)

Here a world in which our instrumental power is insufficient for achieving the ends we desire is magically transformed into one in which no values remain. In this world there is nothing to be done. Hence, we are no longer required to act, and our problems concerning acting in the world are thereby magically annihilated.

Emotion, then, is

> an abrupt drop of consciousness into the magical. Or, if one prefers, there is emotion when the world of instruments abruptly vanishes and the magical world appears in its place. Therefore, it is not necessary to see emotion as a passive disorder of the organism and the mind which comes *from the outside* to disturb the psychic life. On the contrary, it is the return of consciousness to the magical attitude, one of the great attitudes which are essential to it, with appearance of the correlative world, the magical world. Emotion is not an accident. It is a mode of existence of consciousness, one of the ways in which it *understands* . . . its "being-in-the-world." (E, 90–91)

While Sartre's theory of the emotions exhibits many strengths (such as its recognition of the object-directedness and the significative character of emotional consciousness), I think it is open to five powerful, and rather obvious, objections. What all five objections have in common is that they expose Sartre's theory as, not simply mistaken, but rather partial, one-sided, and exaggerated. Sartre's analysis illuminates many aspects of our emotional life, but it ignores or obscures others. While his keenest perceptions are firmly rooted in his phenomenological method (that is, his careful observation of the data of experience, broadly construed), the weaknesses of his theory arise when he distorts the data of experience, interpreting them so implausibly as to suggest that his concern lies less with descriptive fidelity than with making the data conform to his theory.

For example, while Sartre's conception of emotion as an attempt to transform magically an unbearably difficult situation seems plausible over a range of cases, how can it make sense of emotions that arise even when there seems to be no need for magic? How, for example, can Sartre's theory account for such an emotion as joy, which is usually thought to arise from pleasant, rather than difficult, situations? The answer is that, for Sartre, the situations accompanying joy only appear to be pleasant; they are actually quite difficult. To illustrate this, Sartre gives the example of a man who is to be reunited with a loved one whom he has not seen for a long time. The man becomes so excited by the imminent reconciliation that he finds unbearable the time that must pass prior to its occurrence. And when the loved one does appear, he or she is nonetheless an object that, so long as we remain within the instrumental world, can yield itself only by degrees. To overcome this frustrating fact, the instrumental world is overthrown by the magic of an emotion, in this case joy. Thus, "joy is a magical behavior which tends by incantation to realize the possession of the desired object as instantaneous totality" (69).

In response, I would say that, while Sartre deserves credit for anticipating this objection, and for offering a clever solution to it, his solution seems, on phenomenological grounds, implausible on its face. Moreover, it is also objectionable in that it yields the bizarre conclusion that *all* emotions are responses to negative situations. But it is easy to think of counterexamples, and we need not even leave the emotion of joy in order to do so. Consider, then, the joy that is associated with the experience of relief. Here the joy is not connected with the bringing forth of some cherished object, as it is in all of Sartre's examples of joy, but rather with the taking away of, say, some dreaded chore. Thus, the sources of difficulty Sartre describes in his examples of joy (the impossibility of possessing a desired object as an instantaneous totality, the difficulties inherent in preserving and sustaining the object, the insecurity of knowing that the object could be lost at any time, and so on) are not applicable to the joy of relief. This can be easily illustrated. Let us suppose that I have been dreading all weekend the horrible task of picking bagworms off of my grandmother's evergreen trees. I am suddenly presented, however, with the surprising news that I will not have to perform the job after all, that Joe has volunteered to do the chore for me. I am instantly filled with joy, a joy that cannot accurately be described as a response to a difficult situation. Rather, my joy is nothing other than a response to the removal of a difficult experience. It is clear, then, that Sartre's attempt to reduce positive emotions to negative ones flies in the face of our ordinary emotional experience. Still, this does not rule out the possibility that Sartre's theory applies to some emotions, even if it fails as an analysis of others.

A similar criticism applies to Sartre's claim that emotion arises only when instrumentally rational action breaks down. For this appears to be false, not only in the case of positive emotions, such as joy (as we have just seen), but also in the case of such negative emotions as anger and fear. When driving at night on icy roads, for example, I tend to feel fear; and yet this emotion neither stops me from driving, nor prevents me from employing instrumental rationality in doing so. To the contrary, my fear, if anything, tends to focus my concentration on the job at hand more acutely. There is no abrupt transformation to a magical world. But Sartre, because of his conviction that emotion is necessarily incompatible with instrumental action, argues that our lived experience of the coexistence of emotion with rational behavior must be an illusion. The implausibility of this claim is evident from a consideration of one of Sartre's own examples:

> The flight into active fear is mistakenly considered as rational behavior. Calculation is seen in such behavior—quick calculation, to be sure—the calculation of someone who wants to put the greatest possible distance between himself and danger. But this is to misunderstand such behavior, which would then be only prudence. We do not flee in order to take shelter; we flee for lack of power to annihilate ourselves in the state of fainting. Flight is a fainting which is enacted; it is a magical behavior which consists of denying the dangerous object with our whole body by subverting the vectorial structure of the space we live in by abruptly creating a potential direction on the *other side*. It is a way of forgetting it, of denying it. (E, 63)

Here again, Sartre distorts the data of experience in order to support a one-sided theory. For, while Sartre is certainly right in claiming that emotions are *often* ineffective, and stand as obstacles to the successful carrying out of our projects (for example, panicky fear is less effective than calm, rational thought during a fire), any adequate theory of emotions must recognize that the presence of emotions not only is compatible with instrumentally rational action, but even, in some cases, renders such action more effective than it would otherwise be. For example, my irritated response to others' unintentionally annoying behavior might be the most effective means available to me to get them to cease and desist, just as my delighted reaction to their pleasing behavior might succeed in encouraging more of the same.[6] And my evident emotion in these cases is likely to enhance any instrumental action (such as directly requesting that the annoying behavior be stopped) that it accompanies. That, in any case, is part of the explanation of emotions that evolutionary theory offers; so perhaps Sartre's neglect of the physical sciences hurts him here.[7]

A third objection is that Sartre, in insisting that emotions are intentional conscious acts, underemphasizes the involuntary dimension of our emotional experience. To be sure, Sartre's account provides a valuable corrective to earlier theories, most of

---

[6] Sartre evidently recognized later in his career that emotions need not be irrational or instrumentally ineffective. For example, John Gerassi, in his biography of Sartre (*Jean-Paul Sartre: Hated Conscience of His Century* [Chicago: University of Chicago Press, 1989], 6), records Sartre as remarking (probably in the late 1960s or early 1970s), "It is always those who have power who say 'calm down, let's talk rationally, let's be sensible'. . . . It is always those who have power who insist that being emotional is being weak. In the home, the powerful are the male. That's why the best way for a housewife to argue against her calm, rational 'provider' is to throw the plate of rice in his face."

[7] Sartre cannot be blamed, of course, for ignoring scientific developments that have taken place after his death. But, for what it is worth, they do not support him. For example, in radical contrast to Sartre's claim that the emotions are irrational, recent findings of neuroscientists suggest that "healthy emotional responding plays a critical role in guiding reasoning processes and in connecting deliberation to action. Emotional systems allow conclusions to be reached in a timely manner, and they give conviction to our thoughts" (David C. Noelle, "Exorcising the Homunculus," *Free Inquiry* 21, no. 2 [Spring 2001]: 33–34. Noelle here cites Antonio R. Damasio, *Descartes' Error: Emotion, Reason, and the Human Brain* [New York: Putnam, 1994]).

which have maintained that emotions are strictly involuntary phenomena. It is easy to see that this once dominant position is erroneous. I can clearly recall, for example, several incidents in which I suffered a minor injury under the watchful eye of a parent at a very young age, and then faced a moment of decision—to cry and make a fuss, or to shrug off the pain and continue with the game or sport I was engaged in. If I had become bored with my activity, and craved a little parental attention, I would give myself over to the pain, feel it intensely, and then enjoy being comforted. But if the injury had interrupted fun to which I was eager to return, it was not difficult for me quickly to forget my pain, simply by turning my attention away from it and focusing instead on my game. Similarly, many people (perhaps even most) learn, as they mature, techniques that help them to manage their emotions. They learn, for example, how to put a bit of bad luck in perspective, and how to cope with, and rebound from, disappointment and embarrassment. But that doesn't mean, and nor is it true, that we simply choose our emotions voluntarily. Surely there is something involuntary—something that simply happens to one, without it having been in any way chosen—about the deep sadness that strikes a person when a loved one of theirs suddenly and unexpectedly dies, or, for that matter, about the giddy, joyous feeling one gets when receiving a sizeable chunk of utterly unanticipated good fortune.

Since Sartre obviously cannot deny that it often seems to us that an emotion is something which "comes over us," and which we must "endure," he must explain why this appearance is deceptive (always a tricky business for a phenomenologist!). He must explain, that is, why we fail to notice that emotions are rooted in our own intentions. His explanation turns on his distinction between false emotion and genuine emotion. In false emotion I make an external show for the benefit of another, but I am not myself fooled by the performance. Thus, if I am given a gift that does not interest me, I may jump and clap my hands in a demonstration of great joy, knowing all the while that this joy is only an act. I am a magician who tricks only his audience. In genuine emotion, however, my magic fools not only an audience but me as well. Moreover, it is precisely the fact that I believe in my own magic that enables it to serve my intended purpose, that of transforming the instrumental world. Hence, "consciousness is caught in its own trap. Precisely because it lives the new aspect of the world by believing in it, it is caught in its own belief, exactly as in dreaming and in hysteria" (E, 78). True, consciousness would need only to reflect upon its emotion to avoid being trapped in this self-deception.[8] But, as Sartre readily points out, emotional behavior is unreflective, and in the prereflective state consciousness fails to recognize the magical world of emotion as its own creation.

Sartre explains the seemingly involuntary physiological changes that accompany the emotions similarly. They too, he argues, are brought about by consciousness. Sartre refers to them as the results of "using the body as a means of incantation" (E, 70). In other words, "we understand . . . the role of purely physiological phenomena: they represent the *seriousness* of the emotion; they are phenomena of belief" (E, 74). Thus, consciousness brings about bodily changes so as to impress itself with the power of its own magic.

But surely I am not "fooling" myself when my friend's unexpected death makes me sad, when my discovery that my "problem" student is not enrolled in any of my classes this term makes me joyous, or when my sudden encounter with a hostile dog while jogging frightens me. I have no motive to fool myself, and I feel the emotion while staring reality in the face.[9] The death deprives

---

[8] Sartre says that liberation from the "trap" of emotional consciousness "has to come from a purifying reflection or a total disappearance of the affecting situation" (E, 79). But he also cautions that such "reflection is rare and necessitates special motivations. Ordinarily, we direct upon the emotive consciousness an accessory reflection . . . " (E, 91). As the reader may recall from the discussion of *The Transcendence of the Ego*, whereas consciousness often attempts, by means of accessory reflection (also called "impure" reflection) to hide from itself its own freedom and responsibility, it can also, through purifying reflection, confront itself squarely and honestly. The shift from accessory reflection to pure reflection is a prominent theme in Sartre's subsequent work, and is especially crucial to his ethics.

[9] In some of his other works, including his early ones, Sartre shows himself to be aware that there need be nothing self-deceptive about strong emotion. For example, in his story "The Wall," the protagonist discovers, at one point, that he has been perspiring profusely, in spite of being in a cold environment. This was due to his lucid awareness of his own (likely) impending execution. But he is not in the least self-deceived; his emotion seems not to be part of any project of trying to transform the world by magic (except, perhaps, in projecting gloom or indifference over everything). He faces his impending death squarely and honestly.

me of a cherished friend, and thus is sad; the nonpresence of my problem student frees up my time and rescues me from a thousand headaches, and thus is joyous; the dog has the potential to cause me significant pain and injury, and thus is frightening (though my fright, to make the point once again, does not preclude me from engaging in quick, rational thought as to how to maximize my chances of avoiding pain and injury). The emotions, and their accompanying physiological changes, hit me involuntarily, in the very instant in which I grasp the meaning of the situation that gives rise to them. What is needed, then, is a theory of emotion that would investigate the relationship between the voluntary and the involuntary aspects of emotional experience, without slighting either the former at the expense of the latter (as nearly all of the older theories do), or the latter at the expense of the former (as Sartre does.)

Fourthly, Sartre's claim that emotions arise only when instrumental rationality breaks down ignores his own discovery, as articulated in his "Intentionality" essay, that emotions "are merely ways of discovering the world" (INT, 5). Whether emotions reveal real characteristics of objects in the world (as in Sartre's claims, in that essay, that "being dreadful is a *property* of this Japanese mask," or that "if we love a woman, it is because she is lovable" [INT, 5]), or whether they merely expose our own subjective tastes, beliefs, and preferences, the point is that emotions are primarily important to us as the means by which we encounter the world as a positively and negatively "charged" environment. It is because of the emotions that the world is lively and vibrant, and rich in qualitative variation, rather than drab, colorless, and lifeless. And we encounter this qualitative diversity everywhere and all the time, and not merely in connection with our immediate choice of action (let alone merely in connection with our *instrumentally problematic* choice of action).

Finally, Sartre's theory overlooks the fact that many of our projects in life are explicitly emotional in nature. People seek love and joy, and shun fear and pain, for their own sakes, and not as a means to an end (or in order to effect a magical transformation of the world so that it loses its means-end structure). Not all of our goals are pragmatic ones to be pursued instrumentally, with emotions intruding only when things get difficult.

Imagination and *The Imaginary*

Perhaps Sartre's most distinguished early phenomenological work is devoted to the imagination. He wrote two books on the subject. The first, a revision of the first part of his thesis for a diploma in advanced studies (the publisher rejected the second part), was published in 1936 under the title *Imagination*. In this book Sartre explains, and then rather sharply criticizes, several leading modern philosophical theories of the imagination. The book concludes with a detailed discussion of Edmund Husserl's phenomenological approach, which Sartre, without withholding his objections, evaluates much more favorably. He reaches the conclusion, which anticipates his more famous discussion in *Being and Nothingness*, that "it is an ontological law" that "there are only two types of existence": "thing in the world" and "consciousness" (In, 116). The former is "sheer inertness," while the latter is "pure spontaneity, confronting a world of things." "Never could my consciousness be a thing," Sartre writes, "because its way of being . . . is precisely to be *for* itself; for consciousness, to exist is to be conscious of its existence" (In, 1–2).

Sartre later returned to the second, more constructive and original, part of his thesis, which the publisher had rejected. He developed this section further and published it in 1940 (with a substantial chunk having appeared first as an article in 1938) as *The Imaginary* (to give the title as it is rendered in the more recent, and more accurate, of two English translations. It had previously been translated as *The Psychology of Imagination*). In this work Sartre develops many of the methods, and arrives at several of the conclusions, that appear later in *Being and Nothingness*.

Sartre's method is phenomenological. That is, he attempts to describe objects of experience (intentional objects) just as they are experienced, and also to describe the acts of consciousness (intentional acts) by which those objects are disclosed. Accordingly, since Sartre's topic is imagination, he concerns himself both with imagined objects ("imaginaries") and with the act of imagining.

A phenomenological approach seems particularly well suited to the study of imaginaries, since it rejects as a groundless prejudice the idea that the only objects about which we can attain knowledge are those accessible by simple sensory perception. Thus, phenomenology opens the door to the study of numbers, and aesthetic and moral values, for example, in addition to imaginaries. It claims that we find, if we approach the matter without prejudice, that these objects, just as they are given to us in experience, have specific natures, are regulated by identifiable principles, and are related to one another in specifiable ways.

In *The Imaginary* Sartre takes up his task of identifying and clarifying the nature of imaginaries by contrasting them with objects of perception. He points out, for example, that perceptual objects enter into relations with one another whether we know about them or not. (Typically we do not know about these relations at first, but rather have to discover them.) Indeed, the number of these relations is literally infinite—there is always something more to be learned about any perceptual object. Such objects "overflow" consciousness. There is always more to them than we can observe in any one perceptual act (or, indeed, in any number of such acts). We can learn of their size, shape, color, and thickness, of the historical changes they have undergone over time, of the ways in which they typically interact with other objects, of their chemical composition, of their behavior when subjected to heat or cold or light or darkness, of what happens when they are cut in two or submerged in water, and so on infinitely. (This idea that real objects are infinitely "massive" is a major theme of Sartre's novel, *Nausea*, and of the introduction to *Being and Nothingness*.)

Imaginaries, in quite radical contrast, are related to each only in the ways we imagine them to be. There is nothing more to them than what we imagine them to be. Thus, we have a kind of freedom in relation to imaginaries that we lack in connection with perceptual objects (though we are still free to confer various meanings on perceptual objects, by choosing which of their many aspects on which to focus, and/or by choosing the project in the context of which we encounter them—note that the lumberjack, landscape artist, and botanist do not see the same thing when they all look at the same tree). So, to use Gaston Bachelard's phrase, of which Sartre makes much in *Being and Nothingness*, perceived objects present us with a greater "coefficient of adversity" than do imaginaries. Moreover, while objects of perception give themselves as "present" to consciousness, imaginaries are given as "absent," that is, either as utterly nonexistent or as not here now.

Similarly, when we turn our attention away from the objects of our experience and toward the conscious acts by means of which we experience them, we find that imagination differs from perception just as much as imaginaries differ from perceptual objects. We have the data necessary for such a comparison, according to Sartre, because even when our focus is on the object of our experience of perception or imagination, we also have a "nonthetic," or nonpositional, awareness—that is, a peripheral awareness, or an awareness on which we are not explicitly concentrating our attention—of the nature of the experience of perceiving or imagining. Imagining is accompanied by a feeling of spontaneity, creativity, and freedom. Perceiving, by contrast, feels more responsive than creative. We have the sense that we are encountering something independent and real, something that constrains and puts strict limits on the activities of the consciousness confronting it.

Sartre's conclusions run counter to three hundred years of philosophical thought on the imaginary. According to the tradition he inherited, images are literally "in" the mind. They are the residues of objects out in the world that one has perceived. According to this view, images are not qualitatively different from the actual objects that give rise to them, but rather are merely degraded forms of these objects, and behave according to the same principles that govern them, which are beyond our control. Consciousness is said to be passive, not only with regard to perception, but in connection with imagination as well. (Sartre, as we have seen, says it is active in both.)

Clearly, there is no room for freedom in such an account of consciousness and its objects (the objects enter into consciousness against our will, and they obey their own laws over which we have no control). The germ of Sartre's argument that consciousness must be free in order for it to encounter imaginaries is that such entities can only be posited by an act of turning away from what is real and present in favor of the realm of the unreal or absent. Sartre's idea is that being is purely positive and can produce only what is positive. On this level there can be a deterministic order—an order of real, existing, entities bringing forth, or causally altering, others. But imaginaries can emerge only as objects of a consciousness capable of disentangling itself from this positive causal order and turning toward what is not, instead. (A consciousness that could not imagine would be "glued down to," or "sucked" or "bogged down," in what is.) Positive being cannot give rise to this nothingness, but consciousness can. As Sartre puts it, "for consciousness to be able to imagine, it must be able to escape from the world by its very nature, it must be able to stand back from the world by its own efforts. In a word, it must be free" (Iy, 184). Thus, it is only "because we are transcendentally free that we can imagine" (Iy, 186).

At the conclusion of *The Imaginary* Sartre argues that imagination is also deeply connected with all of our encounters with the world from the very beginning. The reason is that we never encounter objects in the world in their brute nudity, but rather always under the color of our projects and interests. Different meanings emerge in our encounters with objects based on the different ways in which we direct our attention at them. Thus, different qualities of a bicycle (for example, "broken") emerge in our perception of it when we are engaged in the project of repairing it than do (for example, "beautiful") when we are making a drawing of it. It is not that we construct these meanings out of neutral "sense data." Rather, what we immediately encounter are meanings and the object. We focus, quite spontaneously and at the very outset of our encounters with objects, with those of their features that are especially relevant to our projects, whether as aids or as obstacles. And these projects, in turn, involve the imagining of desiderata that currently are not.

Finally, Sartre's work on imagination culminates in a criticism of one of Husserl's central doctrines, namely, that only phenomena, as opposed to independently existing objects, are given to us in experience. Husserl's claim, quite simply, is that we encounter only the object-as-experience, and this encounter does not entitle us to know what really exists or does not exist independently. Husserl thus asks us to "bracket" or "suspend" the question of the object's real, independent, existence, so that we might instead focus on precisely how it presents itself as an object of experience. But Sartre denies that our experience is silent on the question of the experienced object's independent existence. His main point is that imaginaries and perceptual objects do not differ only in the nature of the conscious act by which they are apprehended. In other words, it is not that one and the same object, not differing from itself in any way, is an object of perception when it is looked at with the eyes and an imaginary when it is conjured through the imagination. Rather, the objects themselves are different. The object of perception is given as really existing, independently, and as really present. The imaginary is given as absent or as not existing.

This issue—whether or not the independent reality of some intentional objects is a datum of experience—is, without a doubt, abstract, technical, and metaphysical. So it would surely seem a daring (if not foolhardy) idea to base an entire novel on its exploration. But that is exactly what Sartre does in his first, and greatest, novel, *Nausea*. There is no better evidence (nor is any needed) for Sartre's talent as a novelist than the fact that this work succeeds as a darkly comic and grippingly dramatic adventure in spite of the fact that its central concern is to show, in opposition to Husserl, that the real, independent, existence of things can make itself manifest to us in our everyday experience. To that novel we now turn.

2

Nausea

Nausea was published in 1938. Significantly, Sartre wrote much of the novel during his year of studying phenomenology in Berlin. His routine that year was to spend his mornings reading Husserl's *Ideas* and his evenings writing *Nausea*.

There is not much to the plot. *Nausea* is cast in the form of a diary of its protagonist, Antoine Roquentin. This technique is necessary, since the interest of the story is psychological and philosophical—it has to do with the central character's thoughts and feelings, most of which would be difficult or impossible to discern merely from an objective account of the events of his life. He has traveled to the small town of Bouville to research the life of the Marquis de Rollebon, whose biography he is writing. Through his diary we learn of Roquentin's ideas, attitudes, and feelings, and Sartre somehow manages to keep up a sense of suspense and drama through these alone. Roquentin *does* very little. He goes to the library for research, strikes up acquaintances with a few of the locals, and has one brief meeting with his estranged lover. Above all else, though, he *thinks*—mainly about philosophy and art. But in spite of this lack of action, the novel is remarkably atmospheric. Its length is crucial. It wouldn't have worked as a short story, for it takes a certain amount of time for the reader to be gradually pulled into Roquentin's strange, disquieting world, and to learn to live and breathe in it. While the general tone or feel of the work is disturbingly dream-like (in a manner that is reminiscent of Kafka), its menacing atmosphere is periodically relieved by the presence of darkly comic elements.

Roquentin's diary begins with this ominous entry: "Something has happened to me." He goes on to explain:

> There is something new, for example, about my hands, a certain way of picking up my pipe or my fork. Or else it is the fork which now has a certain way of getting itself picked up, I don't know. . . . This morning, at the library, when the Autodidact came to say good-morning to me, it took me ten seconds to recognize him. I saw an unknown face which was barely a face. And then there was his hand, like a fat maggot in my hand. I let go of it straight away and the arm fell back limply. (N, 13–14)

What has happened to Roquentin is that he has started to notice the strange alien abundance of things, the way that there is always much more to them than is relevant to notice about them for our purposes at any given time. When we attach words to them, the words apply only to some aspects of them. The things infinitely overflow our descriptions of them—there is always more to them, more details, than we can ever think of or recount or describe. Roquentin has this vision while looking at the tram seat on which he is sitting:

> I murmur: 'It's a seat,' rather like an exorcism. But the word remains on my lips, it refuses to go and put itself on the thing. It stays what it is, with its red plush, thousands of little red paws in the air, all stiff, little dead paws. This huge belly turned upwards, bleeding, puffed up—bloated with all its dead paws, this belly floating in this box, in this grey sky, is not a seat. It could just as well be a dead donkey, for example, swollen by the water and drifting along. . . . Things have broken free from their names. They are there, grotesque, stubborn, gigantic, and it seems ridiculous to call them seats or say anything at all about them. . . . (N, 180, translation modified)

Roquentin is describing here what Sartre would later call the "transphenomenality" of things—the fact that there is always more to them than can be given in any one experience of them, or even in any finite series of such experiences. Things exist "too much"—they go on forever. They can never be finally summarized. There is always another question to ask of things, another way to approach them, another profile—these are infinite and inexhaustible. Things are, therefore, "contingent," "absurd," "superfluous," "in the way," "excessive," "gratuitous," "overflowing." There is always something more to things, no matter how we look at them, and the something more is typically irrelevant, unnecessary to our current concerns (which is why they are merely additional to the aspects on which we are presently focusing.)

Objects of our perceptual experience thus differ, for example, from a geometer's circle. After all, we know everything about the circle when we know its definition (or, more accurately, everything about the circle is contained within, and is in principle discoverable by thinking about, its definition.) So the circle is not transphenomenal, and contains no excess of detail, and thus no absurdity. But such circles are ideal and do not exist. A "real" circle will be made of a certain material, or be drawn with a certain kind of marker; the line will have a specific thickness; the circle will have a definite diameter and circumference, and so forth. As Roquentin puts it, "a circle is not absurd, it is clearly explicable by the rotation of a segment of a straight line around one of its extremities. But a circle doesn't exist either" (N, 185–86).

The transphenomenality, contingency, and absurdity of perceptual objects (together with their other features which distinguish them from circles and other ideal objects) thus point to their independent real existence. Recall in this context Sartre's work on the imagination. I cannot examine an imagined object, which is a product of my consciousness, so as to learn something about it that I don't already know. If I have imagined a flight of stairs, for example, without having imagined the stairs to be of a specific number or color, I cannot then go back to "look" at the stairs so as to count them or to determine their color. Fixing their number or color would then simply be the result of a new act of imagination on my part, rather than a discovery of already existing properties of the imagined stairs. The imaginary object, in short, contains only what I put into it. But the object of perception is, by contrast, inexhaustibly rich. There is always more to learn about it. This is evidence that it is real, external, not a product of my consciousness.

We are rarely aware of this, because we generally look at things under the color of our interests and projects. As a result, we focus on them in a highly selective manner, and remain oblivious to, precisely because they are irrelevant to our present concerns, the infinite excess of meanings and information that they contain. When consciousness intends objects in its normal ways, it encounters *meanings*, not *existence*. Seeing, typically, indeed almost always, is *seeing-as*. We see the *whatness* of things, rather than their *thatness*. What happens to Roquentin in the novel is that his ability to focus in this way, to elevate parts of his perceptual field to the foreground while relegating others to the background, begins, inexplicably and against his will, to break down, so that he is forced to confront the infinitely excessive abundance of things. In this way he achieves a direct awareness of reality—an awareness of existence itself.

This awareness is, of necessity, nonconceptual. For when we think of a thing in terms of concepts we select only those aspects of the thing that fit the concept. The other aspects are disregarded. The capacity of things to overflow all conceptualization cannot, therefore, as a matter of principle, itself be reduced to a concept. It is for this reason that Roquentin emphasizes, as part of his disquieting vision, that the words that he wishes to apply to things fail to attach themselves to them. It is probably also for this reason that Sartre chose the medium of fiction to convey this point. The best way to get readers to understand that the real independent existence of perceptual objects is a datum of experience is to induce them to *have* the relevant experience. That experience cannot simply be described to readers, since it resists linguistic (and other) conceptual categories. But a psychologically realistic work of fiction, if sufficiently lengthy, can gradually pull readers into its world, so that they come to breathe the same air as does the protagonist. In my judgment, Sartre succeeds admirably in this in *Nausea*.[1]

The entire novel can be read as an extended critique of Husserl's "phenomenological reduction." Husserl had proposed

---

[1] Some think that Sartre's discussion of existence in *Nausea* is pragmatically self-refuting, since he uses words to tell us that words are inadequate to convey the being of things. But he isn't using language to *describe* existence so much as he is using language expressively to prompt us to look in a certain way so as to see it for ourselves. Such an interpretation fits well with many of Sartre's remarks on language. For example, in "What Is Literature?" he argues that "language is elliptical," and offers in support of this conclusion the following example: "If I want to let my neighbor know that a wasp has got in by the window, there is no need for a long speech. 'Look out!' or 'Hey!'—a word is enough, a gesture—as soon as he sees the wasp, everything is clear" (WIL, 71).

that, in order to facilitate gaining clear, accurate access to the data of experience, we should set aside, or "bracket," all questions pertaining to the relation between those data and real, existing objects outside of consciousness. In other words, he wanted us to focus on objects of experience, that is, "phenomena," without worrying about whether (or to what extent, or in what ways) these phenomena correspond to independently existing objects. But Sartre tries to show that this independent existence of the external world is itself an inescapable and irreducible datum of our experience, as opposed to a mere (and dubitable) inference from it. There is a vast difference between the experience of a tram seat (or a chestnut tree—the most famous example from *Nausea*), on the one hand, and a melody or a circle, on the other. Objects of our perceptual experience present themselves as abundantly and undeniably real. (This is also an anti-Cartesian point, since Descartes, like Husserl, had claimed that it was possible, at least in principle, to doubt the existence of an external, physical world.)

Absurdity

These considerations allow us to understand in what ways Sartre affirms what is commonly thought to be an existentialist cliché. When people are asked what they think "existentialism" (the philosophical movement with which Sartre is most frequently identified) is all about, they often reply that existentialism teaches that "life" (or "the world" or "existence") is meaningless or absurd. For the most part, this belief is mistaken. For example, Sartre denies that life and the world are meaningless or absurd. Indeed, the reader may recall from our discussion of his "Intentionality" essay that Sartre credits phenomenology with restoring to the world the rich array of meanings and values that we are constantly encountering in our daily experience. But, on the other hand, there are two technical senses in which Sartre does indeed affirm that existence (as opposed to life or the world) is meaningless and absurd.

Recall that to see something as meaningful is, according to Sartre, to see it *as* something, as opposed to seeing it merely as existing. And to see it *as* something is to focus on it in a selective manner, so that some of its features come into view, with others receding into the background. Typically the way this happens is that we encounter things as colored by our projects and interests, so that the tree as encountered by the botanist differs greatly from the tree as encountered by the farmer, which, in turn, differs from the tree as encountered by the landscape artist. So the world, as we ordinarily experience it, is neither meaningless nor absurd, but rather richly meaningful. But existence itself, the sheer is-ness or thatness (as opposed to whatness) of things, *is* meaningless. The meanings of things emerge when we ask *what* they are, what they are *for*, how they relate to other things, and so forth. Thus, meanings can emerge only by means of a focusing activity which would highlight some features of the things in question (for otherwise only the bare, featureless, fact of existence would emerge) and relegate to the shadows their other, irrelevant, features (for otherwise meaning would be drowned out in a cacophony of infinite, incoherent, and incommensurate meanings, as would happen if, for example, instead of telling a story about an amusing incident that happened during my philosophy class this morning, I were to make an impossible attempt to relate every single true fact pertaining to the events that took place there and then [including the body temperatures of the students, the chemical composition of the chairs on which they sat, the identity of the architect who designed the classroom, the position of my class within the university's general education requirements, and so on infinitely]). When such focusing activity is absent, or (much more rarely), when one manages somehow to focus on the sheer is-ness of things (as Roquentin does), the meaninglessness of existence is manifest. (Thus, to return to our earlier example, notice that one cannot even see a tree as a tree without conceptualizing it in a certain way. Conceived otherwise, it might be seen merely as a "green thing," or a "tall thing," or a "coarsely textured thing," and so forth. But to see it not as colored by any such conceptualization would be to see it as undifferentiated existence itself, which is to say as existence devoid of meaning.) But remember, this is a rather technical claim. It merely means that a necessary condition for the emergence of meaning is the activity of a focusing consciousness. It does not mean that life is bleak, or pointless, or that we would all be better off committing suicide.[2]

---

[2] On the other hand, it must be acknowledged that Sartre occasionally issues such gloomy claims as that "every existing thing is born without reason, prolongs itself out of weakness and dies by chance" (N, 191, translation modified). My

The other sense in which existence is meaningless, for Sartre, is simply that it can't possibly be explained. All explanations presuppose existence. Whenever we explain anything, we do so by referring to some other thing or things that exist. Thus, in explaining the rain, we refer to the clouds; in explaining the election results, we refer to the interests and attitudes of the voters; in explaining an illness, we refer to the presence of a virus, and so forth. What would it mean, then, to explain existence? Existence itself, it would seem, is in principle inexplicable.

Notice that this point follows simply from the logic of explanation, and does not turn on Sartre's atheism. For if one attempts to explain existence by saying that God created it, this just pushes the problem back a step. We are still explaining existence in terms of existence, in this case God's existence. We may then simply ask what explains God's existence. If the answer is that God's existence is inexplicable, then we have abandoned the attempt to explain existence, and have admitted that it remains mysterious and unexplained. If the answer is that God has always existed, we may very well then ask what explains *that*. That is no more explanatory than would be the judgment that the world (or, perhaps, matter-energy) has always existed. Similar remarks apply to the claim that either God or the world (or matter-energy) simply emerged at some point *ex nihilo;* that is, it popped into existence out of nothing, from nowhere, without an antecedent cause. This offers us no insight into the origins of existence, and does not count as an "explanation" as that term is ordinarily understood. (You would not trust an auto mechanic who "explained" your car's failure to run in similar terms.) Thus, existence is absurd in the sense that Sartre's contemporary (and friend, before they had a falling out), Albert Camus, popularized —its indifferent silence frustrates our demand to understand. This absurdity, this maddening lack of fit between our desire for an explanation and the resolute meaninglessness of existence, is most effectively dramatized in Roquentin's encounters with the tram seat and with the chestnut tree. Existence is absurd because no reason can explain it—in principle it defies rational explanation.

---

suggestion is that while such utterances undoubtedly serve Sartre's dramatic purposes, it would be highly misleading to construe them as conveying his central philosophical message.

Life and Art

A related theme of the novel is the difference between life and art. Life is messy, unpredictable, and full of superfluous, irrelevant contingencies. (Thus, to recall an earlier example, if you are running up some stairs to escape a would-be assailant, in real life there will be a precise number of steps, and they will be a specific color.) By contrast, all the parts of a (good) work of art are essential and necessary. As Aristotle has noted, "the events which are the parts of [a] plot must be so organized that if any one of them is displaced or taken away, the whole will be shaken and put out of joint. . . ."[3] (So if the chase up some stairs were to be part of a work of fiction, the number and color of the stairs would be mentioned only if they were relevant.) In telling a story based on real life, one is ruthlessly selective. Inessential details are left out. All that remains is essential and necessary. Similarly, while stories and songs typically have clear beginnings and endings, life does not. Thus, Roquentin remarks in his diary, "I wanted the moments of my life to follow one another in an orderly fashion like those of a life remembered. You might as well try to catch time by the tail" (N, 63).

Incidentally, this underscores a second justification for Sartre's use of the diary form in presenting his novel. A diary is loose and disjunctive, just as life itself, as lived, is. If the story were to be told after the fact, with inessential contingencies left out, it would have the perfection and unreality of art. But Sartre wants something else in order to convey his ideas more realistically and convincingly. A diary also captures the feeling of uncertainty and freedom—we don't know what's coming next; much of it depends on what the protagonist chooses to do. In *What Is Literature?* Sartre criticizes fiction that is written after the fact, from an omniscient point of view: "A past was delivered to us which had already been thought through . . . [but] no art could really be ours if it did not restore to the event its brutal freshness, its ambiguity, its unforeseeability . . ." (WIL, 185).

Notice that Sartre's point about the difference between narrative and life relates to his theories about the reflective constitution of the self in *Transcendence of the Ego*. To tell a story about something that has happened in one's life is to graft structure and form

---

[3] Aristotle, *Poetics* 1452a, trans. James Hutton (New York: Norton, 1982), 54.

onto something that had been amorphous and transphenomenally rich. As more and more stories are told (whether out loud, to others, or simply to oneself, in the quiet of one's own thought), the selective inclusions, exclusions, and emphases gradually result in the construction of a self—an ideal object, similar, in some respects, to a work of art. But we tend to fool ourselves about the nature of this self, taking it to be a natural object, with an essence that we discover, as opposed to a constructed object, with an essence that we determine by choosing to focus on some elements of an infinitely rich transphenomenal field (or series) while disregarding others.

Telling stories creates illusions in other ways too. As events are unfolding, their outcomes are uncertain. But when we tell the story later, knowing how things have turned out, this knowledge colors our understanding of (and our telling about) the events in question. For example, if we tell the story of a marriage that we know to have ended in divorce, we are likely to focus, in our telling, on those aspects of the marriage that prefigure its dissolution. In this way the divorce is made to appear inevitable, determined, when, as lived (and, in Sartre's view, in fact) it was not. Thus, when we tell a story about the past, the contingency of events is artificially removed, and everything that happened is made to have happened necessarily. A life thus becomes like a melody.

(This process is facilitated by the movement from prereflective to reflective consciousness. Life is lived mostly on the prereflective level. But telling a story about one's life is a reflective endeavor. There is no adventure, and very little order, in the former. These appear only in the latter.)

Sartre's example of a work of art that escapes the contingency of ordinary life is a song, "Some of These Days." Not only is every note necessary, but the melody is also indestructible. It cannot be destroyed by demolishing the recording, for example. (Roquentin mentions that the record is scratched, but that the melody is untouched by this imperfection in one copy of one recording of it.) So, while one's life is both finite and full of pointless contingencies (that is, elements that are superfluous, unnecessary, and, in that sense, unjustified), good art is not. It can achieve a kind of perfection, timelessness, purity, and precision that no human life could ever hope to achieve. Accordingly, at the conclusion of the novel Roquentin considers the idea that he might be able to find the missing justification for his existence by creating art. He resolves to write a novel.

Why Write?

While the uncompromising realism of *Nausea* (together with its analysis of existence as transphenomenal and contingent) is retained throughout Sartre's career as a writer and thinker, he would go on to reject the idea that one could or should write in order to achieve personal salvation. (Indeed, his subsequent criticism of it is so severe as to suggest to some readers, rather implausibly in my view, that *Nausea* should be read as ridiculing it satirically.) Sartre's concept of the committed writer—developed most prominently in *What Is Literature?*—better represents his stable position on the purpose and significance of writing. There he suggests that the quest for personal immortality and the pursuit of justification for one's own existence are shallow, selfish motives for writing. There is something contemptible, Sartre argues, about wanting to find salvation in what others think of oneself (in this case, a great writer, a creator of works of enduring value). And in any case, writers cannot control the interpretation that readers will freely give to their works. Moreover, writers who care at all about facing the world realistically must acknowledge the likelihood that their works, and they themselves, as authors of those works, will eventually be forgotten. So writers should, instead, write to disclose the world, reveal the truth, and bring about change. Authentic, or committed, writing is not motivated by a desire to be needed by readers, and to be positively objectified by them. Rather, it is an expression of, and an acknowledgment of, freedom at every turn—that of the writer and of the readers.

Sartre's changing conception of the role of the writer and of the purpose of writing probably stemmed, in part, from his increasing interest in political issues as he grew older. Typically, he himself attributed this change to an improvement in his grasp of reality. For example, in a 1964 interview he remarked, "what I lacked [then] was a sense of reality. I have changed since. I have slowly learned to experience reality. I have seen children dying of hunger. Over against a dying child *Nausea* cannot act as a counterweight" (LBSM, 62). Indeed, it cannot. But the world still needs great art, even if that art is powerless to combat injustice or to ameliorate suffering. And even the later, more radically politicized, Sartre recognized the artistic merits of *Nausea*, as when he said of it, in "Self-Portrait at Seventy," that "from a purely literary point of view, I think it's the best thing I have done" (L/S, 24).

3

Being and Nothingness

Being and Nothingness, a massive philosophical work exceeding 700 pages in length, was published in 1943. Amazingly, it took Sartre less than two years to write this densely complex volume, and he did so during a period in which he also wrote a novel (*The Reprieve*) and a play (*The Flies*), and held a full-time job as a teacher (he was not yet earning enough from his writing to be able to quit teaching and devote himself to writing full time).

The quality of the writing in this book is thoroughly uneven (which is hardly surprising, given the speed with which it was written). In several places Sartre overuses ponderous philosophical terminology, employs needlessly convoluted syntax, and constructs sentences and paragraphs of undue length and complexity. But he also provides intermittent relief from all this abstraction and obscurity by including numerous illustrative examples of rich and brilliant clarity. Many of these examples rank among the most vivid, richly detailed, and memorable in the history of philosophical writing. In them Sartre's literary and dramatic skills are put on full display.

The subtitle of the book is "A Phenomenological Essay on Ontology." Ontology is the study of being, and Sartre here attempts to describe the fundamental categories of being and their interrelations. He does so by means of phenomenology—an investigation into what is given to consciousness. Recall that Sartre shares with earlier phenomenologists the conviction that most philosophers (and scientists) tend to distort (or bury) phenomena because they are concerned to convince us of the truth of their guess about the nature of the reality that (allegedly) underlies and explains these phenomena. But a complete explanation of the physics and physiology of color perception, for example, will not tell us anything about what the experience of seeing the color blue is like, or, for that matter, about the nature of "blue" as an object of perception. Most philosophers tell us nothing about consciousness, little about the qualitative aspects of experience, and nothing about phenomena as such, except insofar as they are alleged to be revelatory of an underlying reality. So philosophy does not tell us much about what our lives are like. Sartre wishes to remedy this.

This raises an immediate problem. How can a book that takes a phenomenological approach deal with ontology, the study of being? After all, phenomenology is concerned with phenomena—that is, with what appears to consciousness—and precisely not (at least in its more orthodox versions) with what really exists. When Sartre speaks of "being," however, he often has in mind not entities or substances, but rather the *way* or *manner* in which something exists. So a discussion of "the being of consciousness" is not about what kind of entity consciousness might be. It is concerned, instead, with the various modalities of being conscious—a subject that *is* accessible to phenomenological description.

In Sartre's introduction to *Being and Nothingness* he presents his fundamental distinction between being-in-itself (as a first approximation, the being of things, of objects for consciousness, of unconscious beings) and being-for-itself (intentionality, the being of consciousness). Being-for-itself is purposive; being-in-itself isn't. A conscious being exists for-itself in the sense that it is aware of itself, stands apart from itself, thinks about itself, and has a relationship with itself. The being of a chair, by contrast, is in-itself, that is, identical with itself, at no distance from itself, having no awareness of, or relation to, itself.

Consciousness also differs from a chair, as we recall from our discussion in the "Phenomenology" chapter, in that it is neither a thing nor a container of things. Nothing is in consciousness, including one's character or ego. These are objects *for* consciousness. Consequently, being for-itself's intentional relation to being in-itself is not that of one thing toward another, but rather that of a negation that articulates being, carving it into a world. On Sartre's view, there is *being* without consciousness, but not a *world*. Consciousness, through its intentionality (that is, its active, focused looking), shapes and articulates the massive, undifferentiated, meaningless plenitude that is being-in-itself. This carving up, this introduction of negation, Sartre calls "nihilation." (The term seems to mean "nothing making.") Being-for-itself is the being by which nothingness enters the world. Being-for-itself makes a world out of being-in-itself through negation, much as a sculptor makes a sculpture through negative carving—by removing part of a slab of stone. To see a world of individual things meaningfully related to one another is to elevate part of the perceptual field to the foreground and to relegate other parts of it to an undifferentiated background.

Interrogation

Sartre offers, as an example of the way in which being-for-itself is related to being-in-itself, the simple act of asking a question. Notice, first of all, that questioning requires selective focusing. Things and states of affairs contain an unlimited number of features, about which an infinite number of questions might be asked. But no one could possibly be interested in pursuing all of these lines of inquiry; and it would, in any case, be impossible to investigate them all at once. Thus, the asking of a question requires a discriminative attention that shines a spotlight on some aspects of a thing while ignoring others. To inquire into the possibility of opening a locked door, for example, is, at least typically, to take no notice of the door's color. In this way the asking of questions facilitates the emergence of meaning, in part by forcing the infinite cacophony of other possible meanings to recede, at least for the moment, to the background.

Thus, the asking of questions introduces negation into the otherwise undifferentiated positivity of being-in-itself. This happens, in part (as we have just seen), from the fact that the selective focusing involved in questioning requires the suppression of some aspects of being so that others might be highlighted for attention. But in addition, as Sartre reminds us, the asking of a question generally requires (rhetorical questions aside) an absence (or nonbeing) of knowledge on the part of the questioner. Moreover, the question brings to light the ever-present possibility of a negative reply. (Sartre points out that this is true of all questions, and not merely those that are explicitly formulated as requiring a yes or no answer. If I ask my guests whether they want cake or pie for dessert, it is always possible that they will answer "neither" or "nothing." Similarly, why-questions always admit, on principle, the possibility of "for no reason" as a reply, just as where-questions might be answered with "nowhere," and who-questions with "nobody.") Finally, even a positive answer implies negation, in that the answer entails that "it is thus and *not* otherwise." Thus, the discovery that it is indeed possible to open a locked door introduces negativity not only by pushing issues concerning the door's color, age, and chemical composition into the background, but also by revealing the door to be *not* impossible to open.

Perhaps most significantly, Sartre argues that questioning is a kind of proof of freedom. His argument is that being-in-itself, which is subject to causal laws, is fully positive, so that the asking of a question, which introduces a multitude of negativities into being, can be accomplished only by wrenching oneself free and clear from the positive realm of deterministic laws of cause and effect. Accordingly, he claims that it

> is essential . . . that the questioner have the permanent possibility of dissociating himself from the causal series which constitutes being and which can produce only being. If we admitted that the question is determined in the questioner by universal determinism, the question would thereby become unintelligible and even inconceivable. . . . Thus in so far as the questioner must be able to effect in relation to the questioned a kind of nihilating withdrawal, he is not subject to the causal order of the world; he detaches himself from Being. (BN, 58)

Sartre's argument that freedom is manifested in questioning is just one of many ways in which he contends that freedom involves the introduction of negation into being. Indeed, the connection between freedom and negation is one of the major themes of the book.

Destruction

Consider, for example, Sartre's seemingly preposterous remark that "man is the only being by whom a destruction can be accomplished," and that "*it is man* who destroys his cities through the agency of earthquakes . . . [and] who destroys his ships through the agency of cyclones . . ." (BN, 39–40). Sartre's point is not that human beings somehow create, control, and direct earthquakes and cyclones, as if these violent forces would never otherwise be able to come into existence. That would be crazy. Nor is he asserting that earthquakes and cyclones only exist "in the mind," and are otherwise unreal.[1] His claim, rather, is that in order for the rearrangement of matter that these natural forces bring about to count as "destruction," nihilating acts of consciousness are necessary. What is required is a conscious witness who can recall the ordered arrangements that presently *are not* (because they have been destroyed by the earthquake or cyclone), and who can evaluate the present arrangement *as not* the city that once existed. Being-in-itself is purely positive. There is one positive arrangement of matter before the storm, and a different positive arrangement afterward. The second arrangement can count as a destroyed city only for a consciousness that can go beyond what is positively given in order to evaluate it in terms of what it is not, of what it no longer is. Thus, the argument for a connection between negativity and freedom is, once again, straightforward. Destruction (a much more violent form of negativity than is mere questioning!) is impossible without nihilation; and nihilation is impossible without freedom; therefore, the phenomenon of destruction stands as evidence for the freedom of consciousness.[2]

Absence

But Sartre's ideas concerning the nihilating powers of consciousness can perhaps most clearly be seen in his discussion of the phenomenon of absence. Sartre offers the following example. I have an appointment to meet my friend Pierre at the café at four

---

[1] Sartre makes it clear that "destruction, although coming into being through man, is an *objective fact* and not a thought." Similarly, he remarks that the destruction of a vase "would be an irreversible event which I could only verify" (BN, 40).

[2] Note, in line with Sartre's comments quoted in note 1 above, that a free consciousness, while a necessary condition for destruction, is not a sufficient one. I must be able to nihilate the given in order to see in the aftermath of an earthquake a destroyed city; but then, it may be that no earthquake comes, and the city remains intact. And while I must be able to foresee a future that currently is not in order to regard a vase as fragile, it remains possible that the vase in question has been constructed in such a way as to render it relatively invulnerable to destructive forces, so that it is, in fact, not fragile.

o'clock. I arrive fifteen minutes late. I know that Pierre is always punctual. As I begin to look for him in the café, I am forced to confront the unpleasant possibility that he may not have waited for me. At the conclusion of an exhaustive search of the café, I reluctantly conclude that he is not there.

On the basis of a richly detailed phenomenological description of the experience of looking in earnest for Pierre only to encounter his absence, Sartre draws several conclusions: (1) Being-in-itself is fully positive and contains no negativities, such as absences. As Sartre points out, "it is certain that the café by itself with its patrons, its tables, its booths, its mirrors, its light, its smoky atmosphere, and the sounds of voices, rattling saucers, and footsteps which fill it—the café is a fullness of being" (BN, 41). (2) Absences require focusing activities of consciousness in order to appear. Thus, my discovery of Pierre's absence from the café depends upon my act of looking for him and expecting him to be there. After all, an infinite number of other people and things are also not to be found in the café at any given time, and yet an inventory of the café's contents presumably would not include these abstract, unexperienced, absences. (3) The freedom of consciousness is illustrated, in part, by the fact that the objects in my perceptual field cannot determine for me what I will see. Rather, what I perceive will largely depend upon the intentionality, or directedness, of my consciousness. For, as Sartre puts it (and note that his method is phenomenological—he is concerned to describe what is given in experience, as opposed to offering a theory about what reality is outside of experience),

we must observe that in perception there is always the construction of a figure on a ground. No one object, no group of objects is especially designed to be organized as specifically either ground or figure; all depends on the direction of my attention. When I enter this café to search for Pierre, there is formed a synthetic organization of all the objects in the café, on the ground of which Pierre is given as about to appear. This organization of the café as the ground is an original nihilation. Each element of the setting, a person, a table, a chair, attempts to isolate itself upon the ground constituted by the totality of the other objects, only to fall back once more into the undifferentiation of this ground; it melts into the ground. For the ground is that which is seen only in addition, that which is the object of a purely marginal attention. Thus the original nihilation of all the figures which appear and are swallowed up in the total neutrality of a *ground* is the necessary condition for the appearance of the principal figure, which is here the presence of Pierre. This nihilation is given to my intuition; I am witness to the successive disappearance of all the objects which I look at—in particular of the faces, which detain me for an instant (Could this be Pierre?) and which as quickly decompose precisely because they "are not" the face of Pierre. (BN, 41)

(4) Pierre's absence is an intentional object (that is, an object of experience, or something actually encountered), as opposed to something that is merely thought about, in an abstract application of the category of negation. As Sartre puts it, "it is an objective fact at present that I have *discovered* [Pierre's] absence, and it presents itself as a synthetic relation between Pierre and the setting in which I am looking for him" (BN, 42). (5) While my conscious expectation of Pierre's presence is necessary for my discovery of his absence, it is not sufficient. Had Pierre actually been in the café waiting for me, I would have discovered his presence, rather than his absence. In that case I surely would have been "suddenly arrested by his face," and the entire café would have organized itself around him (BN, 42).

While the example of Pierre's absence from the café demonstrates that consciousness *can* go beyond what is given, highlighting certain of its aspects, relegating others to an undifferentiated background, and thus, through its nihilating activities, encountering a meaningful world, it would be highly misleading to see such going-beyond merely as one of consciousness's *possibilities*, as opposed to its inescapable and ever-present obligation. For *no* perceptual field or set of circumstances announces its own meaning or instructs us as to how it should be organized for our attention. We are *always* free, Sartre argues, to determine by the direction of our focusing which elements of our perceptual (or conceptual, or imaginary) field will be elevated to the status of figure and which will sink into the ground. Thus, all conscious acts, whether they are acts of looking, thinking, imagining, or what have you, are free. The terms "consciousness" and "freedom" are coextensive. We always *must* go beyond, and nihilate, what is given. This is one of the meanings of Sartre's famous remark that we are "condemned" to be free.

To put the point another way, freedom—a "noetic" freedom, or freedom of focusing and of thought that is even more fundamental than freedom of choice—is manifest in the simple observation that seeing, typically, is seeing-*as*. We encounter a meaningful world, not a meaningless chaos. We do so because of the focusing, selecting, intending, and attentive activities of consciousness, by which we can see an apple as exemplifying "red" or "round" or "fruit," and so forth, or highlight it precisely as an apple, or attend to the fact that it is a particular kind of apple, such as a golden delicious, or notice any one of the infinite number of ways in which it might be combined with other objects in the field of items available for my attention, or, finally, cause it to recede into an unnoticed background by directing our gaze to matters utterly unconnected to it.

A major strength of this analysis of noetic freedom is that it sheds a good deal of light on the phenomenology of freedom of choice. For it is indeed a basic datum of experience that the "givens" that we confront do not affect us mechanistically. They do not stand as simple causes for which our actions would be the effects. Rather their effect on us depends crucially on how we understand them, interiorize them, adopt an attitude toward them, undertake a project with respect to them, and so on. We always act in context, in situation, but the situation is not simply objective. The objective facts that one confronts must be interpreted and understood, and it is this interpretation and understanding that forms the background against which a person acts. It is for this reason that no factual state of affairs can, all by itself, motivate (let alone cause) an action. One must *understand* this factual state of affairs, and one will do so, typically, in the light of one's projects, interests, and background knowledge.

Anguish

All of these themes (the connection between freedom and negation, the refusal of the given to announce its own meaning or to motivate [let alone cause] any action whatsoever, and the constant need for consciousness to go beyond whatever is present to it in the field of its attention, among others) are further clarified in Sartre's extensive analysis of anguish. Moreover, Sartre breaks new ground here in explaining (1) the most direct evidence that consciousness has of its own freedom, (2) the radically ambiguous nature of the relationship between consciousness and its own past or future, and (3) the failure of consciousness to coincide with or be identical with itself, seemingly in violation of the principle of identity. (The principle of identity simply claims that A = A, that is, that anything at all "is what it is," and is the same thing as itself. In quite radical contrast to this, Sartre repeatedly says of consciousness that it "is what it is not, and is not what it is.")

According to Sartre, the phenomena of questioning, destruction, and the perception of absence all stand as evidence, or even proof, of freedom. But the move from these pieces of evidence to the conclusion that we are free requires reasoning, or the drawing of inferences. This raises the question as to whether it is possible to know one's freedom more directly, just as I might know of your presence in this room simply by seeing you there. After all, Sartre's philosophy would seem to imply that it is possible to gain unmediated access to one's own freedom. For, as we recall from the phenomenology chapter, on Sartre's view consciousness is always self-aware, and it can always adopt the mode of reflection, in which it takes itself directly for an object. Thus, if consciousness is, as Sartre maintains, always free, it follows that consciousness should be able to stare its own freedom right in the face through an act of reflection. And indeed, Sartre affirms the reality of this reflective consciousness of freedom. He calls it "anguish," and asserts that "it is in anguish that man gets the consciousness of his freedom" (BN, 65).

Sartre begins his analysis by distinguishing anguish from fear. I am fearful when I am concerned about a threat from without. In one of his examples, I am afraid when I am walking in the mountains and suddenly find myself at the edge of an abyss without a guardrail. My fear is that an external force, such as a sudden gust of wind or the sliding of rocks beneath my feet, might cause me to plunge to my death.

But now suppose that I respond to my fear by resolving to proceed with the utmost caution, paying careful attention to each step and remaining maximally wary of the wind, the rocks, and any other potentially dangerous elements in my surroundings. The problem is that I might then worry about my own future performance. How can I be sure that I won't start to relax and become overconfident after walking a ways without incident? How can I know *now* that I will continue to exercise maximum caution throughout the period in which I will be in danger? This concern about my own future conduct—in this case that I might carelessly expose myself to danger—is what Sartre means by "anguish."

This example tells us much about how we stand in relation to the future. Determinism implies that the future is closed, that what will happen now has been decided by what has happened in the past, and that what will happen next, in turn, will be determined by what is happening now. But our anguish in the face of the future shows that the data of our experience speak powerfully against determinism. Such anguish reveals an open future that we not only can, but must, continually make through our actions.

So I can be anguished about my future. But is it really *my* future? In a sense it is, but in another very real sense it isn't. For notice that if I, right now, could control or determine the future conduct of the mountain walker, there would be no occasion for anguish. That conduct would be fixed and settled, and there would be no basis for worrying about it. But on the other hand, it is clear that the reason why the worrying is so acute is precisely that the future walker is me, and not someone else. So insofar as a self persists through time, I *am* the future mountain walker; but insofar as a self changes over time, and, more to the point, insofar as this future self is temporally separated from me now, and insofar as the conduct of this future self is therefore beyond my present control, I *am not* the future mountain walker. Thus, my relationship to my own future is thoroughly ambiguous. "I am what I am not, and am not what I am." Or, to be more precise, "*I am the self which I will be, in the mode of not being it*" (BN, 68). "Anguish," then "is precisely my consciousness of being my own future, in the mode of not-being," since "the decisive conduct will emanate from a self which I am not yet . . ." (BN, 68–69).

Notice, however, that if I were able to rely on my past to fix my present and future conduct there would be no need for anguish in the face of the future. I could instead simply act now so as to insure that my future conduct would be what I presently desire it to be. Then, when the moment of my future action arose, my future self would find that its conduct had been fixed by the past actions of its past self (that is to say, by my actions in the present). Thus, Sartre, in his description of anguish in the face of the future, is moved to deny explicitly that my present self can rely on my past self or that my future self can rely on my present self. As he puts it, "the self which I am depends on the self which I am not yet to the exact extent that the self which I am not yet does not depend on the self which I am" (BN, 69).

But is it really true that my present self cannot rely on my past self? To show that it is, we must move from anguish in the face of the future (the kind of anguish in which, in Sartre's clever formulation, I make an appointment with myself in the future and then worry that I won't show up to keep the appointment [BN, 73]) to anguish in the face of the past. To illustrate such anguish, Sartre offers a dramatic phenomenological description of the anguish

of the gambler who has freely and sincerely decided not to gamble anymore and who, when he approaches the gaming table, suddenly sees all his resolutions melt away. . . . The earlier resolution of "not playing anymore" is always *there*, and in the majority of cases the gambler when in the presence of the gaming table, turns toward it as if to ask it for help; for he does not wish to play, or rather having taken his resolution the day before, he thinks of himself still as not wishing to play anymore; he believes in the effectiveness of this resolution. But what he apprehends then in anguish is precisely the total inefficacy of the past resolution. It is there doubtless but fixed, ineffectual, surpassed by the very fact that I am conscious *of* it. The resolution is still *me* to the extent that I realize constantly my identity with myself across the temporal flux, but it is no longer *me*—due to the fact that it has become an object *for* my consciousness. I am not subject to it, it fails in the mission which I have given it. The resolution is still there, I *am* it in the mode of not-being. . . . I should have liked so much not to gamble anymore; yesterday I even had a synthetic apprehension of the situation (threatening ruin, disappointment of relatives) as *forbidding me* to play. It seemed to me that I had established a *real barrier* between gambling and myself, and now I suddenly perceive that my former understanding of the situation is no more than a memory of an idea, a memory of a feeling. In order for it to come to my aid once more, I must remake it *ex nihilo* and freely. The not-gambling is only one of my possibilities, as the fact of gambling is another of them, neither more nor less. I *must rediscover* the fear of financial ruin or of disappointing my family, etc., I must re-create it as experienced fear. It stands behind me like a boneless phantom. It depends on me alone to lend it flesh. I am alone and naked before temptation as I was the day before. After having patiently built up barriers and walls, after enclosing myself in the magic circle of a resolution, I perceive with anguish that *nothing* prevents me from gambling. (BN, 69–70)

As this example suggests, I cannot rely on my past self, since my past is no longer me (but is rather an object for me), and since there can be no escaping the constant need freely to surpass, or go beyond, whatever is given as an object for my consciousness. Thus, Sartre's analyses of anguish in the face of the future and of the past mirror his other analyses of my consciousness's nihilation of, and failure to coincide with, items with which it is frequently identified, such as my "self" or ego, my personality, interests and dispositions, and my motives. I *am not* any of these, since they are objects *for me*. Similarly, the objects in my perceptual field do not organize themselves into a situation for my benefit, let alone offer me direction as to how to respond to them. Rather, they become meaningful and comprise a situation only in the light of my surpassing them in reaching toward some end. Anguish arises, then, when I desperately want to escape my ever-present freedom and responsibility to nihilate the given, and wish instead to allow my personality, or resolutions, or motives, or situation to determine for me what I am to do. What I then find is that these objects for my consciousness always fail to perform this desired function, but instead ceaselessly refer me back to my own freedom. I am free because I can exploit (indeed I can't help but do so, even when I wish not to do so—hence my anguish) the gap that always exists between my consciousness and its objects (including my past and my character). One must always choose by exploiting this gap.

In interpreting these claims of Sartre's it is important to recall that he is offering a descriptive, phenomenological account of freedom, rather than a speculative metaphysical theory. His point is that we *directly experience* our freedom. That is, we directly experience such phenomena as our lack of coincidence with ourselves, the inability of factual givens to dictate to us their meanings, the insufficiency of motives to determine what we will do, and our anguish. In short, we experience the unending task of having to choose, and of having to accept responsibility for those choices. These phenomena, according to Sartre, are inescapable elements of human experience, confronted equally by everyone in all situations. They are not conclusions, arrived at by a process of reasoning from other data, but rather are primary data themselves. Thus, we cannot help but think of ourselves as free, not because we have some sort of (determined) psychological compulsion to do so, but rather because our freedom is an omnipresent and inescapable datum of our experience.

Often we find this consciousness of freedom unpleasant, a fact that is reflected in Sartre's choice of "anguish" as a name for it. We are thus motivated to flee our anguish by denying our freedom. In this way we try to rid ourselves of the irksome obligation to act and to take responsibility for our choices. But Sartre insists that we know that we are free, so our denial of this knowledge constitutes an attempt at self-deception. When I tell myself that I am a victim of circumstances, that I had no choice but to do what I did, and that I am not to blame for the mess I've made of things, I am, Sartre claims, lying to myself. His name for such self-deceptive lying is "bad faith."

Bad Faith

Sartre begins his discussion of bad faith by pointing out that it is paradoxical. In order for me to deceive myself I must both know the truth and not know it. For there is no *deception* if I am merely mistaken, and tell myself a falsehood that I fully believe to be true, and there is no *self*-deception if I know the truth and, while retaining for my own benefit a lucid awareness of this truth, deny it solely for the sake of deceiving another. So bad faith requires that I both know the truth (so that my denial of it constitutes a lie, rather than a mere error), and not know it (so that I am genuinely deceived). But that seems obviously contradictory. How can I both know something and (at the same time and within the unity of a single consciousness) not know it?

And yet, it is evident that self-deception is widespread. We've all observed people close to us in the act of attempting (often successfully) to convince themselves of comforting beliefs that we know they know to be false. Indeed, psychological terms for subcategories of this phenomenon, such as "rationalization" and "denial," have become household words. More to the point, I trust that my readers will have no difficulty in recalling such conduct in their own pasts. (If they think that they can remember no such conduct, they might do well to scrutinize that belief itself as a possible instance of bad faith!)

Bad faith thus calls for an explanation, since its existence appears at the same time to be both undeniable and impossible.

Moreover, the puzzle of bad faith presents itself in an especially acute form to Sartre, since he holds that consciousness is always self-aware, and he accordingly rejects Freud's invocation of the unconscious to solve the problem.[3] But Sartre's interest in bad faith goes far beyond a desire to solve a challenging intellectual problem. His main point about it is that the very existence of bad faith provides further evidence for his conclusions, drawn from his analyses of anguish, concerning the ambiguous and non-self-identical being of consciousness.[4] As he puts it, "the condition of the possibility for bad faith is that human reality, in its most immediate being . . . must be what it is not and not be what it is" (BN, 112).

To see why this is so, and to begin to understand how bad faith is possible, I think it is useful to consider the techniques that advertisers, public relations personnel, political propagandists, and other masters of dishonesty use to facilitate their deception of *others*. Consider the following two principles: (1) It is easier to deceive by means of *misleading* statements that are, strictly speaking, true (or at least partially true), than it is by telling outright lies. And the chief instruments of such nonlying deception are *omission* and *emphasis*. They are effective since, while it is relatively easy to question, and then to seek to verify or refute, explicit claims (and those claims themselves often provoke such a response), it requires much more in the way of critical thinking skills to consider what impor-

---

[3] Sartre's critique of Freud on this point is lengthy (see BN, 90–96), and it would take us too far afield to pursue it in detail here. His main point, however, is this. While Freud claims to solve the problem of self-deception by cutting the psychic whole into two (the "id" and the "ego"), so that it is no longer one and the same entity that deceives and is deceived, it still turns out that the ego "in order to apply its activity with discernment must know what it is repressing" (BN, 93). In other words, as Sartre understands him, Freud claims that a person can deliberately repress an idea, burying it in his or her unconscious, and yet be unaware of doing so. Freud's theory contradicts itself, then, by implying that one psychic entity, the ego, can be both aware and unaware of the same thing at the same time.

[4] In subsequent works Sartre also devotes a good deal of attention to bad faith from a moral point of view. He denounces it as a vice, and calls instead for "authenticity," which he says "consists in having a true and lucid consciousness of the situation [and] in assuming the responsibilities and risks that it involves. . . ." He adds that "there is no doubt that authenticity demands much courage and more than courage. Thus it is not surprising that one finds it so rarely" (ASJ, 90).

tant information may have been simply omitted from a message, and how that message may have been distorted by means of a one-sided emphasis. And the (relatively rare) discovery that a piece of communication is indeed a misleading half-truth is unlikely to discredit its source in the same way or to the same degree as would be the case with the exposure of a blatant lie.

(2) *Vagueness* and *ambiguity* aid deception much more than does clear and precise communication. A clear statement is much easier to refute than is a vague (that is, a hazy, indistinct, or imprecise) or ambiguous (that is, one that admits of two or more plausible interpretations) one. For one must expend a good deal of critical energy in the project of attempting merely to understand an unclear utterance. If this preliminary project is skipped, or abandoned prior to its completion, then the subsequent project of attempting to establish the truth or falsity of the utterance cannot even begin. Moreover, since the task of interpreting unclear messages is often a difficult one, and generally less interesting than is the pursuit of verification or falsification, the unclarity of such messages tends to discourage the critical project at the outset. Furthermore, ambiguity and vagueness, when coupled with a skillful appeal to the intended audience's prejudices and interests, can facilitate the successful *suggestion* of a message that would not be received so uncritically if it were stated clearly. Finally, vagueness and ambiguity immunize a claim from refutation, since it can always be plausibly claimed that an attempted refutation rests on a misinterpretation.

Let us return now to bad faith. If Sartre's analysis is sound, the principles just mentioned, which serve advertisers and propagandists so well in their project of deceiving others, are also precisely the ones we use to fool ourselves. For while I cannot believe a blatant lie that I might tell myself (I can't swallow what I know to be a falsehood, especially when I'm staring it right in the face), I can perhaps learn to avert my gaze, scrupulously and consistently, from certain unpleasant matters, while keeping uppermost in my mind (and perhaps exaggerating) others, and thereby convince myself of misleading partial-truths. Similarly, I can become skilled at making sure that unwanted but dimly and hazily perceived truths never receive from me the sustained, clarifying gaze that would remove their vagueness, and that similarly unclear but comforting falsehoods never receive the critical scrutiny necessary to establish their falsehood. And these principles, in turn, are facilitated by (and in some cases require) the nihilating powers, self-division, and ambiguous being that Sartre claims characterize my consciousness.

Consider Sartre's claims about the radical ambiguity of human existence in this light. His main point is that while a table or a chair simply is what it is, I am always engaged in a project, hurtling toward the future (which currently is not), which I move toward by acting (which is to say by negating what currently is). On the other hand, there are facts that pertain to me, and, while I am not them in the same way that a table is a table, it would be wrong to deny that I am them in *any* sense. Whereas a table exhausts itself in the facts that pertain to it (such as its height, weight, color, texture, and so forth), I am always at some distance from the facts that apply to me. I am not my height because I am conscious of it, and have an attitude toward it, and undertake projects dealing with it. (In all of these ways I "transcend" my height, along with all of my other facticities.) So, in one sense, I am not my height. But it would equally be absurd to deny that I am the height I am, and to claim instead that I am a foot taller or shorter. So Sartre says that I "am what I am not and am not what I am," and this ambiguity facilitates a kind of self-deception in which I can play up either the sense in which I am my facticities, or the sense in which I transcend and am not them. In either case I affirm a half-truth and avert my gaze from the full truth. (Alternatively, I might slide back and forth between the two senses.)

Thus, self-deception need not entail the impossible task of making oneself believe a clear and obvious lie that one is staring in the face—that there are 100 elephants in the room right now, for example. Rather, due to the equivocal nature of human existence, bad faith can be accomplished by trading on ambiguities, and through selective looking and avoiding (that is, by emphasis and omission). Sartre argues that we are always in situation—an ambiguous synthesis of the factual givens of our life (facticity) and our ways of living them by surpassing them (transcendence—which involves selectively focusing on some features and not others, interpreting those in a certain way, forming projects with reference to them, and so forth). The ambiguity of this synthesis makes bad faith possible. One can lie to oneself either by denying one's transcendence ("I can't help it; that's just the way I am") or by denying one's facticity ("The evil creep who did that—that's not really me; I'm a church-goer; I give to charities;" and so forth).

Consider, for example, my connection to my social role. I *am* my role insofar as it characterizes me (that is, it is *my* role, rather than someone else's), but I am *not* it insofar as it is an object for me (that is, it is distinct from the consciousness that I presently am, since that consciousness is currently taking it for its object). And, as we have seen, this ambiguity facilitates my bad faith, since it allows me, by means of emphasis and omission, rather than that of bald-faced lying, to affirm misleading half-truths about myself. I can do this by focusing on one or the other of the two ways of looking at my equivocal relationship to my role, while systematically ignoring the other. Thus, if I am ashamed of my role (that of drug dealer, child pornographer, prostitute, or philosophy professor, for example) I can tell myself, with some degree of plausibility, that I *am not* that role, that I am rather the free consciousness that is now contemplating this role (and, perhaps, is also planning to abandon it), and which, by virtue of doing so, swings free of having to identify itself with that role.

On the other hand, if I wish to identify myself with my role, I can do so by emphasizing to my self the (true) fact that this role is indeed mine, by trying to keep my consciousness riveted to the performance of its duties while engaged in that role, and by averting my gaze from the way in which that role becomes distant from me when I focus on it directly. Sartre's example (BN, 101–3) is that of a waiter who attempts desperately to *realize* his role, and thus to be a waiter and *nothing but* a waiter. Sartre makes the further point that this attempt at bad faith is supported by the public at large, which demands of all persons in the service industry that they give up their status as autonomous human beings and exhaust themselves utterly in serving their social function. And the service industry personnel, in turn (perhaps for reasons of economic necessity), seem willing to oblige. Thus we have

> the dance of the grocer, of the tailor, of the auctioneer, by which they endeavor to persuade their clientele that they are nothing but a grocer, an auctioneer, a tailor. A grocer who dreams is offensive to the buyer, because such a grocer is not wholly a grocer. Society demands that he limit himself to his function as a grocer, just as the soldier at attention makes himself into a soldier-thing with a direct regard which

does not see at all, which is no longer meant to see. . . . There are indeed many precautions to imprison a man in what he is, as if we lived in perpetual fear that he might escape from it, that he might break away and suddenly elude his condition. (BN, 102)

It should also be noted that the meaning of my role, like that of my other facticities, is not self-announcing, but rather can emerge only through interpretive acts of consciousness. Here the point, familiar from Sartre's discussion of the phenomenon of the experience of absence, is that perception (and, for that matter, conception) always involves the elevation of some elements in the field of my potential attention to the foreground and the relegation of others to the background. But these elements do not organize *themselves* in this way, so the organization depends on me. Generally what happens is that my interests and projects guide my focusing on items in my perceptual or conceptual field, so that I tend to notice items that are relevant and important to those interests and projects, and to pay much less attention to those that are not. Moreover, I interpret the items to which I do devote my attention in terms of categories that are relevant to my projects and interests (so that what I observe in a bicycle when I am planning to paint it is different from what I notice in it when I am planning to ride it). So I must "go beyond" what is given if that given is to emerge as meaningful in my experience. I make contact with it only as I rush past it in the process of executing an action that has my interpretation of it as its partial foundation. I thus am not my acts, roles, psychic states, and emotions, because by the time these givens emerge as meaningful in reference to me I have already gone beyond them and interpreted them in such a way as to reveal them as the mere background against which I am acting.

My nonidentity with my facticities therefore facilitates my bad faith in at least two ways. First, as already noted, it renders my denial that *I am* the uglier and more reprehensible aspects of my facticity merely a misleading half-truth, rather than an out-and-out lie. Secondly, the fact that the meanings of my facticities do not simply attach themselves to me, but rather depend for their emergence on me, makes it easy for me to present a highly distorted and one-sided picture of myself to myself, and to do so, once again, without resorting to lies, but instead by the tried-and-true method of emphasis and omission. Moreover, the task of convincing myself that I am doing nothing untoward in thinking of myself in this way is made easier by my realization that I cannot help but present the facts concerning myself to myself in a highly selective manner, since all thought and perception, and the emergence of all meaning, depends upon the construction of a figure (what is emphasized) on a ground (what is omitted). So it is not as if I could have given a comprehensive and nonslanted account of myself, but instead merely *chose* to give a selective and slanted one; or that I could have accepted the objective, pre-given meanings of my facticities, but instead *chose* to offer an interpretation of them; or that I could have arrived at this interpretation through passive contemplation, but instead *chose* to cause it to emerge by carrying out a project, directed toward an open future, against which it served as a background. Thus, my recognition of the fact that the meaning of my role (for example) must await my interpretation, and that this interpretation will necessarily be selective, bars me from offering a quick, principled objection to my one-sided story, and thereby makes it easier than it otherwise would have been for me to convince myself that my thoroughly dishonest whitewash is perfectly reasonable and legitimate.

This is not to say, however, that it is impossible to take an honest, accurate, nondistorted view of even such slippery and ambiguous matters as my facticity, my transcendence, and their interrelations. To the contrary, Sartre insists that "these two aspects of human reality are and ought to be capable of a valid coordination" (BN, 98). To show this, he offers the example of a homosexual and his friend, "the champion of sincerity," both of whom he judges to be in bad faith. The homosexual is in bad faith because he denies his facticity. While acknowledging all the facts that would lead an impartial observer to regard him as a homosexual, "he refuses to draw from them the conclusion which they impose" (BN, 107). Rather, his strategy is to emphasize his transcendence, and to develop an interpretation of his past conduct whereby it can be viewed as not indicative of a deeply rooted tendency. The champion of sincerity, on the other hand, who demands only that his friend admit that he is a homosexual, is in bad faith because he denies his friend's transcendence. He sees his friend as a kind of thing, an unfree being with a fixed essence, whose past conduct also constitutes his future destiny. Both of these individuals assert a half-truth. What they each assert is true with respect to one-half of the transcendence-facticity duality, but false with respect to the other half. To avoid bad faith, then, one would have to attain, and then honestly confront, a lucid understanding of the coordinated interplay between these two dimensions of human experience. Thus, the homosexual would not be in bad faith if he were to say, "to the extent that a pattern of conduct is defined as the conduct of a homosexual and to the extent that I have adopted this conduct, I am a homosexual. But to the extent that human reality can not be finally defined by patterns of conduct, I am not one" (BN, 108, translation modified).

Similar remarks apply to other ambiguous structures of human existence. They, too, can either be exploited so as to facilitate bad faith, or else lucidly and honestly comprehended, so as to avoid it. Consider, for example, the senses in which (as we discussed in connection with anguish) I both am and am not my future and my past. In some cases it makes little difference whether a given case of bad faith is analyzed in terms of the facticity-transcendence duality or the past-future duality. For example, if I am ashamed of my past (an aspect of my facticity), I can respond by identifying myself entirely in terms of my transcendence (an aspect of my future). Or if I am afraid of (in anguish about) my own future conduct, I can choose to identify myself in terms of some aspect of my past (for example, a vow, or resolution that I pretend actually binds or determines my present and future conduct). But in other cases, the past-future duality makes a different kind of bad faith possible. For example, why do people so frequently engage in behaviors that put their future health at risk? Why, for instance, do so many people smoke? While some, undoubtedly, exhibit bad faith by going into "denial" about the health risks of smoking, I suspect that many smokers simply fail to identify the future victims of their conduct as themselves. That is, if I am a smoker I can exploit the fact that the future emphysema sufferer or cancer victim is, in some sense, "not me." In this way I can regard my conduct as unthreatening to "me," a person whose identity I fix with reference to the past and present, and perhaps merely feel pity for the old man, so temporally (and therefore, according to my bad faith, essentially and entirely) remote from me, who will suffer the consequences.

It is also worth recalling in this context two other dualities of consciousness. Consciousness may be either in a prereflective or reflective mode, and either thetically or nonthetically aware of a given object. These ambiguities—these ways in which conscious-ness is self-divided—further facilitate bad faith.

Let's begin with the latter distinction. Suppose I am engaged in a practical task, such as washing dishes or changing guitar strings. While performing this task I initially focus intensely on what I am doing. Thus, I am thetically aware of "dishes and soap" or of "strings and tuning pegs," and only marginally aware (that is, non-thetically aware, which is to say aware without focusing my atten-tion on it) of many other things (for example, that the room is a little cold, that I'm getting too much static in my radio reception, that I need to figure out a better way to explain the compatibilism versus incompatibilism debate to my introductory philosophy stu-dents, and so forth). But suppose that I am also nonthetically aware of something complicated and multifaceted, the sort of thing that could only be made clear by a good deal of sustained, focused attention. Writers, for example, often find that ideas creep up on them in this way. They will be doing something else, and concentrating on this other activity, when they begin to notice that they have an inarticulate, unorganized sense of what they might want to say. But they also know, from plentiful and almost excep-tionless experience, that in order to get clear on it, they will have to pay close attention to their thoughts, put them in order, draw out their implications, and so forth. So, if for some reason they wished not to achieve this clarity, all they would have to do is refrain from taking these steps. Similarly, in one kind of bad faith one has a dim, inarticulate awareness of something about which one wants to avoid achieving full, vivid clarity. So one simply averts one's gaze. For example, I might be lucidly aware of numerous instances in my past of some kind of misconduct, and yet make a kind of point of never focusing on them, or of asking myself what sort of pattern they suggest. This is clearly self-deception, but it falls somewhat short of a full-fledged lie to myself. It relies, instead, on the technique of keeping vague things vague, and of exploiting consciousness's self-divisions, in this case by making sure that a certain objective content fails to bridge the thetic/non-thetic divide.

To put it another way, *distraction* is a crucial bad faith skill. In explaining this point, Sartre makes the curious claim that "one *puts oneself* in bad faith as one goes to sleep . . ." (BN, 113). It is diffi-cult to fall asleep by explicitly focusing on that task. Rather, it works much better to focus, and thus make the object of one's thetic awareness, something else—something calming, dull, and absorbing.

The prereflective/reflective duality facilitates bad faith in much the same way. Recall that in the prereflective mode consciousness is directed out toward objects in the world, whereas in reflection consciousness takes for its object its own actions. Painting a distorted, but highly flattering, portrait of oneself (and convincing oneself of its accuracy) can then be accomplished by the simple means of a systematic bias in the adoption of a prereflective or reflective mode of consciousness. That is, when I am doing despicable things, I direct my attention outward, keeping it riveted to the objects with which I am dealing, and I refrain from directing my gaze back toward the shameful acts themselves. But during the (perhaps much rarer) instances when I am doing something laudable, I interrupt my prereflective engagement with external objects frequently, so that I might properly appreciate, and indeed bask in, my nobility and virtue. Over time one can become highly skilled at sliding from prereflective to reflective consciousness in this highly selective manner (and at failing to notice that one has developed this talent)!

But perhaps the most important skill needed for successful self-deception is an ability to allow oneself to be persuaded by weak evidence. The way this works, typically, is not that I first recognize that the evidence for a belief I would like to hold is weak, and only then convince myself to believe it anyway. The much more likely progression is this. First I want to believe something. Then, having already started to believe it, solely on the basis of my desire to do so, I begin to look for evidence in its support. (Notice that this is already a biased and dishonest inquiry; it is not a search for all relevant evidence, as part of an effort to determine the truth, but is rather a highly selective search for evidence that will lend credence to a predetermined conclusion.) Since I have a vague worry (one that I keep vague by scrupulously refraining from focusing on it or interrogating it) that I might not be able to find much evidence, I decide before the inquiry begins (again, without explicitly formulating it this way to myself) to use a low evidentiary standard. As Sartre puts it, "Bad faith does not hold the norms and criteria of truth as they are accepted by the critical thought of good faith. What it decides first, in fact, is the nature of truth. . . . [Bad faith] stands forth in the firm resolution *not to demand too much*, to count itself satisfied when it is barely persuaded, to force itself in decisions to adhere to uncertain truths" (BN, 113).

It is not difficult to understand how such a strategy might be effective. While it would seem to be impossible for me to convince myself of what I *know* to be false, a mere paucity of evidence in support of a belief appears to constitute no such obstacle to my acceptance of it. After all, I don't *know* that it is false; there is *some* evidence that it might be true; and it is not exactly clear *how much* evidence is required to make a belief reasonable in the first place. Still, I will not be able to deceive myself in this way if I frankly recognize that I have made a prior decision to allow myself to be persuaded by nonpersuasive evidence. Thus, to be in bad faith, I must deceive myself not only about the issue with which I am directly concerned to deceive myself, but also about my project of self-deception itself. Thus, "the project of bad faith must be itself in bad faith. I am not only in bad faith at the end of my effort when I have constructed my two-faced concepts and when I have persuaded myself." Rather, the "original project of bad faith is a decision in bad faith on the nature of faith" (BN, 112–13). In order to succeed in deceiving myself about my own project of bad faith, what seems to be required is a strategic refusal on my part to focus on my own conduct in matters of inquiry and belief, including my choices with regard to evidentiary standards. And this refusal, in turn, is made possible, as we have seen, by the division of consciousness into either thetic or nonthetic, and either prereflective or reflective, modes of awareness.

Instead of simply lowering one's standards of evidence, an additional technique of bad faith is to engage in an unscrupulous and inconsistent sliding back and forth between different standards of evidence. Thus, if I am in bad faith I will accept weak evidence in support of views I favor, while simultaneously demanding strong evidence for beliefs that I wish to reject. For example, a fundamentalist Christian who accepts uncritically the miracle stories contained in the Bible may become a tough-minded skeptic when confronted with similar stories in the sacred texts of other religions. (Such a person may say, "how can I be sure these documents are authentic?"; "who were these witnesses?"; "how do I know they were honest and reliable?"; "I'll bet there's a rational, naturalistic explanation"; and so forth). Or again, a U.S. government spokesperson (or "mainstream," that is, pro-corporate, journalist) who condemns an invasion carried out by an enemy state as an unlawful act of aggression may reject as idealistic (if not naively utopian) an identical criticism of a U.S. invasion, claiming that "of course great and powerful nations will use force, if necessary, to achieve their objectives."

Some who make use of double standards like these may do so with a clear understanding of what they are doing. Such people, in Sartre's terminology, are cynics; they are not in bad faith. But the use of such double standards is more likely to indicate bad faith than cynicism. Most people would not like to (and do not) think of themselves as deceitful, cynical manipulators; they would rather (and do) see themselves as fair, objective, and reasonable. So a failure to notice their inconsistent use of evidentiary standards facilitates their maintenance of a positive self-image. Moreover, were they lucidly aware of their double standards they would merely be able to deceive others; they would not be able to use such double standards to enable themselves to believe what they want to believe. And even when the issue is confined merely to that of convincing others, bad faith is in many respects a superior strategy to that of cynicism. I will probably be more convincing, more believable, if I am perceived to believe what I am saying than if I am not so perceived; and I will be more likely to be so perceived if I truly do believe what I am saying.

In many of Sartre's other works he addresses bad faith from an ethical and political standpoint. One of his findings is that bad faith, and especially the employment of evidentiary double standards, underlies racism. For example, in *Anti-Semite and Jew*, he points out that those who complain that "there are too many Jewish lawyers" would never make similar remarks were there an abundance of doctors from Brittany. Instead they would simply say, "Brittany provides doctors for the whole of France" (ASJ, 16).[5]

Since reason and truth, for obvious reasons, are enemies of bad faith, it is not surprising that anti-Semites and other bigots tend to

---

[5] Sartre had anticipated some of these ideas about the bad faith of anti-Semites, and presented them in fictional form, in his early short story, "The Childhood of a Leader." It can be found in *The Wall and Other Stories*, trans. Lloyd Alexander (New York: New Directions, 1975).

hold them in rather low regard, or else to reject them entirely. As Sartre explains, they do so

> because of a longing for impenetrability. The rational man groans as he gropes for the truth; he knows that his reasoning is no more than tentative, that other considerations may supervene to cast doubt on it. He never sees very clearly where he is going; he is "open"; he may even appear to be hesitant. But there are people who are attracted by the durability of a stone. They wish to be massive and impenetrable; they wish not to change. Where, indeed, would change take them? We have here a basic fear of oneself and of truth. What frightens them is not the content of truth, of which they have no conception, but the form itself of truth, that thing of indefinite approximation. It is as if their own existence were in continual suspension. But they wish to exist all at once and right away. They do not want any acquired opinions; they want them to be innate. Since they are afraid of reasoning, they wish to lead the kind of life wherein reasoning and research play only a subordinate role, wherein one seeks only what he has already found, wherein one becomes only what he already was. This is nothing but passion. Only a strong emotional bias can give a lightning-like certainty; it alone can hold reason in leash; it alone can remain impervious to experience and last a whole lifetime. (ASJ, 18–19)

It is clear that Sartre regards this rejection of reason and truth as immoral. For example, he repeatedly points out that we must seek the truth if we are to be responsible (in part because if we do not know the truth about what needs to be changed, or about what means are likely to be effective in changing it, we will be unable to carry out successfully our obligation to change the world for the better), and declares that the courting of ignorance is irresponsible. Here is just one representative passage, from his posthumously published *Truth and Existence*:

> The will to ignore is . . . the refusal to face our responsibilities. Since indeed, Being appears, in principle, as that for which we have to assume responsibility without having wanted it, the For-itself can project the veiling of Being in order not to be obliged to assume it. As a bourgeois I want to ignore the proletariat's condition in order to ignore my responsibility for it. As a worker, I may want to ignore this condition because I am in solidarity with it and its unveiling obliges me to take sides. I am responsible for everything to myself and to

everyone, and ignorance aims to limit my responsibility in the world. (TAE, 52)

Given the burdensome nature of this all-encompassing responsibility, it is not surprising that people often wish to evade it, and that bad faith is, as a consequence, as pervasive as it is. Still, bad faith, like any other project of deception, is difficult and worrisome. One can never escape the threat of being found out. And this danger is especially acute in the case of bad faith. When lying to another, one has the advantage of being able to focus, with laser-like intensity, on every technique one is using to make the deception convincing. But when the person to be deceived is oneself, such explicit focusing would obviously be self-defeating. So the person in bad faith cannot so effectively be "on guard," and thus must constantly run the risk of suddenly encountering, and thereby becoming lucidly aware of, his or her project of self-deception, in which case that project fails. Thus, Sartre points out that "the existence of bad faith is very precarious," and its structure is "metastable" (BN, 90).[6]

In spite of this inherent precariousness, however, Sartre finds that "bad faith is a type of being in the world . . . which by itself tends to perpetuate itself" (BN, 113). Indeed, "it can even be the normal aspect of life for a very great number of people. A person can live in bad faith," in that bad faith characterizes his or her "constant and particular style of life" (even though its metastable character insures that such a person will endure many "abrupt awakenings") (BN, 90). Sartre suggests that bad faith is very pervasive indeed, and many readers take his overall message to be that it is virtually inevitable and inescapable. Only in a footnote, at the very end of his thirty-page discussion of bad faith, does he clearly disavow this reading. There he affirms that one can, after all, "radically escape bad faith." But he immediately adds, rather cryptically, that "this supposes a self-recovery of being which was previously corrupted. This self-recovery we shall call authenticity, the description of which has no place here" (BN, 116, n. 9). The

---

[6] According to translator Hazel E. Barnes, "metastable," a word of Sartre's own invention, means "subject to sudden changes or transitions" (BN, 90, translator's note 2). Sartre also calls the transcendence-facticity duality, which, as we have seen, is a basic instrument of bad faith, a "*metastable* concept" (BN, 99).

proper place for such a description, according to Sartre, is in a consideration of ethics. Later in this chapter I will take up Sartre's ideas on authenticity and the rejection of bad faith in just such a context.

Knowledge

But for now, let's consider instead Sartre's understanding of knowledge. In addition to its intrinsic interest, this topic is important to Sartre's project in BN of attempting to explain the fundamental ways in which consciousness is related to being-in-itself, since, as it turns out, one of the most significant of these is knowledge. Indeed, the first section in BN on knowledge is entitled "Knowledge as a Type of Relation Between the For-Itself and the In-Itself" (BN, 240).

Sartre's most important finding about knowledge is this.

> There is only intuitive knowledge. Deduction and discursive argument, incorrectly called examples of knowing, are only instruments which lead to intuition. When intuition is reached, methods utilized to attain it are effaced before it; in cases where it is not attained, reason and argument remain as indicating signs which point toward an intuition beyond reach; finally if it has been attained but is not a present mode of my consciousness, the precepts which I use remain as the results of operations formerly effected, like what Descartes called the "memories of ideas." . . . Intuition is the presence of consciousness to the thing. (BN, 240)

Intuition, then, is the direct "seeing" or "grasping" of something, whether it be a physical object, a concept, a principle, or what have you, without the intermediary of reasons. To know by intuition that a given principle is true is to attain a lucid understanding that it is true on the basis of directly inspecting it, rather than as a result of surveying evidence or evaluating arguments. Many philosophers deny that there is any knowledge of this kind (or else claim that such knowledge is relatively trivial, informing us only of the ways in which concepts are related to one another, but telling us nothing about what the world is like). Sartre, in quite radical contrast, insists that intuitive knowledge is the only kind of knowledge that there is.

Sartre's claim may strike some readers as irrational, since it seems to denigrate arguments and reasoning. But he does not deny their importance as "instruments which lead to intuition." They are, in fact, crucial, because without them we often cannot get close enough to the knowledge claim in question to see it clearly. Logic, reasoning, arguments, evidence—all of these, when used properly, facilitate this clear insight. They can do so by calling to my attention an aspect of the claim that I had overlooked; or by distinguishing the claim from another, subtly different one, with which I had confused it; or by correcting a mistaken conclusion I had drawn about one of the claim's implications; and so forth. So these instruments—these fundamental tools of critical thought— can lead us to knowledge by, so to speak, bringing us up closer to the object about which we are inquiring, bringing it into a sharper relief and focus, and, in general, allowing us to get a good, long, clear, unobstructed "look" at it. But if after consulting these tools I still fail to achieve such insight into the object in question, then I also fail to acquire knowledge of it. On the other hand, if I am able to get a sufficiently good luck at the object without the use of these instruments, then I am also able to acquire knowledge with- out them. Finally, if I achieve insight only as a result of using the tools of critical thought, it is nonetheless the case that it is the insight that brings me knowledge, not the fact that this or that method, procedure, or tool of inquiry has led me to that insight. To put this last point another way, the tools of critical thought can never replace intuition, even when they facilitate it. That is, they can never, in the absence of intuition, deliver knowledge. In order to know something I still must see it directly (and clearly), and derive my knowledge from this direct inspection, even in those cases in which I need the tools of critical thought in order to achieve such clear and direct access to it.

In defense of Sartre's position, notice that if one denies it, and insists instead on the more orthodox view that it is impossible to achieve knowledge without the intermediary of reasons, the (unwitting) result is clearly skepticism—the doctrine that nothing can be known. The reason is this. If I, in order to know A, must show that A follows from B, then so must I show that B follows from C (for otherwise I could not claim to know B, in which case I also would not know A, which B implies), and (for the same rea- son) that C follows from D, that D follows from E, and so on infinitely. Thus, if I know anything at all (which Sartre, in agreement with common sense, thinks I do), I must know some things directly, as opposed to reasoning to them from other things I know.

Considering the movement from one link to another in a chain of inferences can make the same point. Suppose, once again, that I claim to know A on the basis of the fact that it follows from B, which in turn follows from C, which in turn follows from D, which in turn follows from E. Now, instead of inquiring as to how I know E, let's ask how I know that E implies D. Either I see this directly, that is, by intuition, or I do not. If I do, then intuition plays a crucial role in the acquisition of knowledge, even when the piece of knowledge in question is the conclusion of a rigorously deductive logical argument. If I do not, then I will need a reason to enable me to understand why D follows from E. Perhaps I will be told that E implies F, which then implies D. If I still do not grasp the connection between E and D, then more explanatory premises can be interpolated. I will learn that E implies G, which implies F, which implies D; that E implies H, which implies G, which implies F, which implies D, and so forth. Either this process of adding interpolated premises continues infinitely, in which case the conclusion is never reached and knowledge is never achieved, or at some point one directly "sees" or grasps that one assertion follows from another. So if we know anything, we must, once again, know some things directly, that is, by intuition.

On the basis of these considerations, it would seem, then, that all knowledge is intuitive. Either I clearly grasp and understand a principle by inspecting it directly, or I do not. If I do, then I know it intuitively. (The fact that no process of reasoning was used does not bar it from inclusion in the realm of knowledge since, as we have just seen, all reasoning requires intuition at every point.) If I do not, then I will need an argument; I will need reasons. But my argument will have to make use of premises which are either known intuitively or grounded in other premises that are so known, and the movement from one premise to another will also either depend on an intuitive grasping of the entailment of one point by another or else require additional premises sufficient to prompt this intuitive grasping. For if one premise is not identical to another one, then insight is needed in order to understand that one is entailed by the other (and this point holds no matter how many, or how few, interpolated premises are needed in order to spark this insight). Where this insight is lacking, there is no knowledge. Where it is present, there is knowledge. But in that case, the "methods utilized to attain it are effaced before it." So all knowledge is intuitive.[7]

Others

Sartre's analysis of knowledge is the climax of his nearly 300-page discussion of the basic relations between being-for-itself and being-in-itself. But he closes part two of *Being and Nothingness* with the observation that there is "for human reality another mode of existence as fundamental as being-for-itself . . ." (BN, 298). Sartre devotes part three of BN to a lengthy consideration of this third region of being, that of "being-for-others."

His principal finding is that I get my most vivid and compelling sense of myself when I see myself reflected in the eyes of another, as when I suddenly realize that someone has caught me doing something shameful. When this happens I obtain a powerful and direct intuition both of my own embodied objectivity (my consciousness is revealed to be not only a pure point of view on the world, but also an object within it) and of the other's consciousness.

We do not acquire these intuitions when we encounter the Other merely as an object among other objects. Sartre's example

---

[7] On this point Sartre is a faithful disciple of Husserl, who writes: "*Immediate 'seeing,'* not merely sensuous, experiential seeing, but *seeing in the universal sense as an originally presentive consciousness of any kind whatever*, is the ultimate legitimizing source of all rational assertions. . . . If we see an object with full clarity, if we have effected an explication and a conceptual apprehension purely on the basis of the seeing and within the limits of what is actually seized upon in seeing, if we then see . . . how the object is, the faithful expressive statement has, as a consequence, its legitimacy. Not to assign any value to 'I see it' as an answer to the question, 'Why?' would be a countersense" (Edmund Husserl, *Ideas Pertaining to a Pure Phenomenology and to a Phenomenological Philosophy: First Book*, trans. F. Kersten [The Hague: Martinus Nijhoff, 1977], #19, 36–37).

Accordingly, Husserl states his "principle of all principles" as follows: "*that every presentive intuition is a legitimizing source of cognition, that everything originarily . . . offered* to us in '*intuition*' is to be accepted simply as what it is presented as being, but also *only within the limits in which it is presented there*" (Husserl, *Ideas*, #24, 44).

concerns a man whom I observe passing in front of some benches in a public park. When I regard him merely as an object, I understand him in terms of the same categories that I use to comprehend the objects standing near him, and I construe his relation to those objects as purely additive. He exists in the field of my conscious awareness in the order that my point of view imposes on him. Because I apprehend him solely as an object, I do not perceive any subject-object relationship between him and the other objects present.

But suppose I perceive him, not merely as an object, but as a person. Suppose, for example, that I apprehend him as looking at objects in the park, such as the benches, the lawn, and the Keep Off the Grass signs. To do so is to see him as encountering, and as organizing differently in his world, some of the same objects that I am simultaneously encountering and organizing in mine. As a result, this sort of confrontation with the Other is characterized by "the appearance among the objects of *my* universe of an element of disintegration in that universe . . ." (BN, 343). In this sense the Other steals the universe from me.

> Everything is in place; everything still exists for me; but everything is traversed by an invisible flight and fixed in the direction of a new object. The appearance of the Other in the world corresponds therefore to a fixed sliding of the whole universe, to a decentralization of the world which undermines the centralization which I am simultaneously effecting. (BN, 343)

Even here, however, Sartre insists that I am encountering the Other as an object, albeit one of a special kind (one that "sees what I see," and organizes it differently) rather than as a subject. It is only through my awareness of being seen by the Other that the Other becomes a subject for me. I must become an object for the Other in order to "apprehend the presence of his being-as-subject" (BN, 344-45). Furthermore, it is extremely difficult (and perhaps impossible) for me to remain in the mode of prereflective subjectivity when I am aware of "being-seen-by-the-Other," and it is impossible for the Other to be an object for me at that time. (As Sartre memorably puts it, "It is never when eyes are looking at you that you can find them beautiful or ugly, that you can remark on their color. The Other's look hides his eyes . . ." [BN, 346].) The

Other's being-as-subject appears simultaneously with my being-as-object.

Sartre's name for this third kind of encounter with the Other is "the look." He offers the following (typically literary and dramatic) example. Because of my jealousy, I have just glued my ear to a door and am peeping through a keyhole in an attempt to learn what is going on behind the door. I do not reflect, but rather focus with extraordinary intensity on the external objects with which I am concerned. "This means" [and note Sartre's phenomenological language, in which objects are described from the standpoint of the intentionality of consciousness] "that behind that door a spectacle is presented as 'to be seen,' a conversation as 'to be heard.' The door, the keyhole are at once both instruments and obstacles; they are presented as 'to be handled with care'; the keyhole is given as 'to be looked through close by and a little to one side,' etc." (BN, 347–48). Because I remain in the prereflective mode, and thus do not focus on my actions, I do not characterize them to myself or evaluate them in any way, let alone consider broader issues, such as what they might say about my character. Rather, my consciousness exhausts itself in its concern for "the ends to be attained" and by "the instruments to be employed" (BN, 348). I act as pure subject.

But then I suddenly hear footsteps in the hall and turn to discover a set of eyes witnessing my deeds. My consciousness, having been diverted from its concern for the spectacle to be seen behind the closed door to an awareness of the new presence that is now looking at me, is quickly diverted again to the reflective mode. I take my actions explicitly as objects for my attention, and respond to them with feelings of shame and self-disgust, which had been absent prior to my being seen by the Other. The consciousness which had been acting nonreflectively suddenly becomes inhabited by a self. I see myself as an object, fixed in space and time, with definite, specifiable qualities (as "pathologically jealous," "a stalker," "a voyeur," and so forth), frozen by the gaze of the Other (BN, 349).

It is important to note that "the look," that is, the relation being-seen-by-the-Other, is not contingent on the actual physical presence of a subject encountering me. Thus, while "the look" is usually manifested by the convergence of two eyes in my direction, the look will be given just as well on occasion when there is a rustling of branches, or the sound of a footstep followed by silence, or the slight opening of a shutter, or a light movement of a curtain. During an attack men who are crawling through the brush apprehend as a *look to be avoided*, not two eyes, but a white farmhouse which is outlined against the sky at the top of a little hill. (BN, 346)

Sartre's insistence that the look does not always require even a set of eyes, let alone the presence of another consciousness, may seem surprising, since he simultaneously claims that it is through the look that we most clearly know the existence of the Other as a consciousness. The traditional "problem of other minds" had been based on the assumption that I can have no direct access to any subjectivity other than my own, so that while I can see the bodies and the behaviors of Others, I cannot observe their consciousnesses. On this view, my conclusion that Others are conscious can only be arrived at through an analogy between their behavior and mine. The standard account is that I directly observe the stream of consciousness that accompanies my actions; so, when I observe others behaving similarly in similar circumstances, I conclude that their actions are accompanied by a similar stream of consciousness. Sartre's theory of the look is different, then, in that it claims that I can experience the subjectivity of Others directly—by becoming an object for the Others—and that I perceive my being-as-object (and the Others' corresponding being-as-subject) by means of the look. But if, as we now learn, the look need not require the real presence of the Other's consciousness, then what remains of Sartre's claim that it gives us direct access to the Other's subjectivity?

His reply is that, while it is always open to doubt whether another consciousness is actually present in any given experience of the look, that experience nonetheless makes it impossible to doubt either my own being-as-object for the Other or the existence of Others who (in general and in principle, even if not, in fact, in this particular case) see and objectify me.

To illustrate this, Sartre asks us to consider a variation on his example of the jealous Peeping Tom at the keyhole. Suppose that when I suddenly hear footsteps in the hall (and, as in the original version of the example, respond by feeling a wave of shame sweeping over me), this time, rather than encountering a set of eyes looking at me, my frantic search of the corridor reveals that no one is there. It was a false alarm. I am relieved. No one has seen me.

Still, though in this case no Other was (in fact) actually physically present, the experience nonetheless powerfully refers me to my own objectivity and to the subjectivity (in general and in principle) of the Other. Indeed, as Sartre explains, the false alarm places me in the presence of the Other so powerfully that it may very well result in my giving up on my voyeuristic project. And if I do persist in it, "I shall feel my heart beat fast, and I shall detect the slightest noise, the slightest creaking of the stairs." I will experience the Other as "present everywhere, below me, above me, in the neighboring rooms," and I will "continue to feel profoundly my being-for-others." Indeed, "if I tremble at the slightest noise, if each creak announces to me a look, this is because I am already in the state of being-looked-at." Thus, what is revealed to be false in my false alarm is neither the existence, nor the presence to me, of the Other-as-subject, but rather (and merely) one aspect of the Other's facticity. As Sartre puts it, "what is doubtful is not the Other himself. It is the other's *being-there; i.e.,* that concrete, historical event which we can express by the words, 'There is someone in this room'" (BN, 370).

Sartre's main concern, however, is not with the Other's existence as such, but rather with the role that the Other plays in acquainting me with my own objectivity. Without the other, I am trapped within the confines of my own subjective perspective. To be sure, I can reflect, and thus focus directly on my own conscious actions; but I might, through bad faith, do this in a highly selective and distorting fashion, and, in any case, I still will not escape from my own point of view. But the Other, as "the indispensable mediator between myself and me" (BN, 302), can force me to confront what I would prefer to ignore, and to see myself through the eyes of the Other. For, as Sartre points out, "Shame is by nature *recognition.* I recognize that *I am* as the Other sees me" (BN, 302).

The Body

And what the other sees is, among other things, my body. Moreover, it would appear that my body, far from being a mere inert thing, is conscious. (Think, for example, of what goes on when you type, play tennis, or drive a car.) So consciousness, to put the point another way, is embodied. Thus, Sartre's analysis of the ways in which consciousness is related to the in-itself would be seriously defective if it failed to account for the body, and instead insisted that what confronts being-in-itself is a disembodied consciousness. But Sartre's analysis does not suffer from this defect, as he devotes a seventy-page chapter to the body, and tries to show that being-for-itself is "wholly body" and "wholly consciousness." Thus, he explicitly rejects the idea that consciousness is something separate from a body that might be united with it, and insists instead that "the body is wholly 'psychic'" (BN, 404). And yet, for reasons unknown to me, it is widely believed that Sartre completely neglects or dismisses the body, and favors instead René Descartes's conception of consciousness as "pure," and as utterly separable and distinct from the body. Indeed, so frequently and routinely is Sartre criticized on this score that Hazel E. Barnes has been moved to offer this response: "far from postulating a disembodied consciousness, Sartre seems to me to have examined the ontological complexity of our existence as conscious bodies more thoroughly than any other philosopher, with the possible exception of [Sartre's younger colleague Maurice] Merleau-Ponty, whose work is hardly thinkable without Sartre as his point of departure."[8]

Sartre's first move is to invoke his distinction between being-for-itself and being-for-others, in an attempt to solve what has come to be called "the mind-body problem" (that is, the problem of attempting to explain the relationship between consciousness and the body). To appreciate the force of this problem, consider this. On the one hand, consciousness and the body seem obviously to be connected to one another. For example, the body "knows" how to ride a bicycle or to play the piano; when I consciously decide to get up and make a sandwich, my body follows through; modifications of my body (stepping on a tack) lead to conscious sensations (pain); conscious thoughts (my car payment is overdue) lead to physiological reactions (rise in blood pressure, accelerated heartbeat); a severe blow to the head often at least temporarily alters consciousness (generally for the worse); and the death of the

---

[8] Hazel E. Barnes, "Sartre and Feminism: Aside from The Second Sex and All That," in *Feminist Interpretations of Jean-Paul Sartre*, ed. Julien S. Murphy (University Park, PA: The Pennsylvania State University Press, 1999), 36.

body, so far as we can tell, causes the death of consciousness. But on the other hand consciousness and the body appear to be very different sorts of things.[9] For example, the body obviously exists in space and has a definite size, shape, and location, none of which appears to be true of consciousness—so that the nature of the relationship between the body and consciousness seems thoroughly obscure. (Where, for example, would interactions between consciousness and the body take place?)

Sartre's point about this problem is that it is usually made needlessly difficult by a failure to compare consciousness and the body on the same ontological level. Whereas I approach the body as a thing, which, like other physical objects, is fully accessible to others, I think of consciousness as it is *for me*, reachable only by my own direct inner intuition. So

> if after grasping "my" consciousness in its absolute interiority and by a series of reflective acts, I then seek to unite it with a certain living object composed of a nervous system, a brain, glands, digestive, respiratory, and circulatory organs whose very matter is capable of being analyzed chemically into atoms of hydrogen, carbon, nitrogen, phosphorous, *etc.*, then I am going to encounter insurmountable difficulties. (BN, 401)

The difficulties, then, stem from the fact that I am comparing my consciousness as it is for-me (or for-itself) with the body as it is for others. For "the body which I have just described is not *my* body such as it is *for me*. I have never seen and never shall see my brain nor my endocrine glands" (BN, 401). Moreover, if I were to see them, illuminated on a screen while I am undergoing a medical procedure, perhaps, I would apprehend them as "wholly constituted object[s]," as existing in the midst of the world with other objects. It would only be through a reasoning process that I might come to see them as mine, and even then they would appear more as "my *property* than my being" (BN, 402). To see my body as an object is to see it as it is for others. That object, to be sure, does

---

[9] As we recall from the discussion in the phenomenology chapter above, Sartre would reject this way of conceptualizing the problem, since he thinks of consciousness as something like a force or an activity or a relation, and specifically not as a thing.

not appear to be conscious, and it is difficult to form a clear picture of how it might be related to a consciousness. But my body as it is *for me*, as I live it (rather than observe it), is conscious. When I decide to drink some water, and then do so, it is not the case that my consciousness stands apart from and somehow directs my hand to grasp the glass and bring it to my mouth, or my lips to assume a shape conducive for bringing the water into my mouth and back to my throat, or my throat to swallow. Nor is it the case that my hand, mouth, lips, and throat do these deeds unconsciously. Rather, it seems much more accurate to say that I, an embodied consciousness, drink. My consciousness is diffused throughout my body; my body is wholly psychic.

Moreover, my body, as it is for me, "is *lived* and not *known*" (BN, 427). That is, when I am engaged in activities in the world I generally take notice neither of my "muscles, bones, tendons, or skin," nor even of my own physical effort. Rather, what I perceive is "the *resistance* of things." So, for example, "what I perceive when I want to lift this glass to my mouth is not my effort but the *heaviness of the glass*" (BN, 427). Thus, it is not the case that my knowledge of my body is primary and serves as a kind of foundation for my knowledge of other physical objects. Rather, it is exactly the reverse; "it is the instrumental-things which in their original appearance indicate [my] body to [me]" (BN, 428).

In explaining this idea Sartre makes good use of Gaston Bachelard's concept of the "coefficient of adversity" in objects. The basic point is that we do not typically encounter objects in the world in a neutral way, but rather under the color of their relevance to our projects and interests. Thus, no object is *intrinsically* resistant or adverse. Rather, "it is in relation to an original instrumental complex that things reveal their resistance and their adversity. The bolt is revealed as too big to be screwed in to the nut, the pedestal too fragile to support the weight which I want to hold up, the stone too heavy to be lifted up to the top of the wall, etc." (BN, 428). And objects can reveal themselves as threatening to established ongoing concerns, as when I inadvertently drive into a hailstorm or suddenly discover that my house is on fire. With this in mind, we are in a position to understand Sartre's claim that I do not know my body primarily by focusing directly on it, or even by means of a peripheral awareness of it as I act in the world. Rather, he suggests, "my body is indicated originally by instrumental complexes and secondarily by destructive devices" (BN, 428). For example, "I *live* my body in danger as regards menacing machines . . ." (BN, 428). I live it, in short, as "the center of reference indicated . . . by the instrumental-objects of the world" (BN, 445).

In saying that the body as it is lived, that is, as it is *for me*, is a center of reference, Sartre is claiming, once again, that at this ontological level my body is not something to which I direct my attention. It is better understood as the point of view *from which* I direct my attention to other things. Moreover, since I am constantly hurtling toward the future, and facing the ceaseless obligation to act, my body is also the point of departure from which I do so (BN, 429–30). My body is thus ambiguous in that it is simultaneously both that which I am and that which I surpass through action. In this way Sartre's analysis of the body confirms his findings with regard to consciousness (which is not surprising, given his conception of the body as conscious and of consciousness as embodied): "I *am* my body to the extent that I *am*; I *am not* my body to the extent that I am not what I am" (BN, 430).

For example, suppose I have a specific bodily disability (I am, let us say, blind, or deaf, or confined to a wheelchair). Sartre's claim is that, while it is undeniably true that I am, in a sense, this disabled body (that is, it would be folly to deny my disability and to assert, contrary to fact, that I can see or hear or walk), it is also true, in another sense, that I am not it, since it is, instead, that which I surpass through my actions. Furthermore, the meaning of my disability is not self-announcing, but rather emerges as I engage in projects that are relevant to it. This means, according to Sartre, that "I choose the way in which I constitute my disability (as 'unbearable,' 'humiliating,' 'to be hidden,' 'to be revealed to all,' 'an object of pride,' 'the justification for my failures,' etc.)" (BN, 432).

Here Sartre's distinctive approach to the issue of freedom is on full display. While most people, philosophers and nonphilosophers alike, would be quick to notice the obvious ways in which my physical disabilities limit my freedom, Sartre emphasizes instead that they also serve as the foundation for its exercise. To be sure, my freedom does not require that I possess the precise collection of physical abilities and disabilities that I in fact happen to have. Many of these I have acquired as a matter of chance, principally through the luck of birth. They are not necessary, but contingent. But it is necessary that I have one set of bodily abilities and disabilities or another. Similarly, though it is a contingent fact that I was born in the United States in the twentieth century, it is a necessity (given my existence) for me to have been born somewhere and at some time. The contingencies of my bodily existence (being blind, or short, or a contemporary American), while admittedly closing off some projects that a differently situated person might have chosen (that of being a painter, or a basketball center, or an interlocutor of the living Socrates), nonetheless facilitate my freedom by (1) refusing to announce their meaning, thus requiring me to constitute their meaning in part through my choices of action, (2) helping to comprise the "situation" on the basis of which I act, and (3) preventing me from obtaining everything at once, and thereby *requiring* me to choose (another meaning of Sartre's famous aphorism that we are "condemned to be free"). The body, then, as "the contingent form which is taken up by the necessity of my contingency," is also "precisely the necessity that *there be a choice*, that I do not exist *all at once*. In this sense my finitude is the condition of my freedom, for there is no freedom without choice. . . ." Thus, the body "renders consciousness possible even in its very freedom" (BN, 432).

But the body as lived, that is, the body as it exists for-itself, is only the first of three ontological dimensions of the body that Sartre discusses. The second is the body-for-others. Whereas my body as lived is the unfocused-on and thus unknown contingent center of reference from which I constitute the world and act, and which I transcend in my action (Sartre calls it "the point of view on which I can take no point of view" [BN, 446]), the case is very different when we turn to the way in which my body appears to the Other (or to the way in which the Other's body appears to me).

In one sense it would appear to be quite a simple matter to observe the Other's body and to take it for an object. There it is, in my visual field, right alongside the many and various other physical things that are obviously open to my inspection and evaluation as objects (in a way that my own body, as the standpoint from which I look and evaluate, is not). But this is to ignore the fact that my "primary encounter" with the Other, according to Sartre, is with a consciousness, a center of reference, a "transcendence" which freely encounters other objects in the world and constitutes them according to its own interests and purposes. Sartre gives the example of being in someone else's home and noticing how the various objects in it all refer to the subjectivity of the one who lives there, and take on their meaning by means of their place within his projects: "this easy chair is a chair-where-he-sits, this desk is a desk-at-which-he-writes, this window is a window through which there enters the light-which-illuminates-the-objects-which-he-sees" (BN, 448). Thus, if I were to see his body in his home with his chair, desk, and window, it would not typically appear as just one more object in the room on the same plane with these others, but rather as the center of an instrumental complex, as the conscious standpoint which gives to the other objects in the room their meaning.

To make an object of the Other, then, is to make the Other appear to me as a "transcendence-transcended" (BN, 446). It is to surpass and to put out of play the organization of objects that the Other has effected, and to bring about instead a new arrangement of them from one's own perspective, based on one's own projects, and interests. The Other's body takes its place as one of the items in this new organization (though distinct from them since it, unlike a table or a corpse, is given as a nullified freedom) and ceases to appear as the Sun around which all of the other objects revolve. But the Other's body-for-me is like other objects and unlike my body-for-itself in that I can directly examine and know it and use it instrumentally.

Sartre completes his discussion by considering one final ontological dimension of the body. I can live my body (this is the dimension of the body as it exists for-itself); and the Other can make of my body a perceptual object or a tool (this is the dimension of the body as it exists for-others). But I can also exist "for myself as a body known by the Other" (BN, 460). This is the third (and final) ontological dimension of the body.

The basic idea is that I, through the "shock of the encounter with the Other," can come to recognize that my body, which I had simply lived, is being seen and evaluated by the Other as an object. To put it another way, I begin to understand that my body, which I had experienced as pure subjectivity, has an objective side. My body, which had been simply *me*, becomes instead "a *thing outside my subjectivity*, in the midst of a world which is not mine" (BN, 462). I experience myself as alienated from my body.

As an example of such alienation, Sartre offers an analysis of shyness. Shy people will sometimes describe their state by claiming that they feel themselves blushing or sweating, but Sartre claims that such expressions are inaccurate (presumably because they confuse the first and third ontological dimensions of the body). What the shy person really means, according to Sartre, "is that he is vividly and constantly conscious of his body not as it is for him but as it is *for the Other*" (BN, 463). Part of the shy person's problem—and it is the problem that the rest of us share, even if to a lesser degree—is that one's body-for-the-Other is "on principle out of reach," fully in the hands of the Other, and thus resistant to one's attempts to appropriate and to master it. I find that all my attempts to reach it "in order to give it the form and the attitude which are appropriate" are doomed to failure. This would not be a problem if I could find my objectivity in my body as it is lived, or if I could dismiss my body-for-the-Other as illusory. But my body-for-itself is a conscious center of reference and not an object at all; and it turns out that "we in fact attribute to the body-for-the-Other as much reality as to the body-for-us. Better yet, the body-for-the-Other *is* the body-for-us, but inapprehensible and alienated." As a result, the Other is in a position to accomplish "for us a function of which we are incapable and which nevertheless is incumbent on us: *to see ourselves as we are*" (BN, 463). We thus find ourselves fully at the mercy of the Other, for it is only through the look of the Other that we can access our own objectivity.

Concrete Relations with Others

The problem, however, is that as a consciousness (that is, as a for-itself, a no-thing), I am not an object. Recall that, on Sartre's view, consciousness is a relation, rather than a thing. It is that which reveals and articulates positive being through negation; it is not the in-itself, and it utterly lacks the positive being which characterizes the in-itself. Whereas the in-itself is what it is, the for-itself, as we recall, is what it is not and is not what it is. Consequently, insofar as I, as a conscious being, wish to achieve the hard, stable, permanence of a thing, and to be able to think of myself (truthfully) as having a fixed essence (presumably a good or excellent one), I would seem to be doomed to failure. As a consciousness, I am always on the way. I never arrive (or, if I do arrive, I can't stop, but must move on). The obligation to organize my perceptual field into a figure on a ground, to confront an open future, to choose,

and to act, never ceases so long as I am conscious. Any objectivity that I do manage to achieve becomes merely the starting point
from which I must undertake my next action. And if I attempt to
enjoy my status as a (good) object by reflecting on it, my very act
of doing so reveals to me the separation between my present consciousness and that object. I am not it because I am conscious *of*
it. So I can never be a fixed, unchanging positive entity. But I
want to be one.

Furthermore, this "desire" should not be interpreted psychologically, according to Sartre, but rather ontologically. The for-
itself exists *only* as a nihilation of the in-itself. In its very being it
is oriented toward the in-itself. It pursues the in-itself, structur-
ing it into a world, but it does so only by rushing past it in
undertaking its next free action. So "the for-itself is both a flight
and a pursuit; it flees the in-itself and at the same time pursues
it" (BN, 472). It seeks the permanence, solidity, and stability of
the in-itself, and yet it resists becoming so assimilated to the in-
itself as to lose its freedom. So it attempts to bring about a state
of affairs in which it would both exist as an in-itself and at the
same time freely found and justify itself. In other words, it
attempts to exist as "an in-itself-for-itself—i.e., an in-itself which
would be to itself its own foundation" (BN, 472). So I, as a for-
itself, wish to exist as an in-itself, as an object, without losing my
existence as a free consciousness.

But from my point of view, as a free consciousness confronting
my perceptual field and undertaking actions, I exist as a subject. So
I must turn to the Other for help with this project of becoming an
object, for it is the Other who, through his or her look, holds the
key to my objectivity. (As Sartre puts it, the Other has "the secret
of my being" and "knows what I *am*" [BN, 473].) Consequently,
it is to the other that I must go for assistance in my quest to attain
full being. This helps to explain why relationships with other people are so important to us.

While these relationships could take any of a number of different forms, all of them, according to Sartre, are variations on "two
primitive attitudes" which I might assume when confronting the
Other. One involves attempting to take control of the Other's freedom "without removing from it its character as freedom" (BN,
473). My strategy is to gain access to my objectivity by possessing
the free consciousness of the Other who objectifies me. On the

other hand, this strategy potentially puts me at the mercy of the Other, who might objectify me in ways I dislike. Consequently, I may be motivated to adopt the other primitive attitude toward the Other, that of attempting to deny the Other's subjectivity by making an object of him or her. Since only a free consciousness can look at me and constitute me as an object, the point of this strategy is to prevent the Other from objectifying me. (As Sartre puts it, "the Other's object-ness destroys my object-ness for him" [BN, 473].)

Sartre claims that neither of these strategies can possibly succeed, since their goal, the bringing about of a state of affairs in which I would exist as an in-itself-for-itself, cannot possibly be realized. The concept of being in-itself-for-itself is contradictory, so a project intended to actualize it is as futile as would be an attempt to create a round square. Accordingly, the picture of human relationships that Sartre paints in *Being and Nothingness* is decidedly bleak.

The bleakness is exacerbated, moreover, by the fact that the Other is typically using the same strategies on me that I am employing on him or her. So our projects are done in not only by the intrinsic impossibility and thus utter unattainability of their goals, but also by the fact that we cross one another as we pursue them. Indeed, Sartre claims that "conflict is the original meaning of being-for-others" (BN, 475), and that "the essence of the relations between consciousnesses is . . . conflict" (BN, 555).

To get a sense of what Sartre means by this, imagine two lovers, each of whom reasons as follows:

> The Other's freedom is the foundation of my being. But precisely because I exist by means of the Other's freedom, I have no security; I am in danger in this freedom. It moulds my being and *makes me be,* it confers values upon me and removes them from me. . . . Irresponsible and beyond reach, this protean freedom in which I have engaged myself can in turn engage me in a thousand different ways of being. *My project of recovering my being can be realized only if I can get hold of this freedom and reduce it to being a freedom subject to my freedom.* (BN, 477, emphasis added)

It is clear that the Other must be a subject, hence a freedom, because only a subject is capable of being the foundation of my being. But if I am to achieve full being, if I am to "be what I am" and exist as my own justification, then I must possess the freedom of the Other, which is the foundation of my being. So I might try to fascinate and ensnare the Other in an attempt to possess the freedom which is the foundation of my being. Sartre calls such an attempt "love."

Love is doomed to failure because a freedom cannot be possessed. Only objects can be possessed, but an object cannot serve as the foundation of my being. If I try to control the other's freedom, to make it subject to my freedom, I fail, because a freedom cannot remain a freedom while being controlled. (Alternatively, if it does remain a freedom, I can't control it.) Hence, the attitude which seeks to possess the Other as freedom is a futile one.

To illustrate this point, Sartre discusses the widespread practice or lovers requiring pledges of love from one another, as in the case, for example, of wedding vows. Sartre makes the point that no one would actually be satisfied with "a love given as pure loyalty to a sworn oath." Indeed, no one "would be satisfied with the words, 'I love you because I have freely engaged myself to love you and I do not wish to go back on my word.' Thus the lover demands a pledge, yet is irritated by a pledge. He wants to be loved by a freedom but demands that this freedom as freedom should no longer be free" (BN, 479). We want to be objectified (positively, as "wonderful," as "the whole world" for the beloved) by a freedom, for it would be meaningless to be so objectified by, for example, a robot that we would know had been programmed to do so. And yet, if the Other who objectifies us is truly free, we have no security, and thus are not really in control of the foundation of our being. The Other might at any moment objectify us as loathsome, or else simply go away, perhaps to give his or her love to another. So we want both to possess and control the Other, on the one hand, and for the Other simultaneously to remain free, on the other. So we want an impossibility.

(Let me pause to make one quick, parenthetical, remark to readers who might think, as I do, both that Sartre's claims about the desire to exist as an in-itself-for-itself somehow being ontologically built into the being of consciousness are somewhat dubious and that he tends to exaggerate the darker aspects of human existence. From a purely psychological point of view, surely he is on to something here. Much human misery, especially in the sphere of interpersonal relationships, does result from a widespread tendency to demand both freedom and security in contexts in which each value limits the other.)

In any case, recognizing my inability to capture the Other's freedom (and the consequent failure of love), I may attempt to ground my being by seeking to exist solely as an object for the Other. This is masochism. But masochism, too, must fail:

> It is useless for the masochist to get down on his knees, to show himself in ridiculous positions, to cause himself to be used as a simple life-less instrument. It is *for the Other* that he will be obscene or simply passive, for the Other that he will *undergo* these postures; for himself he is forever condemned to *give them to himself.* . . . The more he tries to taste his objectivity, the more he will be submerged by the consciousness of his subjectivity—hence his anguish. (BN, 493)

The masochist cannot become an object because he cannot lose sight of his subjectivity. He is aware of the fact that it is by his choice that he presents himself to the Other as an object and allows the Other to treat him as one. Sartre gives the example of a man who pays a woman to whip him. In so doing, he treats her as an instrument, thus affirming his freedom in relation to her (BN, 493).

The failure of the fundamental attitude toward the Other that we have been considering gives rise to the adoption of the other fundamental attitude. (Or it could just as well go in the other order. Neither fundamental attitude is logically prior to the other, and the two attitudes might be adopted or described in any order). Since I have failed to appropriate my objectivity through the Other's look, I now turn to look at the Other. "At this instant the Other becomes a being which I possess and which recognizes my freedom. It seems that my goal has been achieved since I possess the being who has the key to my object-state and since I can cause him to make proof of my freedom in a thousand different ways" (BN, 494).

As it turns out, however, this fails as well, because I have merely possessed the Other-as-object, whereas only a subject can serve as the foundation of my being. The problem can be put in the form of a dilemma. My attempt to possess the other will either fail (because the Other is a freedom, and thus is not possessable), or else frustrate my ultimate goal of receiving my objectivity from the Other (because an Other I might actually possess would have to be an object, and only a subject can give to me the objectification I seek).

Moreover, specific examples of this attempt bring about additional problems of their own. Consider, for example, the case of sexual desire. Sartre claims that it is the attempt to incarnate the Other's consciousness and then to possess his or her flesh, so that one might thereby possess the Other's consciousness.

But sexual desire fails for the simple reason that it cannot be sustained. At the termination of desire the Other ceases to be incarnated. As Sartre puts it, "pleasure is the death and the failure of desire . . . because it is not only its fulfillment but its limit and its end" (BN, 515).

The failure of sexual desire may lead to sadism, which is another attempt at the possession of the Other's consciousness through causing his or her incarnation. In this case, however, the incarnation is to be brought about through the infliction of pain.

But sadism fails, too, because there is no way to capture this incarnated consciousness. In desire, I become incarnated so as to possess the Other in his or her incarnation. But if I allow this to happen my project fails for all the reasons desire fails. Yet if I do not become incarnated there is nothing to be done with the incarnation that lies before me. "No goal can be assigned to it. . . . It is *there*, and it is there *for nothing*" (BN, 525).

Sadism fails, also, because it is an attempt to capture the Other's freedom. The glance of the victim proves to the sadist that the victim's freedom has not been captured and that it cannot be captured. Furthermore, in the look of the victim the sadist "experiences the absolute alienation of his being in the Other's freedom" (BN, 525). Far from controlling the victim, and receiving from the victim the objectification that the sadist desires, the sadist discovers instead that the victim is free and uncontrollable, and specifically is free to present to the sadist a highly unflattering self-image—as a cruel, despicable sadist, for example.

The desire to escape from the Other's pitiless gaze can lead to two other ways of relating to the Other. These are indifference, which is the adoption of the attitude that other people are objects exclusively, and hate, which is the attempt to suppress other consciousnesses.

We have all encountered people who are "indifferent" in Sartre's sense. If I am indifferent to other people, I refuse to recognize their subjectivity. They exist for me only as obstacles to be avoided or else as things to be manipulated for my benefit. So my attitude concerning them is similar to that which I direct toward potholes, pencils, or screwdrivers. I tend to see "people" only in terms of their functions: "the ticket-collector is only the function of collecting tickets; the café waiter is nothing but the function of serving the patrons. In this capacity they will be most useful if I know their *keys* and those 'master-words' which can release their mechanisms" (BN, 495).

Sartre maintains that "this state of *blindness*," this obliviousness to the subjectivity of the Other, "can be maintained for a long time, as long as my fundamental bad faith desires; it can be extended—with relapses—over several years, over a whole life; there are men who die without—save for brief and terrifying flashes of illumination—ever having suspected what the *Other* is" (BN, 496).

There are definite advantages to indifference. In this state "I am at ease; I am not embarrassed by myself, for I am not *outside*; I do not feel myself alienated" (BN, 496). But the cost is high. To the extent that I am spared any worry about being confronted with a *negative* image of my objectivity, it can only be because I am cut off from my objectivity *entirely*. Thus, indifference amounts to a complete abandonment of the attempt to ground my being in relations with the Other, and of thereby coming to exist as an in-itself-for-itself. Indifference, therefore, is clearly a failure. Moreover, Sartre maintains that the indifferent person does at times experience a vague, nonthematized sense of the Other's subjectivity, and thus of his or her own status as being-looked-at. This is more unsettling than a clear, explicit awareness of being seen by a particular person, since in the latter case one can turn toward the onlooker and perhaps defend oneself. The blindness of indifference, on the other hand, amounts to a kind of "anxiety because it is accompanied by the consciousness of a 'wandering and inapprehensible' look" (BN, 497).

Perhaps this anxiety could be overcome through hate, the project of suppressing other consciousnesses. The problem, however (aside from the obvious point that it would be virtually impossible, without possessing a near monopoly on weapons of mass destruction, literally to wipe out all other consciousnesses, and that doing so would, in any case, amount to the abandonment of the project of seeking the foundation of one's being through relations with others), is that even the complete elimination of all Others would not "bring it about that the Other had not been" (BN, 534). My prior contact with Others, which would presumably be a prerequisite for my having come to be motivated to want to destroy them, would have already acquainted me with my outside, with my being-for-others. But if the Other has already shown me that I am despicable, killing the Other cannot change my awareness of that fact. I know that I have an outside, even though there is no longer an Other to point it out to me. So "he who has once been for-others is contaminated in his being for the rest of his days even if the Other should be entirely suppressed. . . . He can never recapture what he has alienated." Moreover, the Other's death takes away all possibility that this judgment of what I am might one day be reversed. Rather, the destroyed Other carries "the key to this alienation along with him to the grave" (BN, 534).

Thus, hate is a failure. It does not get us out of the circle of disastrous ways of relating to the Other. Rather, "it simply represents the final attempt, the attempt of despair. After the failure of this attempt nothing remains for the for-itself except to re-enter the circle and allow itself to be indefinitely tossed from one the other of the two fundamental attitudes" (BN, 534).

With these cheerless words, Sartre's discussion of concrete relations with Others comes to a close. However, just as he did at the end of his almost equally devastating analysis of bad faith, Sartre here offers a cryptic footnote in which he suggests that matters might not be quite as hopeless as he has seemingly implied they are. The footnote reads as follows: "These considerations do not exclude the possibility of an ethics of deliverance and salvation. But this can be achieved only after a radical conversion which we cannot discuss here" (BN, 534, n. 13). I will offer an interpretation of this footnote at the end of this chapter, when considering Sartre's views on ethics.

Freedom

Sartre concludes part three *of Being and Nothingness* by noting two important observations. The first is that the for-itself is not merely a force that, through its nihilating activities, reveals and articulates being. Rather, insofar as it is embodied and encounters others, it also has an outside. It exists, for the Other, as in-itself, "present in the midst of the in-itself" (BN, 555). Secondly, despite its desire to do so, "the for-itself by nature is the being which can not coincide with its being-in-itself" (BN, 555).

These two conclusions drive the two chapters of part four of *Being and Nothingness*. In the second of these chapters, Sartre develops the details of the for-itself's project of attempting to coincide with its being-in-itself. It is here that Sartre presents his famous theory of "existential psychoanalysis."

But the first chapter, to which we now turn, is concerned with freedom. It asks how freedom is possible given the for-itself's embodied immersion in the in-itself. Whereas Sartre's earlier discussions of freedom (for example, those undertaken in connection with imagination, interrogation, and the experience of absence) had focused primarily on the freedom of *consciousness* to structure the elements in its perceptual field, to lend meaning to those elements by incorporating them into a project of action, and to go beyond them through an act of imagination, he now expands that discussion to include the full-blooded freedom of *embodied individuals*, existing in a social world with others, to act on and to modify materially the in-itself which they confront.

Sartre begins by returning to the idea that freedom is essentially connected to negativity. He attempts to demonstrate this by analyzing the structure of actions. His main point is that "an action is on principle *intentional*" (BN, 559). That is, when one acts, one does so with purpose. For example, suppose that, after a period of working in silence, it occurs to me that I would enjoy listening to some music while I continue to work. I then get up, go to the stereo, and put some music on. My action thus involves me in at least two negativities. First, in undertaking it I *reject what is* (the state of affairs in which I am working in silence). Secondly, I simultaneously aim, instead, to bring about a state of affairs that currently *is not* (one in which I am enjoying music while I work). And this structure, Sartre argues, is common to all genuine *actions* (as opposed, for example, to instances of altering the world unintentionally through carelessness). For a genuine action "necessarily implies as its condition the recognition of a 'desideratum'; that is, of an objective lack or again of a *négatité*" (BN, 560).

These considerations help us to understand on what basis Sartre can claim that our immersion in physical, historical, and social

structures does not undermine our freedom. To be sure, we typically simply inherit these structures without having done anything
to bring them about. Moreover, they often act on us in ways that
are substantially beyond our control. And it is against the background of them, and with reference to them, that we are motivated to act. (It is not as if freedom, for Sartre, is to be understood
as a wild, capricious thrashing about that makes no contact with
the objective circumstances in which we find ourselves.) Still, these
structures cannot all by themselves deprive us of our freedom, or
even motivate our actions, since external structures are *positive*,
and an action requires the introduction of *negativities*, which only
the for-itself can produce.

Sartre offers the example of a worker whose salary is lowered.
He points out that this cannot motivate an action of revolt if the
worker conceives of his or her salary solely in positive terms, as "X
dollars per week." Rather, the salary can motivate a revolt only
when the worker conceives it negatively, as "not enough," or as
"unjust," or as "unfair." Such a worker "will have to have effected
a double nihilation: on the one hand, he must posit an ideal state
of affairs as a pure present nothingness; on the other hand, he must
posit the actual situation as nothingness in relation to this state of
affairs" (BN, 562). From this analysis Sartre draws two conclusions: "(1) No factual state whatever it may be . . . is capable by
itself of motivating any act whatsoever. For an act is a projection of
the for-itself toward what is not, and what is can in no way determine by itself what is not. (2) No factual state can determine consciousness to apprehend it as a *négatité* or as a lack" (BN, 562).

To put the point another way, we remain free in the face of given
factual states because (a) the way in which a factual state motivates
us to act depends crucially on our understanding of that factual
state, and (b) factual states lack the power to state their own meaning (or to determine how we are to understand them). Rather, the
meaning that a given factual state takes on for us depends crucially
on the way in which it appears to us as we engage it in the context
of intentional action—that is, the context of seeking an end that
currently is not. Thus, "the given is appreciated in terms of something which does not yet exist; it is in the light of non-being that
being-in-itself is illuminated." Indeed, "human reality . . . is the
being which causes *there to be* a given by breaking with it and illuminating it in the light of the not-yet-existing" (BN, 615).

Sartre offers the simple example of seeking a good meal when one is hungry. If my end is a good meal, certain elements of my environment immediately take on meanings that they would not have were I to be pursuing different ends. The meal that lies "beyond the dusty road on which I am traveling is projected as the *meaning* of this road" (BN, 614). And yet, the state in which I am eating this meal does not yet exist. So what *is* depends for its meaning on what *is not*. "Since the intention is a choice of the end and since the world reveals itself across our conduct, it is the intentional choice of the end which reveals the world, and the world is revealed as this or that (in this or that order) according to the end chosen. The end, illuminating the world, is a state *of* the world to be obtained and not yet existing" (BN, 614).

Even if one grants, however, that our immersion in a world of factual givens (or "facticity," in Sartre's terminology) does not undermine our freedom to determine the *meaning* of those factual givens, perhaps it diminishes our freedom in other ways. Sartre asks, for example, whether I can freely "choose to be tall if I am short" or "to have two arms if I have only one" (BN, 619). It would seem not. Indeed, Sartre points out that

> the decisive argument which is employed by common sense against freedom consists in reminding us of our impotence. Far from being able to modify our situation at our whim, we seem to be unable to change ourselves. I am not "free" either to escape the lot of my class, of my nation, of my family, or even to build up my own power or my fortune or to conquer my most insignificant appetites or habits. I am born a worker, a Frenchman, an hereditary syphilitic, or a tubercular. The history of a life, whatever it may be, is the history of a failure. The coefficient of adversity of things is such that years of patience are necessary to obtain the feeblest result. (BN, 619)

In response to this argument Sartre makes three points. (1) First, just as no factual given is intrinsically meaningful, but rather emerges as meaningful only in light of our focusing and intending activities, so does no factual given have the power, all by itself, to stand as an obstacle to the successful completion of our freely projects. Rather, the given can emerge as adverse only if I choose a project with respect to which the existence of that given is (negatively) instrumentally relevant. Thus, "the coefficient of adversity of things can not be an argument against our freedom, for it is *by us*—*i.e.*, by the preliminary positing of an end—that this coefficient of adversity arises." Sartre offers a helpful example to illustrate this point: "A particular crag, which manifests a profound resistance if I wish to displace it, will be on the contrary a valuable aid if I want to climb upon it in order to look over the countryside. In itself—if one can even imagine what the crag can be in itself—it is neutral; that is, it waits to be illuminated by an end in order to manifest itself as adverse or helpful" (BN, 620).

Still, even if crags emerge as aids or obstacles only in the light of our projects, such as that of trying to scale them, the fact remains that "in a world illuminated by our freedom, this particular crag will be more favorable for scaling and that one not" (BN, 620). Indeed, Sartre explicitly concedes that "what my freedom can not determine," once my free choice of action has elevated to the foreground the issue of a given crag's scalability, "is whether the rock 'to be scaled' will or will not lend itself to scaling. This is part of the brute being of the rock" (BN, 627).

(2) But the mere fact that things in the world often stand in the way of the realization of our projects (or even that this is true to a large degree because of the nature of the things themselves, and not merely because of the way that we interact with them) does not, according to Sartre, undermine our freedom. Rather, he argues that "the resistance which freedom reveals in the existent, far from being a danger to freedom, results only in enabling it to arise as freedom. There can be a free for-itself only as engaged in a resisting world. Outside of this engagement the notion . . . of freedom . . . lose[s] all meaning" (BN, 621).

To see his point, one only has to imagine what it would be like if the world offered no resistance to the successful completion of our projects. In such a world, we would only have to choose an end in order for it to be instantly and effortlessly realized. But if we could have anything, and have it at no cost of any kind, and at the very instant we desire it, then we wouldn't have to make any choices. So freedom can only be meaningful for those who can't have everything, and who therefore must make choices; only finite beings with limited power can truly be free. And to say that we are finite beings with limited power is precisely to say that the world that we inhabit resists us when we attempt to realize our projects. As Sartre puts it, "freedom can exist only as restricted since freedom is choice. Every choice . . . supposes elimination and selection; every choice is a choice of finitude" (BN, 636). Thus,

> the very project of a freedom in general is a choice which implies the anticipation and acceptance of some kind of resistance somewhere. Not only does freedom constitute the compass within which in-itselfs otherwise indifferent will be revealed as resistances, but freedom's very project in general is to *do* in a resisting world by means of a victory over the world's resistances.

It might be objected, however, that resistances are one thing, and absolute barriers another. Can a being, such as, for example, a slave in chains, whose circumstances preclude the successful completion of every meaningful project, really be said to be free? The judgment that he or she cannot underlies perhaps the single most widespread criticism of Sartre's early philosophy—that his position on human freedom, as expressed in his repeated declarations that we are "absolutely free" (BN, 653), "totally free" (BN, 709) and "wholly and forever free" (BN, 569), and in his "outrageous" assertion that "the slave in chains is as free as his master" (BN, 703), are objectionably extreme and unrealistic.

(3) In response to such criticism (and to complete his reply to the idea that facticity and the "coefficient of adversity" of things jeopardize or diminish freedom), Sartre draws an often overlooked distinction between "the empirical and popular concept of 'freedom,'" which amounts to "'the ability to obtain the ends chosen,'" and "the technical and philosophical concept of freedom, the only one which we are considering here," which "means only the autonomy of choice" (BN, 621–22). This distinction allows Sartre to agree completely with the commonsense notion that our freedom is not absolute, and that slaves in chains are significantly less free than are the rest of us, if the sense of freedom in question is practical freedom, what Sartre calls "freedom of obtaining" (BN, 622). Only the slave's ontological freedom, that is, "freedom of choice" (BN, 622) is absolute and on a par with our own.

Sartre makes this point clearly in *Being and Nothingness*, and he does so more than once. For example, on page 648 he reminds his readers, precisely in the context of refuting the claim that our limited power entails our limited freedom, that "my freedom *to choose* . . . must not be confused with my freedom *to obtain*." Still, given the frequency with which his readers have ignored this point, we might well conclude that he doesn't emphasize it sufficiently in *Being and Nothingness*. But he does emphasize it in his subsequent works, especially when responding to critics of the analysis of freedom that he offers in *Being and Nothingness*.

Many of those critics objected to Sartre's views on moral grounds. They argued that by insisting that everyone, including slaves and prisoners, is absolutely free, Sartre was implicitly denying that anyone was oppressed and stood in need of liberation. Sartre's replies help to clarify the precise and limited sense in which he thinks that everyone is free, demonstrate his recognition that many people are in another sense very much unfree, and thus provide further evidence of the importance of the distinction between different senses of freedom to the understanding of his thought.

For example, in an essay appearing in 1944, just a year after the publication of *Being and Nothingness*, Sartre addresses his critics as follows.

> You call us social traitors, saying that our conception of freedom keeps man from loosening his chains. What stupidity! When we say a man who's out of work is free, we don't mean that he can do whatever he wants and change himself into a rich and tranquil bourgeois on the spot. *He is free because he can always choose to accept his lot with resignation or to rebel against it.*[10]

Or again, consider Sartre's response to his Marxist critics, published in 1946: "But, say the Marxists, if you teach man that he *is* free, you betray him; for he no longer needs to *become* free; can you conceive of a man free from birth who demands to be liberated? To this I reply that if man is not originally free, but determined once and for all, we cannot even conceive what his liberation might be" (MR, 244). Similarly, Sartre asks, "but what would it mean to liberate a man whose actions were determined? *If man were not free, it would not be worth moving a finger for him.*"[11] And in his unfinished and posthumously published

---

[10] "A More Precise Characterization of Existentialism," trans. Richard C. McCleary, in *The Writings of Jean-Paul Sartre, Vol. 2: Selected Prose*, ed. Michel Contat and Michel Rybalka (Evanston: Northwestern University Press, 1974), 159.

[11] Sartre, speaking in an interview with Jean Duché, "A la recherche de l'existentialisme: M. Jean-Paul Sartre's explique," excerpt quoted and translated by

Notebooks for an Ethics, composed in the late 1940s and originally intended to serve as a sequel to *Being and Nothingness*, Sartre argues at length that "only a freedom can be oppressed," and that "if we pretend that man is not free, the very idea of oppression loses all meaning." After all, "[a] stone does not oppress, [and] one does not oppress a stone" (NFE, 327).

The implication of these passages is that Sartre holds ontological freedom to be a necessary, but not a sufficient, condition for practical freedom. On his view, while one can perhaps satisfy the desires of a thoroughly determined being, that being is still in no sense "free." We are practically free, according to Sartre, only to the extent that we are able successfully to realize our freely (in the ontological sense) chosen projects.

Another way to approach Sartre's point is by means of his analysis of situation. While many critics, perhaps misled by his use of the phrase "absolute freedom" and by his claim that the slave in chains is as free as his master, have claimed that Sartre denies or neglects the situated character of human freedom, in fact nothing could be further from the truth. For Sartre repeatedly and consistently maintains that "I am never free except *in situation*" (BN, 653), that "for the for-itself, to exist and to be situated are one and the same" (BN, 408), that "'being in situation' . . . characterizes the For-itself" (BN, 701), that "being in situation defines human reality" (BN, 702), that "*being situated* is an essential and necessary characteristic of freedom" (WIL, 133), and so on endlessly.

But what does Sartre mean by "situation"? One might guess that my "situation" refers to the objective facts about me and about my environment as they exist in a particular time and place. But that is what Sartre means by "facticity." "My situation," by contrast, refers to the result of the confrontation, in a particular time and place, between my facticity and my free consciousness. Consequently, "the situation is neither objective nor subjective," and "can be considered neither as the free result of a freedom nor as the ensemble of the constraints to which I am subject; it stems from the illumination of the constraint by freedom which gives to it its meaning as constraint" (BN, 704).

Dagfinn Føllesdal in his "Sartre on Freedom," in *The Philosophy of Jean-Paul Sartre*, ed. Paul Arthur Schilpp, 404–5, emphasis added.

To see the force of Sartre's point, let's return to his crag example. Suppose that I have undertaken, and am in the middle of completing, the project of climbing a crag. This is my situation. But it is not simply reducible to facticity (for example, the height of the crag, its angle of incline, my ability as a climber, and so forth), since these factors would not have come into play had I chosen a different project (such as drawing the crag or attempting to clear it away). Indeed, these different projects, while causing the facticities just mentioned to recede into insignificance, would have brought others (such as the shape and texture of the crag, my artistic abilities, the weight of the crag, the quality of my heavy-duty rock-moving equipment, and so forth) to the forefront. Nor is the situation simply reducible to my freedom, since I would likely not have been motivated to choose the project of climbing, or perhaps even to think of it, had I been confronted with a significantly different crag (such as a short one, or an impossibly steep one, or one that is covered with ice, or one with gunmen visible at the top and signs saying "trespassers will be shot" at the bottom). Granted, Sartre claims that we never encounter brute facticity as such, but rather always as colored by our freely chosen projects. Still, this does not mean that we can color the facticity that we confront in every conceivable way, or in any way we might want. Rather, there is still an involuntary dimension to our uncovering of the meaning of the brute existent. Given our project, its meaning is constrained by its nature. Thus, both elements of the situation, in their interplay with one another, comprise my situation. Facticity makes up my situation, but only as that facticity is illuminated and made relevant by my free project; and my free project constitutes my situation, but only as it confronts a facticity which constrains and enables it. As Sartre puts it, this is "the paradox of freedom: there is freedom only in a *situation*, and there is a situation only through freedom. Human-reality everywhere encounters resistance and obstacles which it has not created, but these resistances and obstacles have meaning only in and through the free choice which human-reality *is*" (BN, 629).

Moreover, it is often, and perhaps generally, unclear which element, my freedom or the facticity it faces, is dominant in the constitution of my situation. Do I choose to climb the crag (rather than draw it or try to move it) because certain of its features (such as its height and angle of incline) are somehow (objectively?) more prominent or significant than others (such as its shape or weight)? Or is it rather that I notice some features of the crag rather than others because of the project I already have in mind (or, perhaps, because of my general interests, which in turn predispose me both to undertake certain projects [like climbing or drawing] whenever I find myself in an environment conducive to the successful completion of such projects, and also to pick out, from the limitless features of my environment that could become objects of my attention, precisely those that are relevant to my projects and interests)? Sartre's answer is that these two factors are so thoroughly intertwined that we cannot possibly disentangle them accurately. Thus, "the *situation*, the common product of the contingency of the in-itself and of freedom, is an ambiguous phenomenon in which it is impossible for the for-itself to distinguish the contribution of freedom from that of the brute existent" (BN, 627).

Sartre also highlights this ambiguity by calling to our attention the "coefficient of adversity" in things, that is, the tendency of external objects and states of affairs to "resist" me as I attempt to complete my freely chosen projects successfully. We have already discussed Sartre's point that nothing can count as an obstacle in an absolute sense, since the emergence of features in my environment as harmful (or helpful or neutral) to me depends crucially on the nature of my project. (The fact that the extreme steepness of a crag stands as an obstacle to me depends on my adoption of the project of scaling it [as opposed to that of drawing it, for example]). It also depends, of course, on the objective features of the crag, as some crags are steeper (and thus more difficult to climb) than others. But in spite of Sartre's initial claim that my freedom cannot determine whether a given crag will or will not lend itself to scaling ("this is part of the brute being of the rock," he tells us [BN, 627]), and his implication that my freedom's role in establishing the degree of resistance in a given thing is exhausted in my selection of a project with respect to which that thing emerges, due to its objective features, as adverse to me, his final position is that the two elements, freedom and facticity, are inextricably (and ambiguously) intertwined. For if, in addition to considering (1) my freedom in choosing a project and (2) the objective steepness of the crag (which emerges as relevant because of the particular project I have chosen), we deepen our analysis by adding (3) the degree to which I desire to climb the crag, we find that the rock will not be an obstacle if I wish at any cost to arrive at the top of the mountain. On the other hand, it will discourage me if I have freely fixed limits to my desire of making the projected climb. Thus the world by coefficient of adversity reveals to me the way in which I stand in relation to the ends which I assign myself, so that I can never know if it is giving me information about myself or about it. (BN, 628)

And our sense of the complexity and ambiguity of this situation deepens further when we consider that the coefficient of adversity of the crag's steepness also depends on (4) the strength and endurance of my body, and my skill as a climber (all aspects of facticity), which in turn depend on both (5) the choices I have made with regard to training versus neglecting my body (freedom), and (6) my genetic endowment (facticity). In the light of this complexity, and in consideration of the multiple ways in which freedom and facticity interact with and affect one another, it is impossible to determine with any degree of precision the role of freedom and of facticity in any particular case of adversity.

Because facticity does play a role in defining my situation, and because my freedom is always situated, it follows, contrary to the popular caricature of Sartre's position, that my freedom is always limited. I can never do just anything that I might want to do. Rather, my situation constrains me in that it rules out certain projects even as it makes others possible. For example, suppose that I decide to become an actor, and that nothing in my situation prevents me from pursuing this project—I am young when I start; I have no familial or other obligations that would stand in my way; I have time and money available for acting classes, and so forth. Suppose further that I achieve great success in pursuing this project and become a world-famous movie star, so that the public recognizes me wherever I go. If I then find this fame a horrible burden, and begin to long for an utterly different kind of life, one in which I can enjoy my privacy and move about freely in public without being recognized, I may find, to my horror, that the project of pursuing such a life is now utterly closed off to me (or else available to me only at a great cost—that of having to change my name, and of either undergoing radical cosmetic surgery to alter my appearance or of constantly having to wear elaborate disguises when going out). I no longer have the option, as I once did, of simply and easily going about my business and blending in with the crowd. And I can no longer choose never to have been famous, or to have returned to me now for use in pursuing a new career the youth that I have spent on acting.

This is not to say, of course, that my situation as a constantly recognized celebrity *forces* or *determines* me to stay in the public eye and to continue to ply my trade as an actor. While I may, in surveying the options open to me, choose to do so, I also retain other options (those of going into seclusion, or of having the cosmetic surgery, or of entering into another profession while hoping that my fame will eventually wear off, or of committing suicide, and so forth). So my situation, while serving as the *basis* for my choice, is never, for Sartre, sufficient to *compel* my choice.

Thus, we are now in a position to understand Sartre's claim that the slave in chains is as free as his master. There is no evidence at all that he means by this statement that the slave's life is as good as the master's, or that the range of options open to the slave is as rich and varied as is the master's (if that means that the values to which the slave has access by successfully completing a freely chosen project are as numerous and qualitatively good [whether assessed subjectively or objectively] as those to which the master has access). To think otherwise would be to confuse practical freedom (freedom of obtaining) with ontological freedom (freedom of choice).

Nor does he mean merely that the slave enjoys an inconsequential inner freedom, that is, a freedom of attitude, of desiring, of judging, and of wishing. Rather, he explicitly condemns such an "inner freedom" as "a pure idealist hoax," on the grounds that "care is taken never to present it as the necessary condition of the *act*" (MR, 237). On Sartre's conception, by contrast, ontological freedom is neither "a license to do whatever one wants" nor an "internal refuge that would remain to us even in our chains" (ILTM, 264). For ontological freedom

> supposes a commencement of realization in order that the choice may be distinguished from the dream and the wish. Thus we shall not say that a prisoner is always free to go out of prison, which would be absurd, nor that he is always free to long for release, which would be an irrelevant truism, but that he is always free to try to escape (or get himself liberated); that is, that whatever his condition may be, he can project his escape and learn the value of his project by undertaking some action. (BN, 622)

So the point of Sartre's claim is simply that slaves, no less than masters, fail to coincide with themselves, are undetermined by their motives (which are accessible to their reflective conscious-nesses), must give meaning to their facticity by surpassing it, and so forth. The oppressed, no less than the oppressors, experience anguish, and must ask: "What shall I do?" "What is important to me?" "What do I stand for?" "What are my values?" "Who am I?"

Similarly, Sartre does not deny that physical disabilities, such as blindness, or an inability to walk, limit possibilities, stand in the way of the realization of certain important values, diminish one's prospects for successfully carrying out various valuable projects, and, in general, are bad things, best avoided if possible. But it is not clear that they diminish ontological freedom. If I am physically disabled, I still have to choose how to constitute my disability; and I still must decide which projects to undertake within the range of possibilities it presents to me (and I must also choose from among the vast array of options open to me that are not especially relevant to my disability). The general point is that "to be free is not to choose the historic world in which one arises—which would have no meaning—but to choose oneself in the world whatever this may be" (BN, 668). That is a task that everyone, equally, must face.

Existential Psychoanalysis

But if ontological freedom is as pervasive as Sartre claims, how can a human life be *comprehended*? And if all human actions are indeed undertaken freely, what remains of psychology, understood as the attempt to *explain* human behavior? After all, psychology, like any other science, has historically understood its task of explanation in terms of discovering underlying *causes*. But if Sartre is right in asserting that all human actions are free, that is to say, uncaused, it would seem that a causal account of human behavior is thereby ruled out. Must we conclude, then, that Sartre's account renders human behavior simply random, haphazard, lawless, and thus, utterly unpredictable and incomprehensible?

Sartre explicitly denies this, and insists, instead, that freedom must not be understood as "a pure capricious, unlawful, gratu-itous, and incomprehensible contingency." Though "each one of my acts, even the most trivial, is entirely free," it simply doesn't follow that "my act can be anything *whatsoever* or even that it is *unforeseeable*" (BN, 584). The reason, in short, is that my actions, though undertaken freely, are interrelated in multiple ways: (1) Many of the facticities that are relevant to my actions remain constant throughout my life. For example, I have never acted from within the situation of being a woman, or a sixteenth-century figure, or a Chinese man, or a blind person, and so forth. (2) My actions are directly connected with one another in that my past actions comprise part of the facticity I confront in choosing my present action, just as my present actions help to make up the facticity I will face in choosing my future actions. (3) As we recall from our discussion of *The Transcendence of the Ego*, it is largely on the basis of reflecting on my past actions that I develop my sense of myself (that is, of my personality, character, values, and priorities), and it is largely on the basis of this sense, in turn, that I regulate my future conduct. (4) Finally, and most importantly, my actions are related to each other in that their ends can be organized into a coherent hierarchy, according to which some are pursued for the sake of more fundamental ones, which, in turn, are pursued for the benefit of even more primary ones. Thus, for example, I respond to my alarm clock by getting out of bed only because I want to get to school on time; but I want this, in turn, only because I want to pass my courses (which I want only because I want to get my degree, which, in turn, I want so that I can pursue my chosen career, and so on).

As a result, it is possible, at least in principle, to understand a human life. Just as a scientist might explain a seemingly diverse assortment of physical events (for example, the rising and falling of the tides, the movements of celestial bodies, and the behavior of material objects near the surface of the earth) by showing that they all flow from one fundamental physical law (for example, that of gravity), so, Sartre claims, is it possible in principle to explain a human life by showing that (and in what ways) all of the free actions comprising it are manifestations of one fundamental choice. Since no existing psychological theory takes up this task, Sartre assigns it to a new intellectual discipline of his own invention. He calls this new discipline "existential psychoanalysis."

The name clearly invites comparison with Freudian psychoanalysis, which shares with Sartre's dissident version the goal of understanding a human life. Still, the two psychoanalytic approaches clearly differ in at least two crucial respects. First, as just noted, Sartre's version, in radical contrast to Freud's, rejects determinism. Thus, while Freud attempts to explain a life by identifying underlying causes (drives, complexes, instincts, and the like), Sartre tries to do so by identifying the internal coherence and logic unifying the series of seemingly disparate choices of action that comprise a life. Secondly, while perhaps the most significant theoretical innovation of Freudian psychoanalysis was its invocation of the unconscious to explain what otherwise had seemed inexplicable, Sartre, as we have seen, not only denies the unconscious, but goes to the opposite extreme in positing a perpetually lucid and self-aware consciousness. It is important to recall here that, for Sartre, consciousness of something is not the same thing as knowledge of it. To look at something, let alone be merely nonthetically aware or conscious of it, is obviously not always sufficient for understanding and knowing it. Accordingly, even on Sartre's view that I am always self-aware, it does not follow that I have a deep understanding of my choices, my projects, or, in general, my life. For such an understanding would typically require, at the very least, a sustained focusing on (as opposed to mere awareness of) those choices and projects, together with a critical probing of various hypotheses concerning their possible interrelations. It would also require a degree of courage and honesty that, on the evidence of the widespread nature of bad faith, is evidently highly unusual. Thus, existential psychoanalysis, no less than its Freudian predecessor, can have the goal of helping a person to understand his or her project, choices, hopes, fears, and intentions. And this is so in spite of the fact that Sartre's existential psychoanalysis proceeds from premises (especially those of freedom and lucid self-awareness) that Freud would claim render this goal utterly unattainable.

From a more purely philosophical standpoint, the rationale for Sartre's project of existential psychoanalysis lies in the recognition that human reality "identifies and defines itself by the ends which it pursues," and that "a study and classification of these ends" is, therefore, "indispensable" (BN, 712). Recall that, for Sartre, I am not to be understood solely in terms of what I *am*, for this leaves out of the equation all of the ways in which I transcend, or go beyond, all factual givens, including those that might be thought to constitute my identity. To act is to negate what is and to try to bring about what is not. Moreover, as we have seen (recall the crag example), the meaning of the factual givens that I confront in acting depends, to a large degree, on the ways in which I highlight some of their aspects by attending to them, while relegating other aspects to the background by neglecting them. I do not confront the items in my perceptual and conceptual field in a neutral way. Rather, they typically appear to me under the color of their relevance to my interests and projects. Their meaning emerges only as I hurtle past them in thrusting toward a desired but currently nonexistent future.

One of Sartre's most important criticisms of existing psychological approaches, then, is precisely that they "avoid everything which could evoke the idea of transcendence" (BN, 712). This is true, Sartre claims, even of those psychologists who seem to recognize the importance of ends, as when they claim that "a particular man is defined by his desires." For these psychologists remain "victims of the illusion of substance," viewing "desire as being *in* man by virtue of being 'contained' by his consciousness," and believing "that the meaning of the desire is inherent in the desire itself" (BN, 712). Sartre, of course, rejects these beliefs, maintaining (1) that consciousness is neither a substance nor a container of things, but rather an activity of focusing on objects that are external to it, and (2) that the meanings of intentional objects are not self-announcing, but rather emerge only as the objects are transcended through the activities of consciousness. It is thus a mistake to think that desires are "little psychic entities dwelling in consciousness." Rather, "they are consciousness itself in its original projective, transcendent structure, for consciousness is on principle consciousness *of* something" (BN, 712–13).

All of these themes—that my actions, though free, are nonetheless understandable and even predictable; that these actions relate to one another in a coherent way; that the key to understanding them lies in grasping the ways in which they help to constitute my pursuit of my most fundamental project(s); that the meanings of the factual givens against the background of which I act are not self-announcing; that the emergence of these meanings depends crucially on my focusing and interpretive acts in the context of my pursuit of freely chosen ends; that these givens are not forces acting on me from *within* my consciousness, but rather are objects *for* my consciousness; that they, as a direct consequence, do not act on me mechanistically, and do not *cause* my actions; and so forth—are clearly illustrated in his famous example of the tired hiker:

I start out on a hike with friends. At the end of several hours of walking my fatigue increases and finally becomes very painful. At first I resist and then suddenly I let myself go, I give up, I throw my knapsack down on the side of the road and let myself fall down beside it. Someone will reproach me for my act and will mean thereby that I was free—that is, not only was my act not determined by any thing or person, but also I could have succeeded in resisting my fatigue longer, I could have done as my companions did and reached the resting place before relaxing. I shall defend myself by saying that I was *too tired*. Who is right? (BN, 584–85)

The debate seems clear. My critic, in blaming me for my action, is implying that I am free, that I could have, and should have, continued on the hike with my friends. (For it would make no sense to hold me responsible for doing what I did if I was *determined* to do it, and could not have done otherwise.) I, on the other hand, in insisting that I was "too tired" to continue hiking, am arguing that I was *not* free to do so, and thus should not be blamed or held responsible for failing to do so.

But Sartre, instead of simply taking sides on this disagreement, argues that the entire debate is "based on incorrect premises." He explains:

There is no doubt that I could have done otherwise, but that is not the problem. It ought to be formulated rather like this: could I have done otherwise without perceptibly modifying the organic totality of the projects which I am; or is the fact of resisting my fatigue such that instead of remaining a purely local and accidental modification of my behavior, it could be effected only by means of a radical transformation of my being-in-the-world—a transformation, moreover, which is *possible*? In other words: I could have done otherwise. Agreed. But *at what price*?" (BN, 585)

In order to clarify Sartre's point, let's begin by considering the role of fatigue in my decision to stop hiking and in my friend's decision to continue hiking. My argument is that the fatigue exerts causal pressure on me, *forcing* me to stop. Because of the fatigue, I am simply *too tired* to continue. My friend counters that since my body is in roughly the same condition as his (we are both in equally good health, and have undergone practically the same training), it is likely that I am no more fatigued than he is—our experience of fatigue is essentially the same. Thus, he regards my refusal to continue hiking simply as a free choice on my part. The proof that my fatigue did not cause me to stop is simply that he, with a body no stronger or healthier than mine, is both able and willing, in the face of the same fatigue, to continue.

Sartre's argument, of course, is that both of us are wrong. I am wrong because my fatigue, far from causing my decision, is merely an aspect of the facticity of my consciousness. Thus, its meaning is not self-announcing. The very fatigue that I regard as "intolerable" my friend finds quite bearable. On this point my friend is right.

But my friend is wrong in thinking that my decision to quit hiking and his decision to continue it are simply divergent responses to the same facticity. For facticity, as it is lived or experienced, is *meaningful*. Whereas I experience my facticity simply as a burden, as pain, my friend experiences his as

> the privileged instrument for discovering the world which surrounds him, for adapting himself to the rocky roughness of the paths, for discovering the "mountainous" quality of the slopes. In the same way it is this light sunburn on the back of his neck and this slight ringing in his ears which will enable him to realize a direct contact with the sun. Finally the feeling of effort is for him that of fatigue overcome. (BN, 586–87)

Thus what I reject and what my friend embraces are far from the same thing.

Moreover, although it may be true, in a certain abstract, ontological sense, that the meaning of my facticity, in-itself, is neutral, it does not follow that the meanings of the respective fatigues that my friend and I first encounter are initially identical (because neutral), and only diverge subsequent to our acts of interpreting those fatigues. Rather, we experience our fatigues, right from the beginning, as meaningful, because we encounter them within a context established by our projects and interests. Thus, if my project of hiking is part of an underlying project of relatively little importance or value to me (such as, say, the pursuit of novelty, or the experimental trying out of different kinds of exercise), it is easy to see that my fatigue would manifest itself, quite spontaneously, as simply a cost attached to that project. And if the project, in turn, is not important to me, the cost will present itself, even without any new or special interpretive acts on my part, as excessive and unbearable.

The case is vastly different with my friend, because his project is different. His fatigue

> is given as a way of appropriating the mountain, . . . and [of] being victor over it. . . . Thus my companion's fatigue is lived in a vaster project of a trusting abandon to nature, of a passion consented to in order that it may exist at full strength, and at the same time the project of sweet mastery and appropriation. It is only in and through this project that the fatigue will be able to be understood and that it will have meaning for him. (BN, 587)

But that is not the end of the analysis, because it can always be asked whether this "project of sweet mastery and appropriation" might itself be embedded in a more fundamental project. Thus, if we are truly to understand the way in which my friend suffers his fatigue, we must, Sartre insists, "undertake a regressive analysis which will lead us back to an initial project" (BN, 588). This, then, is the task of Sartre's new "existential psychoanalysis": "to disengage the meanings implied by an act—by every act—and to proceed from there to richer and more profound meanings until we encounter the meaning which does not imply any other meaning and which refers only to itself" (BN, 589).

Sartre's principal finding in this area is startling, given the diversity, and indeed the opposed nature, of the different projects that different people undertake—differences to which Sartre appeals in explaining such phenomena as my friend's and my utterly dissimilar responses to fatigue when hiking. For Sartre claims to find that we are all alike in that we share a fundamental desire and a fundamental project, so that our differences arise only at the secondary and applied level of the particular way in which we *pursue* that project and attempt to *satisfy* that desire. He argues that, as for-itselves, we desire what we lack: the in-itself. But we want, at the same time, to remain conscious and free. Thus, we want to be in-itself and for-itself at the same time. As Sartre puts it,

> the fundamental value which presides over this project is exactly the in-itself-for-itself; that is, the ideal of a consciousness which would be the foundation of its own being-in-itself by the pure consciousness which it would have of itself. It is this ideal which can be called God. Thus the best way to conceive of the fundamental project of human reality is to say that man is the being whose project is to be God. . . .

To be man means to reach toward being God. Or if you prefer, man fundamentally is the desire to be God. (BN, 723–24)

To understand Sartre's odd-sounding claim, consider the fact that consciousness is related to being-in-itself in an essentially negative way. Its freedom necessarily involves negation. To act is to attempt to bring about what currently is not, and to negate and go beyond what currently is. Indeed, to exist is to posit ends and to pursue them. There is no escape from our condition as a flight toward or pursuit of projected *desiderata*. This, in part, is what Sartre means by his oft-stated claim that we are "condemned to be free;" and it seems to imply that we are doomed to frustration. We are always on the way and never arrive. Consciousness is always a flight from being even as it is also always a quest for being. We would like, instead, for our quest for being to result in our actually coinciding with it (as opposed to being always alienated from it, because of the nihilating activities of consciousness). And yet, at the same time, we wish to remain free, conscious beings.

From another angle, Sartre's point is that we wish to escape from the burden, responsibility, and anguish of freedom by becoming finished, complete, something that is what it is, like a thing, even as we remain free. We desire, moreover, to exist justifiably and necessarily, rather than contingently. We want to be our own foundation, and to overcome permanently the self-division and alienation inherent in being what one is not and in not being what one is. We seek "to have the impermeability and infinite density of the in-itself" (BN, 723), even as we retain the freedom and lucid consciousness of the for-itself. Thus, we wish to be in-itself-for-itself, like God. Indeed, the chief merit that Sartre attributes to his "existential psychoanalysis" is that it clearly reveals to us that this is our project.

This illustrates an interesting feature of Sartre's philosophy—its engagement with, and reworking of, popular belief systems that it rejects. We are presently considering Sartre's "existential" revision of Freudian psychoanalysis. This has led us to consider the idea of God, and his treatment of that idea underscores the fact that, although Sartre is an atheist, much of his thought can be understood as a reworking of theistic (particularly Christian) thought on atheistic terms. Thus, while he completely rejects belief in the existence of God, he is not content merely to point out inconsistencies and paradoxes inherent in the conception of God and logical flaws in arguments defending God's existence. Nor does he attribute theism merely to ignorance, or to superstitious or wishful thinking, on the part of believers. Rather, he suggests that the conception of, and longing for, God, is essentially built into the human ontological condition. On this point he agrees with many prominent Christian thinkers, including Saint Thomas Aquinas and Søren Kierkegaard (though of course he disagrees with them in that he holds that God, far from actually existing, is merely the projection of that which we wish to achieve but cannot). Moreover, Kierkegaard even anticipates Sartre's claim that the concept of God is self-contradictory. Indeed, Kierkegaard champions Christianity in part because the extremely paradoxical nature of many of its key claims requires extraordinary faith on the part of its believers. But Sartre, as we have seen, is a critic of faith, and is too much a rationalist to countenance the knowing acceptance of logical absurdities.

Indeed, for Sartre the main problem with the project of attempting to be God is that the very idea of God—a being who would be in-itself-for-itself—is contradictory. As for-itself, God would be divided. But whatever is divided isn't in-itself, since being-in-itself is an undifferentiated plenitude. And being free is incompatible with having a fixed essence of any kind, let alone that of perfection.

The idea that the concept of God is contradictory is an old one, and many theists have wrestled with it. For example, there are paradoxes of omnipotence—if God can do anything, can he make a stone so heavy that even he can't lift it? If he can make such a stone, then he can't lift that stone—hence there is something he can't do, and he therefore isn't omnipotent. So then it must be that he can't make such a stone, since he, being omnipotent, can lift any stone. But then his inability to make such a stone is proof of his lack of omnipotence. Similarly, how can a free being be omniscient? For an omniscient being knows the future. Thus, such a being would have no choices to make. To a clear-thinking person, then, "the very nature of God forbids us to believe in him" (NFE, 146).

Moreover, Sartre argues that this is so not only because the concept of God is contradictory, but also because this concept "is opposed to the psychological structure of belief," since it cannot be the object of experience or intuition: "We can neither see him nor grasp his infinite nature through rational intuition. Therefore, we cannot found ourselves on any concrete operation, and so our belief is a belief *in nothing*. To be legitimate, it has to borrow from the sensory world of intuitions (nice old man, Christ on the cross), which is only possible for children or those who have a shoemaker's faith." Thus, Sartre concludes that "the Christian's faith is bad faith" (NFE, 146).

All of this entails the disturbing conclusion that our fundamental desire, to be God, is in principle unsatisfiable, and that our fundamental project, that of becoming God, is doomed to failure. And Sartre does not flinch from drawing this conclusion, but rather states it with dramatic flare: "The idea of God is contradictory and we lose ourselves in vain. Man is a useless passion" (BN, 784).

Before considering whether or not there might be a way to evade this disturbing consequence of Sartre's analysis, let me pause to point out a couple of ways in which his existential psychoanalysis seems in tension with the rest of his thought. First, since Sartre is in most contexts among the first to emphasize the role of accident and contingency in human affairs, it is difficult to understand his insistence that my every act, and even my every *gesture*, is so intertwined with the rest of them as to be revelatory, to the skilled existential psychoanalyst, of my entire hierarchy of projects. One might have thought, to the contrary, that some of my habits and enthusiasms would be attributable to separate, utterly unconnected, historical accidents. But Sartre maintains that "[a] gesture refers to a *Weltanschauung* [world view] and we *sense* it" (BN, 589). Indeed, he goes so far as to identify as "the *principle* of [existential] psychoanalysis" the idea that "man is a totality and not a collection." He explains that this means that "he expresses himself as a whole in even his most insignificant and his most superficial behavior. In other words there is not a taste, a mannerism, or a human act which is not *revealing*" (BN, 726).

Secondly, what remains of my freedom if the implications of my most basic choices are so far reaching as to entail even my "most insignificant and most superficial behavior"? After all, it certainly *seems* to me that I am confronted, on a daily basis, with the need to make a number of significant choices; and indeed it is chiefly on the basis of this powerful datum of experience that Sartre develops his rich and intricate phenomenological account of freedom. But if he is correct in claiming that all of my actions are predictable because they are merely the mutually interconnected products of my most fundamental choices, it would appear to follow that my experience of freedom is largely illusory. For it certainly seems to me not only that my future is open, and thus unpredictable, since its content must await my decision, but also that my decision is not determined by my prior choices.

To be fair, we must note that Sartre would agree that my decision is not *determined* by my prior choices. For, to return to the hiking example, while Sartre's main point is that my acts of giving in to my fatigue and of quitting the hike are fully comprehensible and even predictable, he still allows that it would have been "possible" for me to have resisted my fatigue and to have continued with the hike. What would have made such an act extremely unlikely (though not impossible) is the fact that it could not have been accomplished by means of "a purely local and accidental modification of my behavior" (BN, 585), but rather only through "a radical conversion of my being-in-the-world; that is, by an abrupt metamorphosis of an initial project—*i.e.*, by another choice of myself and of my ends" (BN, 598).

But this account, in addition to failing to square with my experience of my freedom, seems to imply that there are fewer issues with respect to which I am called on to make a free decision than is commonly thought—a decidedly odd position for Sartre, of all people, that great champion of freedom, to be defending. For it suggests that the choices one makes without altering one's fundamental choice, that is, without undergoing a radical conversion, aren't real choices—they all simply flow from the fundamental project. So the only real choice is whether to continue one's project or to undertake a radical conversion. After all, if even my "most insignificant and most superficial behavior" is entailed by my fundamental choice, it would seem that the *only* choice that I ever face concerns that fundamental one—shall I continue with it, or shall I overthrow it and effect "a radical conversion of my being-in-the-world?" But it seems to me that the choices confronting me are much richer, more varied, and more multi-leveled than that. For example, even if Sartre is right (as I suspect he is) in his analysis of the meaning of my fatigue as I experience it, it is far from clear that I could resist my fatigue only by undergoing a radical transformation. The reason, I suggest, is that my projects and interests are not as intricately and hierarchically related to one another as Sartre's existential psychoanalysis says they are. Rather, I can have conflicting projects, based on unrelated (and perhaps even incommensurable) interests, and these regularly put me in the position of having to make difficult choices. For example, while my fatigue may indeed strike me as nothing but pain, and thus fail to convey to me any of the positive meanings that my friend finds in it (such as mastery, appropriation, the establishment of intimate contact with nature, and so forth), I may still have other reasons, based on interests having nothing to do with finding a positive meaning in fatigue, for wanting to continue with the hike. For example, I may have an ethical interest in not spoiling the hike for my companions, or perhaps merely a selfish desire not to alienate my companion's friendship by annoying and disappointing him. If so, I am likely to experience these interests as competing with my desire to escape the pain of the fatigue, and as requiring me to make a choice—and a choice that is by no means necessitated by a fundamental choice, so that it could be avoided only by radically altering that fundamental choice. The existential drama of having to make such choices on a daily basis is ordinarily one of the driving forces underlying all of Sartre's thought. So it is strange that his existential psychoanalysis seems to diminish this drama, if not to explain it away entirely.

And he does so not only with respect to ordinary, day-to-day choices, but also in connection with more fundamental ones. One might have thought, to the contrary, that persons who had read and been persuaded by Sartre might at least experience a heightened sense of freedom with regard to these basic choices. For such persons, now recognizing that their daily choices are rooted in more fundamental ones that they had previously not even recognized, let alone critically examined, would perhaps as a result come to see the need for regular, persistent, careful reevaluation of such choices, and for serious consideration of the possibility of reversing them through a radical conversion. But Sartre disagrees, on the grounds that "our actual choice is such that it furnishes us with no *motive* for [reversing it] by means of a further choice." The reason is that "it is this original choice which originally creates . . . all motives which can guide us to partial actions; it is this which arranges the world with its meaning, its instrumental-complexes, and its coefficient of adversity." Indeed, Sartre even goes so far as to say that fundamental choices other than our own, though possible, are "incomprehensible" to us from our standpoint of having made a different choice. Thus, "to 'understand' them in fact would be already to have chosen them" (BN, 598–99). It is difficult to see, then, how one could seriously consider different possible fundamental choices, critically evaluate them, and then, in any meaningful sense, choose from among them. And this bleak conclusion is only underscored by Sartre's seemingly sweeping, exceptionless claim that the fundamental project of *all* humans is to strive to become in-itself-for-itself, or God.

Ethics

However, just as he had done in connection with his disturbing analyses of bad faith and of concrete relations with others, here again Sartre drops a brief hint that there might be a way out after all—in this case that the fundamental choice which he had seemed clearly to identify with the human condition might instead turn out to be optional and avoidable.

He first makes this point (briefly, and without calling much attention to it) in the context of offering a sketch of the project that he calls "play." He defines play as "an activity of which man is the first origin, for which man himself sets the rules, and which has no consequences except according to the rules posited" (BN, 741). In play

> the function of the act is to make manifest to *itself* the absolute freedom which is the very being of the person. This particular type of project, which has freedom for its foundation and its goal, deserves a special study. It is radically different from all others in that it aims at a radically different type of being. It would be necessary to explain in full detail its relations with the project of being-God, which has appeared to us as the deep-seated structure of reality. But such a study can not be made here; it belongs rather to an *Ethics* and it supposes that there has been a preliminary definition of nature and the role of purifying reflection (our descriptions have hitherto aimed only at *accessory* reflection); it supposes in addition taking a position which can be *moral* only in the face of values which haunt the For-itself. (BN, 742)

In these terse, tantalizing remarks, Sartre seems to be implying (1) that play, perhaps uniquely, differs radically from the project of being-God, (2) that it is possible to choose play instead of choosing the project of being-God, (3) that Sartre's earlier descriptions and analyses, which had led to the conclusion that it is simply the human condition to choose the project of being-God, were one-sided and incomplete, and (4) that this one-sidedness, to be corrected in the study and description of play, had consisted specifically in the neglecting of the realm of ethics.

While Sartre does not again take up the topic of play in *Being and Nothingness*, he does close the book by returning to the idea that we might be able to renounce the project of being-God. This discussion takes place in the last two pages of the book, in a brief, concluding section entitled "Ethical Implications." And it follows a passage the bleakness of which perhaps exceeds all others in the book, including those describing the ubiquity of bad faith and the futility and misery of interpersonal relationships. For here Sartre issues the despairing, nihilistic proclamation that "all human activities are equivalent," since "all are on principle doomed to failure." "Thus," he concludes, in one of his most famous and most shocking utterances, "it amounts to the same thing whether one gets drunk alone or is a leader of nations" (BN, 797).

Attention to the context in which this statement occurs, however, removes from it much of its shocking quality. For the statement arises in the midst of a discussion of the fact that existential psychoanalysis reveals to us "the real goal of [our] pursuit, which is being as a synthetic fusion of the in-itself with the for-itself;" and this context strongly suggests that Sartre's harsh judgment concerning the equivalent futility of all human actions is intended to apply only to actions undertaken in pursuit of that unattainable goal.

Moreover, in the final two paragraphs of the book he raises again the possibility that we are not doomed to choosing the futile project of trying to be in-itself-for-itself, or God. He speaks of the need to reveal to moral agents that this project is only one possible project among many. While he then immediately notes that in his previous discussion all of the possible choices had appeared to be unified in that all of them were attempts, by different routes, to arrive at the supreme value of being in-itself-for-itself, he now suddenly asks a series of questions concerning the possibility of overthrowing this supreme value. He asks, for example, "What will become of freedom if it turns its back upon this value? . . . Will freedom . . . be able to put an end to the reign of this value? In

particular is it possible for freedom to take itself for a value as
the source of all value . . ." (BN, 797–98)? Unfortunately, rather
than answering these questions, Sartre merely remarks, "All these
questions, which refer us to a pure and not an accessory reflection, can find their reply only on the ethical plane. We shall devote
to them a future work" (BN, 798). With these words, *Being and
Nothingness* comes to a close.

Unfortunately, Sartre never completed his promised book on
ethics (although a substantial portion of this unfinished and abandoned work was published posthumously as *Notebooks for an
Ethics*). Nonetheless, I think the resources available to us are more
than adequate for determining how Sartre intended the questions
posed at the conclusion of *Being and Nothingness* to be answered.
Can freedom "turn its back upon" and "put an end to the reign
of" the value of being in-itself-for-itself, and instead "take itself for
a value as the source of all value?" It seems clear that Sartre's
answer to these questions is yes.

Recall, first of all, that Sartre has already announced, in *Being
and Nothingness*, that there exists one project (play) that differs
radically from the project of being-God "in that it aims at a radically different type of being," and takes "freedom for its foundation and its goal." Moreover, the fact that he makes a point of
reserving full discussion of this project for a planned future work
on ethics further suggests that it is this project that he has in mind
when he poses his questions at the conclusion of *Being and
Nothingness*. After all, he says there that these questions, too, must
await a book on ethics to receive their answer.

Secondly, notice that this understanding of Sartre's message
enables us to make sense of the brief, puzzling "radical conversion" passages in *Being and Nothingness* that we have noted. For
example, recall Sartre's terse footnote informing us that "a radical
conversion," to be discussed and explained elsewhere, may provide
us "deliverance and salvation" from the hellish circle of mutually
antagonistic and unsatisfying "concrete relations with Others" that
he has described in such vivid and nightmarish detail. Could this
radical conversion be the abandonment of the project of being-
God and the adoption, instead, of a project based on recognizing
and embracing (and perhaps maximizing and intensifying) freedom? It would seem that it could, since Sartre's analysis of concrete relations with Others identifies the project of attempting to

be in-itself-for-itself as the source of the futility, hostility, and misery that typically characterizes these relations. Were we to give up the impossible project of being-God, and with it the attempt to take control of the Other's freedom and make it a freedom subject to our freedom, there would be no need for so much interpersonal warfare. (And it is worth pointing out, in this regard, that many other of the gloomier pronouncements in *Being and Nothingness*—that "man is a useless passion," and that "it amounts to the same thing whether one gets drunk alone or is a leader of nations," for example—are issued in the context of stating the implications of the project of being-God. Thus, it is entirely possible that they are not intended to apply to individuals who are not pursuing that project.)

If this interpretation is correct, Sartre's approach to ethics in *Being and Nothingness* is indirect and dialectical. Rather than arguing straightforwardly for an ethics centered on the pursuit of freedom, Sartre attempts to persuade us to take this route by showing us the intolerable consequences of doing otherwise. He tries to demonstrate both that it is our ontological condition to yearn for something utterly unattainable, and that if we act on that yearning, our inescapable lot will be bad faith, endless interpersonal conflict, and futility. What is needed, then, is a "radical conversion" from the project of being-God to a project based on recognizing freedom as the highest value.

Thirdly, and perhaps most importantly, Sartre's subsequent writings support this interpretation. In them Sartre consistently speaks of freedom, not being in-itself-for-itself, as the highest value. Moreover, he occasionally calls this change a "radical conversion," and in *Notebooks for an Ethics* he explicitly affirms that "*Being and Nothingness* is an ontology before conversion" (NFE, 6).

Consider, as an example of Sartre's post–*Being and Nothingness* rhetoric, his declaration, in a lecture delivered three years after its publication, that "freedom . . . can have no other end and aim but itself," and that "freedom" is "the foundation of all values" (EH, 51). Readers of *Being and Nothingness* are likely (unless they notice the way in which it seems designed to answer the questions posed at the end of that book) to find this pronouncement puzzling, since it appears to contradict one of the book's central tenets, namely that one can (and indeed typically, and, in a sense, *naturally*, does) take the idea of God, of being in-itself-for-itself, as the supreme value. Thus, it is highly significant that Sartre immediately qualifies his new claim that freedom is the highest value by noting that "the actions *of men of good faith* have, as their ultimate significance, the quest for freedom itself as such" (EH, 51, emphasis added). This strongly suggests that those who seek, instead, to become God are living inauthentically, that is, in bad faith. Therefore, given that *Being and Nothingness* (aside from the brief radical conversion passages) presents both bad faith and the project of being-God as ubiquitous, this reference to the actions of "men of good faith" indicates that we have now moved to a new territory, largely left unexplored in *Being and Nothingness.* And that, in turn, implies that the focus of that book is narrower than is generally supposed. Far from simply describing the human condition, Sartre in *Being and Nothingness* is describing the situation of human beings living inauthentically. Little wonder that their interpersonal relationships are unsuccessful!

(In fairness to those who read *Being and Nothingness* as addressing the human situation, it is important to note that Sartre sees bad faith, the futile quest to be God, interpersonal conflict, and misery to be, as it were, our natural, or default, condition. This is why a radical conversion from the situation toward which our ontological condition inclines us is needed. Here again we find in Sartre's philosophy an atheistic analogue to Christian doctrines—in this case that of original sin. It is as if he were saying that we are in a fallen state, and stand in need of salvation! This, I propose, is the key to understanding Sartre's footnote placed at the end of his discussion of bad faith, in which he tells us that we can "radically escape bad faith," but that this requires "a self-recovery of being which was previously corrupted." This self-recovery, which Sartre calls "authenticity," requires a radical conversion from the project of being-God to a project based on freedom.)

Sartre's most detailed discussion of the radical conversion is to be found in his *Notebooks for an Ethics.* There he explains its motivation: The "conversion may arise from the perpetual failure of every one of the For-itself's attempts to be.[12] Every attempt of the

---

[12] Here Sartre appears to be abandoning his claim, discussed in the final paragraph of the "Existential Psychoanalysis" section above, that "our actual choice is such that it furnishes us with no *motive* for [reversing it] by means of a further choice."

For-itself to be In-itself is by definition doomed to failure." This failure, according to Sartre, leads to a kind of "Hell," which he defines as "that region of existence where existing means using every trick in order to be, and to fail at all these tricks, and to be conscious of this failure." And this failure can then

> push the For-itself to ask itself the . . . question of the meaning of its acts and the reason for its failure. Then the problem gets posed as follows: Why is the human world inevitably a world of failure, what is there in the essence of human effort such that it seems doomed in principle to failure? This question is a solicitation for us to place ourselves on the plane of reflection and to envisage human action reflectively in terms of its maxims, its means, and its goals. . . . Reflection is born as an effort by consciousness to regain itself. (NFE, 472)

Recall, in connection with this reference to reflection, that in Sartre's discussion of play in *Being and Nothingness* he distinguishes between "accessory reflection" and "purifying reflection." He tells us there that his descriptions in *Being and Nothingness* have aimed only at accessory reflection, but that play, a project "which has freedom for its foundation and its goal," demands purifying reflection.

In *Notebooks for an Ethics* Sartre clarifies the nature of these two kinds of reflection and their relevance to the radical conversion. Accessory reflection fails to address fundamental issues, but rather confines itself to secondary matters. It takes my fundamental ends for granted, and merely aids in the deliberation over the means to attain them. Insofar as it falsely assumes that I have no choice over my basic goals, taking them instead simply as given, it is in bad faith. Purifying reflection (also called "nonaccessory reflection"), by contrast, does explicitly focus on fundamental ends, calling them into question, revealing them not to be necessary or inevitable, but rather as optional, that is, as possibilities. Purifying reflection thus facilitates authenticity and the escaping of bad faith. Through purifying reflection one achieves a true and lucid understanding of how one stands in relation to his or her ends, and acquires the ability to accept or reject them, not passively, by default, but rather by free, conscious choice.

This distinction helps us to understand the role of reflection in the radical conversion. Of course, I do not begin with reflection. Rather, prereflective consciousness is primary. At first I direct my consciousness outward, at the objects with which I am dealing as I pursue my projects. But at some point it dawns on me that things aren't working out. I find myself in "Hell." So I withdraw from my projects so as to reflect on them. How else might I go about pursuing my ends? Are there other ways that might work better? This is accessory reflection. But it fails to produce better results. This may finally lead me to focus explicitly on, and to reevaluate, my fundamental project (this is purifying reflection), and, perhaps, to change it (this is the radical conversion). Thus, "conversion comes . . . from the failure of accessory reflection. . . . This failure of accessory [reflection] can serve as a motivation for turning to nonaccessory reflection. . . . In a word, the very structure of alienation . . . , the failure of the For-itself's attempt to be in-itself-for-itself, and the failure of accessory reflection make up a bundle of solicitations that may lead to pure reflection," which, in turn, leads to a "new, 'authentic,' way of being oneself and for oneself, which transcends . . . bad faith" (NFE, 472–74). And Sartre makes it clear that this new authentic way of being can only come about through "a conversion from the project to-be-for-itself-in-itself . . . to a project of unveiling and creation" (NFE, 482).

These ideas—that human beings are ontologically inclined toward inauthenticity, that this inauthenticity leads to a hellish life, that we consequently stand in need of salvation, that this salvation requires a radical conversion, that this radical conversion involves renouncing the project of being-God and embracing instead a project based on freedom, and that this conversion requires a move to the mode of reflection (and then a move from accessory reflection to pure reflection)—are crucial to the understanding of Sartre's thought. Moreover, they appear throughout his intellectual career. Recall from chapter 1, the phenomenology chapter, that Sartre invokes them even in his very early works, *The Transcendence of the Ego* and *The Emotions: Outline of a Theory*. (In the former his point is that our belief in the transcendental ego is part of our tendency to deceive ourselves about the extent of our freedom and responsibility—an inauthentic belief that is sustained by accessory reflection, but which must be overthrown by purifying reflection; while in the latter the inauthentic belief to be overcome through purifying reflection is that we are passive victims of our emotions, and not responsible for them. As these examples indicate, these concepts do not originate, as some suspect, only in

Being and Nothingness, and then only as part of a pathetic, ad hoc attempt to paper over the disturbing results of Sartre's phenomenological investigations there.) And he carries them over to the very end. In his last major work, a series of discussions he carried out with Benny Lévy shortly before his death, he remarks: "I think there is a modality other than the primary modality. . . . It's the ethical modality. And the ethical modality implies . . . that we stop wanting to have being as a goal, we no longer want to be God, we no longer want to be *ens causa sui* [our own cause]. We're looking for something else" (HN, 59). The fact that Sartre holds fast to these ideas even in this work, one in which he seems willing to renounce or modify many other notions that had been important to him, demonstrates their centrality to his thought, from beginning to end.

But what, more concretely, do they mean? What does Sartre's proposed freedom-ethic entail? Recall that, for Sartre, our inescapable freedom carries with it the consequence that we never arrive, can never rest, can never coincide with ourselves. We cannot stop exercising our freedom. So our values must also always be dynamic, never static. Thus, if our goal is scientific or philosophical knowledge, for example, our success in such a project can never be final. Any answers we find will just give rise to new questions. The key, then, is to recognize this and to appreciate it. The value lies in the doing, and not in the arriving at a permanent stopping point. As Sartre puts it, "Authenticity reveals that the only meaningful project is that of *doing* (not that of being). . . . So, originally, authenticity consists in refusing any quest for being . . ." (NFE, 475).

And it also consists in recognizing that the highest values are those that are most closely connected to freedom. Sartre argues that "values reveal freedom," and that "any ordering of values has to lead to freedom." Accordingly, he calls for a classification of "values in a hierarchy such that freedom increasingly appears in it" (NFE, 9). In Sartre's classification, the highest values, in ascending order, are passion, pleasure, criticism and the demand for evidence, responsibility, creation, and, at the very top, generosity (NFE, 470).

Though Sartre never completed to his satisfaction a book solely devoted to ethics, his many attempts to clarify and to elaborate on these (and other) ethical ideas may be found scattered throughout most of his post–*Being and Nothingness* writings. To these writings we now turn.

4

No Exit

Sartre's play, *No Exit*, appeared in 1944. It immediately achieved spectacular success, not only in France, but worldwide. (For example, it received the Donaldson Prize, awarded to the best play performed in New York, for the 1946-1947 season.) Now firmly established as a classic of twentieth-century theater, it has been repeatedly filmed, televised, performed on radio, and produced as an audio recording. It is perhaps the most widely performed French play of the twentieth century, and continues to be revived regularly.

The immediate stimulus for the play was a practical problem. Sartre had three vain actor friends who wanted him to write a play for them. Sartre knew there would be trouble if any one of the actors had more lines or more stage time than the others. Thus, he hit upon the solution of putting them all in one room together for the duration of the play, with none of them ever exiting. From this idea it was but a short step to think of putting them all together in hell, trapped in a room together for all eternity.

The three main characters (there is also a valet, who makes a brief appearance at the beginning) are Garcin, Estelle, and Inez. As one might expect of characters in hell, none of them is admirable.

Garcin, a pacifist journalist who has been executed for fleeing military service, is callous and vain. While he claims to be in hell only for having treated his wife "abominably" (NE, 24), we quickly learn that what really troubles his conscience is his concern that his refusal to fight may have stemmed more from cowardice than from genuine conviction.

Estelle is wealthy, vapid, self-absorbed, and obsessed with class and status. She had married an older man, whom she did not love, for his money, and then treated him unkindly. More importantly, she had murdered her daughter, the product of an extramarital affair with a man of a lower economic and social class, by drowning her right in front of her father, who proceeded, in response, to commit suicide by shooting himself in the head.

Inez, an admitted sadist, had seduced her cousin's wife (she was living with the couple), making his life miserable. When he was subsequently run over by a tram, she tortured her lover (his widow) with daily reminders that "we killed him between us" (NE, 26). After six months of such provocations, the lover got up late one night to turn on the gas, killing herself and Inez in their bed.

Fairly early in the play, Inez, the most intelligent and clear-thinking of the three, figures out why they have been placed together in hell:

> **Inez:** I understand now. . . . You'll see how simple it is. Childishly simple. Obviously there aren't any physical torments. . . . And yet we're in hell. And no one else will come here. We'll stay in this room together, the three of us, for ever and ever. . . . In short, there's someone absent here, the official torturer.
>
> **Garcin:** I'd noticed that.
>
> **Inez:** It's obvious what they're after—an economy of man-power—or devil power, if you prefer. The same idea as in the cafeteria, where customers serve themselves.
>
> **Estelle:** What ever do you mean?
>
> **Inez:** I mean that each of us will act as torturer of the two others. (NE, 17–18)

And these three are indeed ideally suited to carry out this role of torturer for one another. Their situation is this: Inez desires Estelle; Estelle desires Garcin (mostly because she wants to be admired and desired by men); and Garcin desires the moral approval of Inez. But Inez's desire for Estelle must go unfulfilled, since Estelle needs Garcin, and has no use for Inez. Estelle, in turn, cannot attract Garcin's attention (not for long, anyway), because she cannot give him what he desperately wants (but which only Inez, for reasons to be discussed in due course, can deliver)—assurance that he is not a coward. And Garcin cannot get Inez's moral approval because she has no motive, either in terms of her honest assessment of the evidence or in terms of her self-interest, to give it to him. Indeed, even aside from the evidence, she has two strong reasons to hurt him by withholding the positive judgment that he craves: First, she wants revenge against Garcin, since she sees her pursuit of Estelle as being thwarted by Estelle's desire for him. Secondly, she is a sadist ("When I say I'm cruel, I mean I can't get on without making people suffer" [NE, 27]), and thus is motivated to take advantage of her situation as affording her a unique opportunity to make him suffer for all eternity.

The plot of *No Exit*, as befits a short, one-act play, is rather slight. We witness several attempts by each of the characters to get what he or she wants from one of the others, only, in every case, to be frustrated in this quest, usually because of the words and actions of the third character. At the play's climax, Garcin utters one of the most famous lines in Sartre's enormous body of writings: "So this is hell. I'd never have believed it. You remember all we were told about the torture chambers, the fire and brimstone. . . . Old wives' tales! There's no need for red-hot pokers. Hell is— other people!" (NE, 46-47)

But the minimal plotting of *No Exit* does not prevent one from fully enjoying and appreciating it. It holds a viewer's or reader's interest from start to finish. In part, this is a tribute to the play's concision (a virtue rarely found in Sartre's writings!). The plot is more than adequate for a play of this brevity. Moreover, all of the characters are fascinating, in a grotesque way; and one can, if so inclined, thoroughly enjoy the play simply as a darkly comic character study. But *No Exit* is, above all else, a philosophical play, a play of ideas, and it is at this level that it truly shines.

A Philosophical Play

It is ironic, then, that Sartre himself, in "The Purposes of Writing," makes the preposterous claim that *No Exit* "doesn't contain a word of philosophy." As he explains, "I had no wish to 'repeat' *Being and Nothingness* in different words. What would have been the point?" (BEM, 10)

One can, of course, agree that there would have been little point in writing a play which did *nothing else but* repeat *Being and Nothingness* in different words, and which did not concern itself *at all* with, for example, aesthetic considerations (such as pacing, the development of characters, the building up of tension, the occasional injection of humor, and so forth), that are central to dramatic works and less important in (if not utterly irrelevant to) lengthy, abstruse philosophical treatises. But Sartre seems to be advancing the much stronger and more dubious thesis, especially in his claim that *No Exit* contains not even *a word* of philosophy, that there would have been no point in including, in different words, *any* ideas from *Being and Nothingness*, even merely as one element among many in a literary work that also exhibits several other features of aesthetic interest.

Still, Sartre's question stands in need of an answer. What would be the point of repeating some ideas from *Being and Nothingness* in a play? Well, for one thing, as his own frequent use of examples in *Being and Nothingness* amply demonstrates, Sartre's philosophical ideas are abstract and difficult, and tend to come to life, to become clear and vivid, only when they are conveyed concretely. A play is an ideal vehicle for accomplishing this. (And perhaps it goes without saying that the ideas will reach far more people this way— short, entertaining plays are much more popular than are dense, lengthy philosophical works.)

Coming at it from another direction, it has been widely recognized since at least the time of Aristotle that the inclusion of interesting ideas to ponder and discuss is an element that can greatly enhance the enjoyment of a play.[1] Moreover, since philosophical ideas address fundamental issues (for example, the nature of reality, of truth, of value, and so forth), any play is bound, however loosely, indirectly, or unwittingly, to convey a certain number of philosophical theses. (And this point seems especially clear in the case of Sartre's philosophy, which takes as its subject matter human existence as it is lived, and which employs a descriptive, phenomenological method.) Thus, Sartre could not have written a play devoid of philosophical ideas even if he had wanted to do so. So

---

[1] See Aristotle's *Poetics*, especially sections 6 and 19. A good translation is that of James Hutton (New York: Norton, 1982), 50–52, 65.

why shouldn't the ideas be, as is so obviously the case anyway, *his*, rather than, say, those he opposes?[2]

Bad Faith Dramatized

One Sartrean idea that the play vividly illustrates is bad faith. Garcin, for example, is in bad faith about his cowardice. He has both an obscure, nonthetic awareness of his many past cowardly actions, and a clear, focused awareness of his lifelong aim of being a hero. Thus, he wishes to avoid confronting the pattern of his past actions ("facticity," in the language of *Being and Nothingness*), and chooses instead to define himself in terms of his aspirations ("transcendence"). He seeks the aid of Estelle in this project, trying to persuade her to objectify him as a hero, or at least as not a coward, so that he might receive, through her eyes, confirmation of his self-image. Estelle in turn, who wishes to be seen by a man as attractive, is eager to oblige. But the cynical, and in this case fully clear-sighted, Inez is also present to poke holes in their cooperative bad faith venture. Consider this bit of dialogue:

Estelle: . . . you refused to fight. Well, why shouldn't you?

Garcin: I—I didn't exactly refuse . . . I—I took the train. . . . They caught me at the frontier.

Estelle: Where were you trying to go?

Garcin: To Mexico. I meant to launch a pacifist newspaper down there. [*A short silence.*] Well, why don't you speak?

Estelle: What could I say? You acted quite rightly, as you didn't want to fight. [*Garcin makes a fretful gesture.*] But, darling, how on earth can I guess what you want me to answer?

Inez: Can't you guess? Well, *I* can. He wants you to tell him that he bolted like a lion. For "bolt" he did, and that's what's biting him.

Garcin: "Bolted," "went away"—we won't quarrel over words. (NE, 37–38)

---

[2] It should be noted that Sartre did not consistently maintain that *No Exit* is devoid of philosophical ideas. In a preface to *No Exit* that he wrote for an audio recording of the play he discusses at some length what he takes to be its main philosophical themes. This preface can be found in SOT, 198–201.

While Garcin's bad faith is obvious here, elsewhere in the play Sartre handles it with greater subtlety. For example, he leads his audience to infer, at first, that Garcin, far from being in bad faith, is extraordinarily honest in his self-evaluation. After all, Garcin does not merely admit to having mistreated his wife, but rather seems to make a point of describing that mistreatment with maximum clarity, thus underscoring its full horror: "Night after night I came home blind drunk, stinking of wine and women. She'd sat up for me, of course. But she never cried, never uttered a word of reproach. Only her eyes spoke. Big, tragic eyes. I don't regret anything." Then, after noting that this explanation might be too vague to convey the full extent of his callousness, he continues by offering "something you can get your teeth into. I brought a half-caste girl to stay in our house. My wife slept upstairs; she must have heard—everything. She was an early riser and, as I and the girl stayed in bed late, she served us our morning coffee." When Inez responds to this story by calling Garcin a "brute," he cheerfully agrees: "Yes, a brute, if you like. But a well-beloved brute. . . . Yes, a brute. Certainly. Else why should I be here?" (NE, 25)

At this point we begin to see the deceptive, self-serving purposes underlying Garcin's seemingly admirably candid confession. His story of humiliating his wife with other women is intended (1) to demonstrate how attractive and "well-beloved" he is, and, more importantly, (2) to distract attention away from what really concerns him, namely, the issue of his cowardice. When Inez had first brought up the fact that he had been a deserter, he had replied, "Let that be. It's only a side-issue. I'm here because I treated my wife abominably. That's all" (NE, 24). It is in this context that his quick admission to being a brute, and his even quicker addendum, "Else why should I be here?," are to be understood.

Garcin also clearly illustrates the point that one usually cannot succeed in lying to oneself if the lie is too blatant, as when the evidence against what one wants to believe is clear, unequivocal, and overwhelming. Thus, Garcin does not go so far as to claim to be a hero, or even not to be a coward. Rather, he grasps at straws in order to cling to the belief that the matter has been "left in suspense, forever" (NE, 39), since a life can't be judged by a single action (NE, 44). And he tries to convince himself that, had he had time, he would have acted courageously in the future. Here Garcin uses the tried-and-true bad-faith tactic of employing inconsistent standards of evidence, for we learn (NE, 38) that he would have been happy to judge himself by a single act if it had been a courageous one.

But his pathetic attempts to enlist the aid of others in his bad faith project (that of attempting to convince himself that he is not a coward) all fail, of course, and this brings us to a second theme from *Being and Nothingness* that *No Exit* graphically illustrates: Sartre's distinctive analysis of human relationships.

Hell Is Other People

Recall that in *The Transcendence of the Ego* Sartre argues that the original and dominant mode of consciousness is not reflection, but rather a prereflective, outwardly directed engagement with its objects. Consciousness is not controlled by a "self" that inhabits or stands behind it. Rather, the self is a construct that is built up when consciousness adopts a secondary mode, that of reflection, directing its attention away from the objects with which it is ordinarily concerned and instead focusing back on itself and on its own activities. By noticing patterns in its own past actions, consciousness then begins to attribute to itself characteristics, tendencies, dispositions, and the like. By synthesizing what had been discrete, unconnected moments in its history, consciousness fabricates a "self."

But as Sartre's analysis of "the look" in *Being and Nothingness* makes clear, the Other plays a crucial role in this process.[3] Whereas I live my life "from the inside," looking out at the world (and away from myself), the Other looks directly at me, taking me for an object, noting my features and evaluating me, just as he or she might do with any other object. Thus, when I see myself as reflected in the eyes of the Other, I get a powerful sense of my own objectivity, far more so than is possible through my own unaided acts of reflection.

---

[3] In his preface to *No Exit*, Sartre explains: "other people are basically the most important means we have in ourselves for our own knowledge of ourselves. When we think about ourselves, when we try to know ourselves, basically we use the knowledge of us which other people already have. We judge ourselves with the means other people have and have given us for judging ourselves. Into whatever I say about myself someone else's judgment always enters. Into whatever I feel within myself someone else's judgment enters" (SOT, 199).

This is so for at least three reasons. First, when I reflect, my consciousness is divided. While we can say, loosely, that in reflection consciousness takes itself for an object, this is not strictly accurate, since the consciousness that is looking is in this case not identical to the consciousness that is looked at. There is, for example, a temporal separation. The conscious acts on which I am presently reflecting must all have already taken place. They are in the past. My present act of reflecting cannot take that very act of reflection for its object. Consciousness cannot catch itself in the act.

The Other, by contrast, while he or she cannot literally observe my consciousness, can observe its outside "in the moment," right as it is carrying out its prereflective acts. Thus, it is in the psychic jolt, the shock of recognition that I receive when I suddenly become aware of the Other's look and see myself from the outside, just as I am, in the midst of acting, that I receive my most powerful and direct awareness of my own objectivity.

Secondly, my freedom, the dimension of transcendence that characterizes my being, guarantees that I am always somewhat at a distance from my objectivity. I only encounter my facticity as I am hurtling past it in undertaking an action and pursuing a project. To observe that I am in some way cruel, or impolite, or awkward, is, typically, to notice it only in passing, in the context of pursuing a project at the conclusion of which I will not be (or so I tell myself) cruel or impolite or awkward. And indeed, in a sense I *am not* these things (or any other of my facticities), because I am an activity—that of pursuing a *desideratum* that does not currently exist. Thus, my ceaseless, inescapable obligation to transcend the given (part of what it means to be "condemned to be free") makes it extremely difficult for me to evaluate myself disinterestedly, or from a purely contemplative, point of view. Rather, my evaluation presents itself to me as "to-be-surpassed" through my action. My facticty does not strike me simply as "what I am."

But once again, things are very different when the Other looks at me (and when I gain access to the Other's perspective by means of seeing my reflection in his or her look). The Other can take note of my characteristics without experiencing any sort of obligation to do anything about them. Moreover, the Other who observes my facticities is not in any sense at the same time my transcendence of those facticities. Thus, not only is the Other much better positioned than I am to see my objectivity (in the sense of "object-ness," seeing me as an object, rather than as a subject); he or she also can do so more objectively (in the sense of "disinterestedly") than I can.

Finally, I am likely to be in bad faith about my own objectivity. By the simple technique of selective focusing—making a point of noticing, emphasizing, and reminding myself of my admirable deeds and traits while simultaneously learning to stay locked into the prereflective mode when my conduct is shameful—it is easy for me to convince myself that I am better than I really am. The bad faith of selective omission and emphasis gives almost all of us an unrealistically lofty opinion of ourselves. Others see us more clear-sightedly, with less deception. When they reflect this more accurate picture back to us, it punctures our illusions.

As *No Exit* brilliantly illustrates, however, even characters who are in bad faith (and who, as is typically the case, are also in bad faith about the very fact that they *are* in bad faith), are usually will-ing to acknowledge that others are better positioned to judge their characters fairly than they themselves are. That is why such persons crave the approval of others. They hope that if they can persuade others to see them as virtuous (or at least as not vicious), this will help them to arrive at the same belief themselves. Thus, even Garcin, who at first urges that he and his two companions should work out their respective salvations on their own, without so much as speaking to one another (NE, 18), eventually comes around to the view that "none of us can save himself or herself" (NE, 29).

At first he turns to Estelle:

> If there's someone, just one person, to say quite positively I did not run away, that I'm not the sort who runs away, that I'm brave and decent and the rest of it—well, that one person's faith would save me. Will you have that faith in me? Then I shall love you and cherish you for ever. Estelle—will you? (NE, 40)

The pathetic quality of this plea reveals how desperately Garcin wants to be seen as not a coward. And in Estelle, he appears ini-tially to have found a willing accomplice. But Inez is there to ruin this transaction. She points out that Estelle's esteem is not freely given on the basis of sincere conviction, but rather, insincerely and self-servingly, in exchange for Garcin's attention and admiration.

(Estelle also wants him to see her as a victim of circumstances, rather than as a murderer.) As Inez puts it to Garcin, in ridiculing Estelle's claim that he can "trust" her declaration that she does not consider him a coward:

> That's right! That's right! Trust away! She wants a man—that far you can trust her—she wants a man's arm around her waist, a man's smell, a man's eyes glowing with desire. And that's all she wants. She'd assure you you were God almighty if she thought it would give you pleasure. (NE, 41)

Though he'd like to deny it, it is obvious even to the self-deceiving Garcin that Inez is right: approval offered in exchange for love can't be trusted to be sincere. Moreover, Estelle makes it far too clear that she just wants a man, not particularly caring whether he is a hero or a coward. So her approval clearly would prove nothing. Reluctantly, he turns to the sadistic Inez, who delights in disappointing him. In desperation, he turns to Estelle one last time, only to find that his efforts at receiving the favorable justification that he desires from her are at every turn thwarted by the hostile (but honest) eyes of Inez, which reflect back to him the deceptive nature of this enterprise. Moreover, Inez incessantly reminds him of her presence, and of her readiness to puncture any self-serving illusions he might be able to generate with the help of Estelle. "I'm watching you," she tells him. "I'm a crowd all by myself. Do you hear the crowd? Do you hear them muttering, Garcin? Mumbling and muttering. 'Coward! Coward! Coward! Coward!'—that's what they're saying. . . . It's no use trying to escape, I'll never let you go" (46).[4]

---

[4] Here Sartre dramatically illustrates one of his most important claims from the section of "Concrete Relations with Others" in *Being and Nothingness*: "Such is the true reason why lovers seek solitude. It is because the appearance of a third person, whoever he may be, is the destruction of their love" (BN, 491). Recall that in *Being and Nothingness* "love" refers to my attempt to appropriate the Other's freedom as freedom, so that I might gain access to my own (favorable) objectivity by controlling the Other who "freely" delivers it to me. Sartre's point here is that this attempt is doomed to fail because (among other reasons) I cannot control the third person, and he or she will have no motive to confirm the unrealistically positive picture of myself that I might be able to extract from my "lover."

Little wonder, then, that Garcin finds his interactions with Estelle and Inez to be so excruciating as to make the physical tortures that are traditionally said to take place in hell seem preferable. Indeed, at one point he pounds on the door and screams:

> Open the door! Open, blast you! I'll endure anything, your red-hot tongs and molten lead, your racks and prongs and garrotes—all your fiendish gadgets, everything that burns and flays and tears—I'll put up with any torture you impose. Anything, anything would be better than this agony of mind, this creeping pain that gnaws and fumbles and caresses one and never hurts quite enough. (NE, 42)

And, of course, the most famous line of the play, also uttered by Garcin, underscores the same point: "Hell is—other people!" (NE, 47)

But is this, as many readers apparently believe, simply the *message* of the play? Is Sartre saying that there is literally "no exit," no way out, from a condition in which our relations with others are hellish?

There are several reasons to doubt this interpretation. First, recall that in *Being and Nothingness* Sartre makes a point of saying that, despite the negative tone and emphasis of his discussion in that book, it is indeed possible to achieve authentic, positive, and mutually satisfying relationships with others. Secondly, we have Sartre's subsequent testimony that "'hell is other people' has always been misunderstood. It has been thought that what I meant by that was that our relations with other people are always poisoned, that they are invariably hellish relations. But what I really mean is something totally different" (SOT, 199). Finally, the play makes far more sense, both aesthetically and philosophically, if taken as an allegory, and as a cautionary tale (or morality play), than as an attempt simply to describe the human condition. If it were interpreted merely as a dramatization of our unavoidable plight, it would come off as grotesque and depressing. But as it stands, it fills the reader or viewer with the desire to learn from the mistakes of Sartre's characters, so as not to end up in their predicament.

Death

In order for the play to have this effect, readers or viewers must see themselves both as like Sartre's characters (so that they recognize the hellish condition of Garcin, Estelle, and Inez as their own possibility, as well) and as unlike them (so that they see that possibility as avoidable). But, how, specifically, do the members of Sartre's audience differ from his characters? One of the most obvious ways is that the latter, unlike the former, are dead. (And, indeed, the fact that Sartre, an atheist who does not believe in an afterlife, sets his play in hell gives as further evidence that the play is best understood as an allegory.) Thus, we should consider the possibility that the play, far from simply describing our inescapable situation, is instead dramatizing some of Sartre's ideas on death.

The most important of these, with regard to *No Exit*, is that my death closes off my possibilities and puts me at the mercy of others. So long as I am alive, I can, through my actions, alter the meaning, not only of my future, but even of my past. If, for example, I have written some novels that are universally regarded as mediocre, there is still something I can do to change the way in which those novels are evaluated. For suppose I now go on to write some good or even great novels. Surely this would result in my earlier novels no longer being read simply as "mediocre," but rather as "youthful," as works leading up to my finding my voice and developing my style and achieving greatness. But if I am dead, this possibility is closed off to me. My books remain what they are, and I can do nothing to change their meaning. Nor can I do anything to convince the living to remember me as anything other than the writer of undistinguished works. As Sartre puts it in *Being and Nothingness*, "To be dead is to be a prey for the living" (BN, 695).[5]

If Garcin were still alive, he could cease being a coward by simply engaging in courageous actions. But he is dead, so this path is closed to him, and he finds himself at the mercy of the living, as he himself notes: "I'm locked out; they're passing judgment on my life without troubling about me, and they're right, because I'm dead. Dead and done with" (NE, 40).

Since we are alive, our situation is significantly different from that of Sartre's characters, and he frequently reminds us of that,

---

[5] Or again, "at my limit, at that infinitesimal instant of my death, I shall be no more than my past. It alone will define me. . . . At the moment of death we *are*; that is, we are defenseless before the judgments of others. They can decide *in truth* what we are. . . . By death the for-itself is changed forever into an in-itself in that it has slipped entirely into the past" (BN, 169).

sometimes in subtle ways. For example, the characters complain, in two or three different places in the play, that all mirrors have been removed from their room, so they cannot look directly at themselves and must instead rely on others for information about their physical appearance. But our situation is different. Because we are free, and thus ceaselessly obligated to transcend the given through action, we not only can but must evaluate the meanings of our own past actions for ourselves, even if we make use of input from others in doing so.

> Thus from this point of view we can see clearly the difference between life and death: life decides its own meaning because it is always in suspense; it possesses essentially a power of self-criticism and self-metamorphosis which cause it to define itself as a "not-yet" or, if you like, makes it be as the changing of what it is. . . . [But in death] there is a radical transformation: nothing more can *happen* to it inwardly; it is entirely closed; nothing more can be made to enter there; but its meaning does not cease to be modified from the outside. (BN, 694–95)

So one of Sartre's messages in *No Exit* may be simply that we should not emulate the dead—we should not delegate to others the task of determining the meaning of our own lives. And indeed, Sartre himself interprets the play as saying that "there are a vast number of people in the world who are in hell because they are too dependent on the judgment of other people" (SOT, 199).

But the most important difference between ourselves and the dead is that we, unlike them, are free, and thus have some capacity to change our situation (or at least to attempt to do so) if it is bad. Similarly, if we ourselves are bad in some way—if we have behaved in a cowardly fashion, for example—we can do something about this by changing how we act in the future. Sartre's characters cannot do this, of course, because they are dead. But in keeping with the allegorical nature of his play, Sartre informs us that "'dead' symbolizes something here. What I was trying to imply specifically is that many people are encrusted in a set of habits and customs" which cause them misery, but which they make no attempt to change.

> In point of fact, since we are alive, I wanted to show by means of the absurd the importance of freedom to us, that is to say the importance

of changing acts by other acts. No matter what circle of hell we are
living in, I think we are free to break out of it. And if people do not
break out, again, they are staying there of their own free will. So that
of their own free will they put themselves in hell." (SOT, 200)

This is a harsh message, and *No Exit* abounds in them.
Consider the following exchange between Garcin and Inez:

Garcin: . . . Can one judge a life by a single action?

Inez: Why not? For thirty years you dreamt you were a hero, and con-
doned a thousand petty lapses—because a hero, of course, can do
no wrong. An easy method, obviously. Then the day came when
you were up against it, the red light of real danger—and you took
the train to Mexico.

Garcin: I "dreamt," you say. It was no dream. When I chose the hardest path, I made my choice deliberately. A man is what he wills
himself to be.

Inez: Prove it. Prove it was no dream. It's what one does, and nothing else, that shows the stuff one's made of.

Garcin: I died too soon. I wasn't allowed time to—to do my deeds.

Inez: One always dies too soon—or too late. And yet one's whole life
is complete at that moment, with a line drawn neatly under it,
ready for the summing up. You are—your life, and nothing else.
(NE, 44–45)

This passage encapsulates several of the play's central ideas—ideas
about bad faith, human relationships, death, freedom, and responsibility—and all of them are tough. For example, one clear message
is that we are, and are properly defined by, what we *do*. Many people are like Garcin in that they make excuses for their actual
actions, and want credit for their good *intentions*, or for some kind
of internal essence that is (allegedly) distinguishable from their
deeds.

In this respect, and in many others, Sartrean existentialism is a
much more demanding philosophy than, say, Christianity as it is
commonly understood. There is no Christ to pay for our sins, or
God to forgive us for them. If we do wrong, this is an ineradicable
fact. If it is possible to make amends and receive forgiveness, this
is an affair between us and our victims. A forgiving God is not a

party to the transaction. While we can escape bad faith and hellish interpersonal relationships, there truly can be "no exit" from our freedom and from our responsibility for what we do. This point is central not only to *No Exit*, but to all of Sartre's writings.

5

The Devil and the Good Lord

Sartre's play *The Devil and the Good Lord* appeared in 1951, opening on June 7 of that year and playing continuously until March 1952. It was then revived in September for thirty more performances, and yet again in November 1968. Of his own dramatic works, it was Sartre's favorite.[1] It is an extremely lengthy and complex play, perhaps his most ambitious. Whereas *No Exit* is a one-act play, requiring only one set, and lasting less than an hour in performance, *The Devil and the Good Lord* is a three-act play, with eleven scenes, requiring ten sets, and lasting more than four hours in performance.

The action is set in Germany at the time of the Peasants' War in the sixteenth century. One of the central issues in the play is that of the morality of violence in political struggle, and Sartre may have felt that the partisan commitments of his audience members would make it difficult for them to grasp and to appreciate his points if they were made in connection with the intense political conflicts of the current time.

In the play's first act we encounter the protagonist Goetz doing evil for its own sake. He is a ruthless warrior who lives for conquest and destruction. He takes great pride in his evil deeds until he is one day persuaded by a priest that there is nothing special about doing evil. The world is so permeated with evil, the

---

[1] Sartre, interviewed by Simone de Beauvoir in her "Conversations with Jean-Paul Sartre," in her *Adieux: A Farewell to Sartre*, trans. Patrick O'Brian (New York: Pantheon, 1984), 187.

priest argues, that "if you want to deserve Hell, you need only remain in bed. The world itself is iniquity; if you accept the world, you are equally iniquitous. If you should try and change it, then you become an executioner" (DGL, 63). Goetz, impressed by the priest's oration, presses him as to whether it could really be true that *everyone* does evil, and that *no one* does good. The priest assures him that this is the case. Thereupon Goetz lays a bet that *he* will henceforth do nothing but good.

For most of the remainder of the play we find Goetz attempting to carry out his vow, but invariably failing. He begins by deciding to give away his land and his wealth to thirty thousand peasants who are dying of hunger. But he is immediately implored by Nasti, the leader of the peasants' movement, to keep his gifts to himself. If he were to give away his land and his wealth at once, Nasti claims, he would precipitate a revolt at a time when the peasants are not prepared for one. Thus, his gift would simply cause the violent destruction of those whom he had wished to save. Goetz refuses to hold back, however, asserting that he "cannot do Good by installment" (DGL, 73). He proceeds not only to give his land immediately to the peasants, but also to set up a model community for them, to be based entirely on fraternity and common ownership. As a result, the premature revolt that Nasti had feared breaks out. Nasti begs Goetz to save the situation he has unwittingly created, and make the revolt succeed, by becoming the peasants' general. But Goetz refuses, claiming that he has abandoned the way of violence, and now lives only for love. He goes to the peasants' camp and urges them to give up their fight and join him in renouncing violence. The peasants jeer at Goetz and ignore his advice. They go ahead with their revolt and are soundly defeated.

Finally, near the end of the play, Goetz learns his lesson. He goes back to Nasti and tells him "I want to be a man among men" (DGL, 145). He goes on to explain that in order to become a man he must begin at the beginning, and that means beginning with crime, since

> men of the present day are born criminals. I must demand my share of their crimes if I want to have my share of their love and virtue. I wanted pure love: ridiculous nonsense. To love anyone is to hate the same enemy; therefore I will adopt your hates. I wanted to do Good: foolishness. On this earth at present Good and Evil are inseparable. I agree to be bad in order to become good. (DGL, 145)

Nasti responds to Goetz's oration by again offering to make him the leader of the peasants' army. This time Goetz accepts, and promptly issues an order that all deserters will be hanged. The curtain closes as Goetz utters the following lines:

> A fine start! Nasti, I told you I would be hangman and butcher. . . .
> Never fear, I shall not flinch. I shall make them hate me, because I
> know no other way of loving them. . . . I shall remain alone with this
> empty sky over my head, since I have no other way of being among
> men. There is this war to fight, and I will fight it. (DGL, 149)

As should be clear from this short summary, *The Devil and the Good Lord*, like Sartre's other plays, is a serious work concerned with serious philosophical issues. Because such intellectual depth is the most striking aspect of Sartre's literary works, however, many readers tend to overlook the comic touches on frequent display in them. For example, in *The Devil and the Good Lord* there is a very funny scene in which Goetz, while engaged in his project of doing good, makes a public show of his willingness to embrace a leper. As Goetz approaches him, the leper suddenly realizes that Goetz intends to kiss him, and responds by admonishing him: "Not on the mouth!" (DGL, 82)

Let's now turn to a consideration of the central issues discussed in *The Devil and the Good Lord*, bearing in mind, as we do so, Sartre's remark that "when I write for the theatre, it's not to resolve a problem, it's to present it."[2]

One of the first things one notices about *The Devil and the Good Lord* is that it, in contrast to *Being and Nothingness* and *No Exit*, is concerned with large-scale social issues. Whereas *Being and Nothingness* had discussed extensively dyadic relationships between oneself and "the Other," and *No Exit* had addressed the complicated and agonizing relationships among three persons struggling to resolve highly personal salvation issues, *The Devil and the Good Lord* expands this social concern to include political, historical, and economic social structures affecting interactions among large groups of people. Consider, for example, the follow-

---

[2] Sartre, in conversation with a reporter during rehearsals for *The Devil and the Good Lord*, as quoted in *The Theatre of Jean-Paul Sartre*, Dorothy McCall (New York: Columbia University Press, 1969), 37.

ing line, which Sartre puts in the mouth of Nasti: "When the rich fight the rich, it is the poor who die" (DGL, 11). This concern for the plight of the poor, and indignation at the injustice of their treatment at the hands of the rich, will appear prominently in Sartre's work for the rest of his life.

Atheism

Another important theme in the play is atheism. While *The Devil and the Good Lord* is sometimes read as being primarily about the nonexistence of God, it contains, as one might expect from a play (as opposed to a philosophical essay), very little direct argumentation in support of atheism. We find a brief discussion of the classical "problem of evil" (DGL, 10–13)—the idea that the existence of evil stands as evidence against the existence of an infinitely powerful and infinitely good God. (The argument, in brief, is that since an infinitely good being would be infinitely opposed to evil, and an infinitely powerful being would be able to eradicate evil, it follows that the existence of an infinitely good and infinitely powerful being should be sufficient to preclude the existence of evil. But there is evil. Therefore, no such infinitely good, infinitely powerful being [God] exists.) And we find repeated statements (and dramatic illustrations) of the idea that God is silent and appears to be absent. (Sartre also points out that God's absence serves the power interests of the churches since, in the words of Nasti, "when God is silent, you can make Him say whatever you please" [DGL, 71].)

Still, even if the argumentation on behalf of atheism in *The Devil and the Good Lord* is scanty, there is no denying that Goetz's conversion to atheism, which occurs near the end of the play, is one of its dramatic highpoints:

> I supplicated, I demanded a sign, I sent messages to Heaven, no reply. Heaven ignored my very name. Each minute I wondered what I could BE in the eyes of God. Now I know the answer: nothing. God does not see me, God does not hear me, God does not know me. You see this emptiness over our heads? That is God. You see this gap in the door? It is God. You see that hole in the ground? That is God again. Silence is God. Absence is God. God is the loneliness of man. . . . God doesn't exist. (DGL, 141)[3]

---

[3] Later in the play Sartre has Goetz utter Nietzsche's famous pronouncement: "God is dead" (DGL, 143).

As the balance of the play makes clear, Sartre's concern in *The Devil and the Good Lord* is not so much with the ontological question of the actual existence or nonexistence of God as it is with the psychological, ethical, and political consequences of belief or nonbelief in Him. Throughout most of the play, Goetz understands himself only in terms of his relation to God. Other people are of little significance to him. The play can be seen as an indictment of this common attitude. (Think, in this context, of all those who see immoral acts that harm persons as essentially offenses against God—who alone has the power to forgive wrongdoers and to absolve them of the stain of wrongdoing.) When Goetz does evil, he does it because of God, with little concern for humans. But the same is true when he does good. He seems able to engage himself with people deeply, directly, and concretely only when he gives up his belief in God.

Thus, God and the Devil are symbolically roped together in the play. Insofar as they both represent absolutes, and the realm of the inhuman, their commonalities are presented as being much more important than their differences. Sartre seems to be saying not that we should reject God in favor of the Devil (or the reverse), but rather that we should reject both God and the Devil, and live instead in a world of humans, that is, in a world of context, history, and finitude—a world without such absolutes.[4]

Conversion

This brings us to another important theme of the play, that of conversion. In light of our discussion of "radical conversion" in the *Being and Nothingness* chapter, the fact that Goetz arrives at his atheistic, humanist, contextualist world view (the one that Sartre appears here to be endorsing) only after undoing an abrupt transformation seems especially noteworthy. Recall that Goetz had already undergone one conversion, earlier in the play, from a project of doing evil to one of doing good. But, as Sartre subsequently

---

[4] As Sartre remarks in an interview about *The Devil and the Good Lord*, " your relations with God may be good or bad, but in any case they isolate you from other men, even if your principle is the love of men" (SOT, 231). Similarly, in the play itself, Goetz, following his conversion to atheism, remarks to another character, "how REAL you have become since He no longer exists" (DGL, 143).

explained, this leads to a "dead end," which Goetz escapes only by making

> a more radical choice: he decides that God does not exist. That is Goetz's conversion, the conversion to man. Breaking away from the morality of absolutes, he discovers a historical morality, human and particular. He had cherished violence formerly in order to defy God, and had then abandoned it in order to please God. He now knows it is necessary at some times to engage in violence and to behave peaceably at others. So he leagues himself with his fellow men and joins the peasant revolt. Between the Devil and the Lord, he chooses man.[5]

While the radical conversion Sartre describes here is not identical to the one hinted at in *Being and Nothingness* and discussed more fully in *Notebooks for an Ethics* (it is not a conversion from a project of attempting to be God to a project based on affirming, maximizing, and intensifying freedom), it does resemble it in at least three important respects.

First, in both cases the conversion requires a rejection of comforting illusions, and a clear-sighted acceptance, instead, of the harsh, bracing aspects of our human condition (the inescapability of freedom and responsibility, in the earlier works, the "loneliness" stemming from the "silence" and "absence" of God, in *The Devil and the Good Lord*).

Secondly, Goetz's conversion, fully in keeping with Sartre's analyses of the radical conversion in the earlier works, involves a rejection of a project of *being* in favor of a project of *doing*. Moreover, in both cases the renunciation of a project of being requires at the same time an abandonment of any attempt to acquire an essence, a fixed state of being, by means of being objectified by the Other. In *The Devil and the Good Lord*, however, this Other is not another human being, but rather God. Thus, Goetz explains his preconversion project: "Each minute I wondered what I could BE in the eyes of God." He then remarks, from his postconversion perspective: "Now I know the answer: nothing" (DGL, 141).

Finally, in both cases the conversion demands a rejection of God as an ideal that is unsuitable for human beings. In the play,

---

[5] Sartre, in yet another interview about *The Devil and the Good Lord*, as quoted in SOT, 227–28.

"God" and "The Devil" seem to function as symbols for all absolutes, such as good and evil, for example. Sartre's argument is that these absolutes should be rejected on the grounds not only that they are unreal (so that belief in them requires a life lived in bad faith), but also that they represent attempts to evade the responsibilities confronting us as finite, context-bound, beings.

Good and Evil

This discussion of good and evil as absolutes brings us to another central theme of the play, that of ethics. Sartre's claim that we should reject good and evil as absolutes seems to mean that neither good nor evil can stand alone and remain pure, unmixed with its opposite. All of the goods and evils with which we deal are good or evil only in a restricted, or qualified, sense. Similarly, sound general moral principles will have to admit of exceptions since, in the world in which we live, a world of concrete historical circumstances, full of messy complications, good is often inextricably bound up with evil.

To see the point of this, consider just a few of the ways in which good, in real life, here on Earth, is tied up with evil: (1) We have finite knowledge. In our ignorance, our efforts to do good often cause evil instead of or in addition to good. (2) We have finite power. Consequently, many of our actions that produce good also bring about unintended evil side effects. (3) Sometimes we know beforehand that the only means available to us for producing good are evil ones. This is the famous means/end problem. In the practice of medicine, for example, sometimes the only means available to us to combat a disease are surgical procedures that are dangerous, painful, invasive, and expensive. (4) There is the problem of participation in the world's many evil systems (an economic system in which some work in sweatshops for inadequate wages, while others inherit billions for doing nothing; a military system of perpetual war; a system of ruthless exploitation of animals; and so forth). To participate in them is to participate in evil. To refuse to participate in any of them is to withdraw from the world and live a monkish existence that leaves everything as it is. One can fight against some of these evil systems, but not against all of them at once. (5) Finally, as just indicated, there is a problem of selection. This is not merely due to the fact that we have limited time and energy, and thus can't do everything at once. The problem is much more radical than that. It is that we are often confronted with situations in which different values, each of which would ordinarily warrant our support, are set in opposition to one another.

Goetz's mistake, after his conversion to doing good but prior to his conversion to atheism and humanism, was that he failed to understand this. In doing good by giving away his land to the peasants, he refused to consider, despite receiving ample warning on this point, that his action might inadvertently hurt the peasants. And in refusing to participate in evil in the form of violence, he abandoned what may have been the only means available for helping them. He wanted to be pure, to do every good at once, and to do nothing but good, while scrupulously refraining from any involvement in evil. No wonder that he failed so spectacularly!

Sartre illustrates several of these ideas most vividly in a famous story that he tells in his lecture, *Existentialism Is a Humanism*:

A pupil of mine . . . sought me out in the following circumstances. His father was quarrelling with his mother and was also inclined to be a "collaborator"; his elder brother had been killed in the German offensive of 1940 and this young man, with a sentiment somewhat primitive but generous, burned to avenge him. His mother was living alone with him, deeply afflicted by the semi-treason of his father and by the death of her eldest son, and her one consolation was in this young man. But he, at this moment, had the choice between going to England to join the Free French Forces or of staying near his mother and helping her to live. He fully realized that this woman lived only for him and that his disappearance—or perhaps his death—would plunge her into despair. He also realized that, concretely and in fact, every action he performed on his mother's behalf would be sure of effect in the sense of aiding her to live, whereas anything he did in order to go and fight would be an ambiguous action which might vanish like water into sand and serve no purpose. For instance, to set out for England he would have to wait indefinitely in a Spanish camp on the way through Spain; or, on arriving in England or in Algiers he might be put into an office to fill up forms. Consequently, he found himself confronted by two very different modes of action; the one concrete, immediate, but directed towards only one individual; and the other an action addressed to an end infinitely greater, a national collectivity, but for that very reason ambiguous—and it might be frustrated on the way. At the same time, he was hesitating between two kinds of morality; on the one side the morality of sympathy, of personal devotion and, on the other side, a morality of wider scope but of more debatable validity. He had to choose between those two. What could help him to choose? Could the Christian doctrine? No. Christian doctrine says: Act with charity, love your neighbor, deny yourself for others, choose the way which is hardest, and so forth. But which is the harder road? To whom does one owe the more brotherly love, the patriot or the mother? Which is the more useful aim, the general one of fighting in and for the whole community, or the precise aim of helping one particular person to live? Who can give an answer to that *à priori*? No one. Nor is it given in any ethical scripture. The Kantian ethic says, Never regard another as a means, but always as an end. Very well; if I remain with my mother, I shall be regarding her as the end and not as a means: but by the same token I am in danger of treating as means those who are fighting on my behalf; and the converse is also true, that if I go to the aid of the combatants I shall be treating them as the end at the risk of treating my mother as a means. (EH, 35–36)

Here Sartre attacks ethical absolutism in several different (though overlapping) ways. First, Sartre's example makes a powerful case for the importance of context, of circumstances, in ethics. It suggests that moral rules or principles cannot be absolute, since they will, of necessity, have to be abstract and general, and thus they will not be able to cope with all of the morally relevant considerations that concrete situations might present. As Sartre puts it, such principles tend to "break down when we come to defining action" (EH, 52).

Secondly, the example shows that moral duties cannot be absolute, since they can conflict, and it is therefore impossible, in principle, to honor all of them. Sartre's student's duty to care for his mother, stemming from his specific relation to her and from the details of her situation, obviously conflicts with his more general duty to resist the Nazis.

Thirdly, the example shows that our limited power renders an absolutistic ethic unsuitable and unrealistic for us. The student's finitude in this regard leaves him utterly unable to carry out both of his obligations, uncertain of his ability to discharge the broader one with any significant degree of effectiveness, and more certain of success only with respect to the one that concerns a single person.

Finally, the example strongly suggests that our finitude renders us incapable of knowing, at least in many circumstances, what morality demands of us. Sometimes we simply don't, and can't, know what we should do. This is not merely because there is a lack of consensus as to which moral theory (if any) is the correct one. Rather, the messiness and complexity of life, coupled with our limitations, often renders us incapable even of *applying* whatever moral theory we might think is right to the situation at hand. Thus, if morality requires us to do the act which will (or is likely to) bring about the best consequences, this does not tell us how to weigh, for example, an act that brings with it a small chance of positively affecting millions against an act that is virtually certain to enhance the life of one person. And the same point holds if we think of morality in terms of doing our duties or acting virtuously (that is courageously, kindly, honestly, and so forth). The complexity of situations, with their numerous morally relevant features pointing in different directions, seems to mean, when put in tandem with our cognitive finitude, that often we can do no better than simply to "choose—that is to say, invent" (EH, 38).[6]

Sartre's ethical contextualism should not be confused with subjectivism or relativism, however. To say that there are no simple, absolute, exceptionless moral principles, that situational variables sometimes matter greatly, that they can place different moral duties in conflict with one another, and that we sometimes cannot

---

[6] Though Sartre, as is to be expected, makes the point with considerably more flair and drama, he is basically echoing Aristotle's observation that, while general and approximate knowledge of ethics is possible, our limitations and the intrinsic complexity and difficulty of that subject make precise and exact knowledge of it unattainable. Thus, Aristotle claims, "our discussion will be adequate if it achieves clarity within the limits of the subject-matter. For precision cannot be expected in the treatment of all subjects alike, any more than it can be expected in all manufactured articles. . . . The problem of the good . . . presents a . . . kind of irregularity, because in many cases good things bring harmful results. There are instances of men ruined by wealth, and others by courage. Therefore, in a discussion of such subjects, . . . we must be satisfied to indicate the truth with a rough and general sketch: when the subject and the basis for a discussion consists of matters that hold good only as a general rule, but not always, the conclusions reached must be of the same order. The various points that are made must be received in the same spirit. For a well-schooled man is one who searches for that degree of precision in each kind of study which the nature of the subject at hand admits: it is obviously just as foolish to accept arguments of probability from a mathematician as to demand strict demonstrations from an orator" (*Nicomachean Ethics*, trans. Martin Ostwald [Indianapolis: Liberal Arts Press, 1962], 5 [1094b]).

know what is right and thus must improvise and do the best we can, drawing on all of our resources of understanding and creativity, is not to say that what is right is whatever I (or my "culture") *thinks* is right, or that "anything goes," or that one opinion is as good as another, or anything even remotely like that. To say that it is unclear whether Sartre's student should stay with his mother or should instead go off to fight Nazis, or even to say that, in this case, there *is* no right answer, so that he is free to choose, is not to say that it would be perfectly fine for him to choose to *murder* his mother, then go off to *join* the Nazis, and then devote his retirement to the hobby of collecting string. Rather, in *Existentialism Is a Humanism* (where the example of the student is presented) Sartre sketches a moral theory that coheres very well with the line he takes in *Notebooks for an Ethics* (and in *Being and Nothingness*, according to the interpretation that I offer above in the chapter on that book). Thus, while he maintains, in conjunction with examples like that of his student, that "the content of morality is variable," he immediately adds that "a certain form of this morality is universal" (EH, 52). Similarly, while he advises his student to "choose—that is to say, invent," he also insists that "the one thing that counts, is to know whether the invention is made in the name of freedom" (EH, 53).

Violence

In any case, Sartre's attack on ethical absolutes sets the stage for a discussion of one final major theme of the play, that of violence. If there are no moral absolutes, then there can be no absolute prohibition against violence. Sartre seems to be arguing that the ethics of absolute nonviolence is an ethics of passivity and contemplation, not of action; it is essentially a religious morality, appropriate for heaven, not for Earth.

The point is not to deny that violence is evil, or that peace is good. But frequently the alternative to violence is not peace, but rather another kind of violence. This appears to be Nasti's point when he remarks, "men like me have only two ways to die. Those who are resigned die of hunger. Those who are not resigned die by hanging" (DGL, 52).

Another problem flows from the fact that nonviolence is not the only good, and it can come into conflict with other goods, such as freedom. Thus, the insistence that slaves should abstain from fighting for their freedom would seem, at least in some circumstances, tantamount to the demand that they remain slaves. This point is forcefully made by Karl, an advocate for the peasants' revolt:

> **Karl:** And tell me, good people, what will you do if this war breaks out?
>
> **A Peasant Woman:** We shall pray.
>
> **Karl:** Ah! I'm afraid you may be obliged to join the fight.
>
> **Teacher:** Oh, no!
>
> **All the Peasants:** No! No! No!
>
> **Karl:** Is this not a holy war, this war of slaves fighting for the right to become free men?
>
> **Teacher:** All wars are ungodly. We shall remain as guardians of love and martyrs of peace.
>
> **Karl:** The barons pillage, violate, kill your brothers at your gates, yet you do not hate them?
>
> **A Peasant Woman:** We pity them for being wicked.
>
> **All the Peasants:** We pity them.
>
> **Karl:** But if they are wicked, is it not just that their victims should rebel?
>
> **Teacher:** Violence is unjust, no matter what the source.
>
> **Karl:** If you condemn the violence of your fellow men, then you approve the conduct of the barons?
>
> **Teacher:** No, of course not.
>
> **Karl:** But you must, since you have no desire that it should cease.
>
> **Teacher:** We want it to cease by the will of the barons themselves.
>
> **Karl:** And who will give them that will?
>
> **Teacher:** We shall.
>
> **The Peasants:** We shall!
>
> **Karl:** And until then, what should the peasants do?
>
> **Teacher:** Submit, wait, and pray.
>
> **Karl:** Traitors, now you are unmasked! You have no love except for yourselves. (DGL, 107–8)

Karl's last remark suggests that a personal refusal, no matter what the circumstances, to engage in violence, can only stem from a selfish motive, such as a desire to maintain personal purity. Granted, if we knew how to, and had the actual ability and available means, to carry out our duties, defend our rights, and achieve the good things of life without violence, we should do so. But if we don't, what should we do? Should we let other people, whom we otherwise could have helped, suffer because of our unwillingness to soil ourselves?

These problems—the general problem of whether or to what extent it is justifiable to use evil means in pursuit of good ends, and the specific problem of the morality of violence—command Sartre's attention for the balance of his career. Moreover, these concerns mark an evolution in his thought away from an emphasis on personal salvation (as in an individualistic conversion to authenticity), and toward a greater emphasis on large-scale social concerns. To be sure, *Being and Nothingness* and *No Exit* dealt with the social dimension of human experience, but they confined this social focus to dyadic and triadic relationships, and, moreover, did so primarily in the context of considering the role such relationships play in the individual's quest of a personal life project.

But one can't liberate the peasants by acting alone, or by acting in concert with one or two others. Rectifying social injustices requires coordinated group activity. Thus, Sartre's concern for social injustice requires him, throughout his later works, to undertake an analysis of social collectives to complement his simultaneously emerging analysis of violence and the means/end problem. These themes receive their most detailed and sustained treatment in Sartre's *Critique of Dialectical Reason*, to be discussed in due course.

But first, let's return to the individual one final time to consider what is simultaneously Sartre's finest biography and clearest application of his theory of existential psychoanalysis: his book-length discussion of the writer, Jean Genet.

6

Saint Genet

Saint Genet, a massive biography of the French writer Jean Genet, appeared in 1952. While Sartre had written, and would go on to write, other biographies of writers, these works all fall under the familiar heading of "a great writer's studies of his predecessors," as Sartre directs his attention to such giants of the nineteenth century as Charles Baudelaire, Stephané Mallarmé, and Gustave Flaubert. *Saint Genet* is unique among these works in that its subject is a contemporary of Sartre's—a writer who was actually younger (by five years) than Sartre himself.

In *Saint Genet*, perhaps more so than in any of his other works, Sartre's versatility and virtuosity as a writer are put on full display. On the large canvas of a book of over 650 pages in length, Sartre skillfully assembles a dizzyingly intricate collage comprised of biographical story-telling, philosophical analysis, psychological and sociological theorizing, and literary criticism, all put to the service of a deeply sympathetic account of a writer whose explicit accounts of homosexuality and of criminality were sufficiently provocative as to result in his works being banned in the United States at the time of the publication of Sartre's book. The sheer audacity, complexity, and intensity of Sartre's effort tend to dazzle the reader, and so does the warmth of his defense of his younger, less celebrated, and more despised (quite a feat, on Genet's part!) literary colleague.

One measure of Sartre's success in this book is that, in spite of the fact that it was written by a radical opponent of respectable bourgeois culture, and in praise of another writer who was, at the time of writing, even more of an outcast from that culture, it nonetheless received lavish praise from the mainstream press. This is documented on the paperback edition of the English translation, which contains several blurbs from such publications proclaiming Sartre's book as "brilliant," "magnificent," and "masterly." *Newsweek*, for example, declares that "the brilliance and humanity and erudition and unsentimental compassion that have gone into this work are literally unbelievable. . . . *Saint Genet* is biographical exegesis carried to the point of high art." Indeed, this work, which *Chicago News* calls "unquestionably the most thorough . . . examination of a living author ever attempted," is also widely regarded as one of finest biographies ever written.

Existential Psychoanalysis Illustrated

One of the noteworthy features of *Saint Genet* is that it illustrates the method of existential psychoanalysis that Sartre first sketched in *Being and Nothingness*. He tries to show, at great length, that a life can be comprehended without recourse to the hypothesis of determinism. To put it more positively, Sartre attempts to demonstrate that free actions can manifest a coherent logic. At the same time, while he argues that Genet's life is a product of his free choices, Sartre also acknowledges that it is conditioned by social, cultural, and historical circumstances. Much of the book is devoted to explaining the logic of this interaction between freedom and facticity. Sartre says that his purpose is

> to indicate the limit of psychoanalytical interpretation and Marxist explanation and to demonstrate that freedom alone can account for a person in his totality; to show this freedom at grips with destiny, crushed at first by its mischances, then turning upon them and digesting them little by little; . . . to learn the choice that a writer makes of himself, of his life and of the meaning of the universe, including even the formal characteristics of his style and composition, even the structure of his images and of the particularity of his tastes; to review in detail the history of his liberation. (SG, 628)

In Sartre's analysis, the crucial event in Genet's life happened early in his childhood. He liked to imitate adults, and noticed that they invariably owned many objects and used them freely. So young Genet liked to take things. But one day he was caught stealing, and heard an adult's judgment of him: "you are a thief."

(Note how this fits Sartre's discussion of "the Look" in *Being and Nothingness*.) For many people, such an event might have had no lasting impact. It is not uncommon for young children to steal, and to be caught, scolded, and punished for doing so. But Genet had been born out of wedlock, and then was made a state orphan and given to a new family for adoption. Consequently, he saw himself as an outcast, and as one whose position within his new family and in respectable society was tenuous at best.

Indeed, on Sartre's analysis, the explanation for Genet's subsequent comparison of himself with filth and waste lies in his awareness of his having been given up for adoption by his natural mother. Genet saw himself as his mother's discarded excrement, rather than as her beloved son. He, in turn, struck back at respectable society by rejecting it and discarding its mores, becoming a thief and a homosexual prostitute, and going on to spend much of his life first in reformatories and then in prisons.

Genet, in realizing that foster parents raised him, came to resent any generosity exercised toward him, since he felt that it caused him to assume a debt he could never repay. Kindnesses done to him by his biological parents would be due him; those done by his foster parents, because they, prior to taking him on, were under no natural (or other) obligation to undertake them, were supererogatory. He had no "natural right" to anything. Little wonder, then, that he took the "thief" verdict to heart, concluded that he would not be allowed a place within lawful society, and undertook the project of *being* an outlaw.

Referring to the decisive moment when young Genet hears the accusation, "you are a thief," Sartre comments:

> He who was not yet anyone suddenly becomes Jean Genet. . . . It is revealed to him that he *is* a thief and he pleads guilty, crushed by a fallacy which he is unable to refute; he stole, he is therefore a thief. . . . What he *wanted* was to steal; what he *did*, a theft; what he *was*, a thief. . . . What happened? Actually, almost nothing: an action undertaken without reflection, conceived and carried out in the secret, silent inwardness in which he often takes refuge, has just *become objective*. Genet learns what he *is objectively*. . . . He is a thief by birth, he will remain one until his death. . . . *Genet is a thief*; that is his truth, his eternal essence. And if he *is* a thief, he must therefore always be one, everywhere, not only when he steals, but when he eats, when he sleeps, when he kisses his foster mother. (SG, 26–28)

This, of course, is bad faith, similar to that of the waiter in *Being and Nothingness*. Genet's project, at first, was to "be" fully what others saw him as being. Thus, he interiorized and made subjective the objectivity that others gave him. He then repeatedly reenacted, as a ritual, the scene that had initially objectified him as a thief.

On Sartre's view, Genet himself eventually came to interpret his behavior in this way—as an attempt to realize himself symbolically as evil. But once Genet realized that he was living by symbol and myth, he decided to turn to the proper medium of the symbolic—art, and more specifically, literature.

This decision began, in common with many other turning points in Genet's life, in an incident in which he was made acutely aware of his alienation from the society in which he found himself. Genet had been put into a prison cell with other prisoners. He and they were awaiting sentence, but, due to a mix-up, only Genet was clothed in a prison uniform. This caused him to stand out, and led to his being ridiculed by the other convicts. Then, when one of the prisoners whiled away the time by composing and reciting a short poem, Genet declared that he could do better. When his first poetic effort received further insults from his peers, Genet resolved to continue with his writing. Several factors were at work here. One was the general sense that, while he was not finding success in the "real" world, perhaps he could fare better in the fictional world of the imagination. Another is the idea that, while not escaping the scorn of others, at least now it would be based on his free, creative actions, rather than on his static essence as a thief. Finally, Genet delighted in seducing his right-thinking bourgeois readers—the beauty of his writing could draw them into a world they wished to ignore, and force them to see that the ugly realities about which he wrote were part of their world as well.

At first Genet's main purpose in his writing was simply to express himself. He wanted to shock and to seduce his readers, but he took little interest in communicating seriously with them. Eventually he did develop an interest in such communication, however, and its purpose, according to Sartre, was to defend criminality, to show that there was beauty and poetry in a life of crime. Above all he sought to show that criminals choose crime freely and are not victims of society, or of other deterministic causes, nor are they in need of cure or rehabilitation. Thus, Genet at this time of his career was still on the side of evil. Still, his writings were so good, and so effective in drawing his readers into his strange and repulsive world, that they also compelled these readers to extend the effort to understand the criminal, rather than to reject him summarily.

But, according to Sartre, Genet's "ten years of literature" turned out to be "equivalent to a psychoanalytic cure" (SG, 585). Once Genet's literary ambitions included the desire to be understood, he had to obey the rules that enable successful literary communication. Therefore, Sartre argues, he reintroduced "into himself order, truth, reciprocity and the universal, which are, if I am not mistaken, characteristics of Good" (SG, 588). But the aspect of Genet's new choice that most interests Sartre is not the fact that it is now a choice of what society deems "good," as against his earlier choice of "evil," but rather that in choosing to be a writer, a creator, a communicator, Genet was choosing a project of freedom, of free creation. He was no longer trying to *be* something (in his case, "Evil," or "a thief," but that is not the point at present) in the sense of trying to inhabit a fixed essence, but rather was embarking on a free and open-ended project, the only authentic kind of project for a human being, according to Sartre. He moved from a project of *being* to one of *doing*.

Genet's books, written in prison, were smuggled out and privately published. Many French intellectuals, Sartre prominent among them, read these works, admired them, and concluded that Genet was no longer the same man who had committed the crimes for which he was incarcerated. The criminal had given way to the writer. They agitated for, and won, his release from prison. The president of France granted him clemency from the life sentence he was serving for ten convictions for theft. Upon his release, he continued to write, and did not return to his earlier life of crime. Indeed, many who came to know him during these years have remarked that they found him to be extraordinarily sweet and gentle.

Thus, Genet's life, on Sartre's analysis, illustrates the folly of society's tendency to absolutize its customs and mores, and to divide all of its members into two neat categories: the "respectable" people who conform, and the evil scum who do not. Such thinking is objectionable on multiple grounds: (1) it transforms a continuum into a hard and fast dichotomy; (2) it cuts off

those condemned as evil from any human sympathy or understanding; and (3) it falsely sees the "evil" ones as *being* evil, as having an evil *essence*, as opposed to seeing them as free beings (and
thus capable of changing), acting in the context of specific external circumstances (which could also be changed).

Inventing the Homosexual Subject

And it is not only Genet's life, but also his works, which make
these points. What was new and distinctive about these works was
not their subject matter. Other writers had written about criminality and homosexuality before. But Sartre points out that such writings, unlike those of Genet, invited us to consider their subject
matter only from the outside. As a result,

> we "normal" people know delinquents only from the outside, and if
> we are ever "in a situation" with respect to them, it is as judges or
> entomologists. . . . One is willing to allow a repentant culprit to con-
> fess his sins, but on condition that he rise above them; the *good* homo-
> sexual is weaned away from his vice by remorse and disgust; it is no
> longer part of him. He was a criminal but no longer is. He speaks of
> what he was as if he were *Another*, and when we read his confession
> we feel ourselves *absolutely other* than the poor wretch he is speaking
> about. . . . [Genet, however,] never speaks to us *about* the homosex-
> ual, *about* the thief, but always *as* a thief and *as* a homosexual. His
> voice is one of those that we wanted never to hear. . . . He invents the
> homosexual *subject*. (SG, 630–32)

Sartre points out, further, that, just as we tend to take credit for
the achievements of scientists, inventors, and artistic geniuses, and
take them to reflect positively on all humanity, so must we, on pain
of inconsistency, see ourselves in Genet. We don't want to, and are
usually successful in avoiding doing so in connection with other
criminals. But Genet's talent compels us to do so.

Freedom and Facticity

And it also compels us to think about the relationship between
freedom and facticity. Sartre points out that in Genet's fictional
works he has written of children who had freely chosen to embrace

something unpleasant that had been thrust upon them, just as Genet himself had done. For example, in one of his novels Genet writes of a boy who accidentally put a maggot into his mouth: "He found himself caught between fainting from nausea and dominating his situation by willing it. He willed it. He made his tongue and palate artfully and patiently feel the loathsome contact. This act of willing was his first poetic attitude governed by pride. He was ten years old" (SG, 67).

On Sartre's view, Genet's life, like that of his maggot-eating character, cannot be explained simply in terms of deterministic causes. Rather, it can only be understood as a free, creative response on Genet's part to his unique circumstances. Indeed, in a 1969 interview in which Sartre reflects on his entire career to that point (the piece is entitled, appropriately enough, "The Itinerary of a Thought"), he comments that *Saint Genet* is "perhaps the book where I have best explained what I mean by freedom." He explains: "For Genet was made a thief, he said, 'I am a thief', and this tiny change was the start of a process whereby he became a poet . . ." (BEM, 35). The meaning of freedom, then, is

> that in the end one is always responsible for what is made of one. Even if one can do nothing else besides assume this responsibility. For I believe that a man can always make something out of what is made of him. This is the limit I would today accord to freedom: the small movement which makes of a totally conditioned social being someone who does not render back completely what his conditioning has given him. Which makes of Genet a poet when he had been rigorously conditioned to be a thief. (BEM, 34–35)

And in 1974, Sartre elaborates:

> That homosexual child, beaten, raped, and overwhelmed by young sodomites and treated rather like a toy by the toughs around him, did become the writer Jean Genet. There was a transformation here that was the work of freedom. Freedom is the metamorphosis of Jean Genet, the unhappy homosexual child, into Jean Genet, the great writer, a pederast by choice, and if not happy, then at least sure of himself. This change might very well not have taken place. Jean Genet's change came truly from the use of his freedom. It transformed the meaning of the world and gave it another value. It was indeed that freedom and nothing else that was the cause of this rever-

sal. It was freedom choosing itself that brought the transformation about.[1]

On the basis of such passages as these, many have argued that Sartre's views on freedom in *Saint Genet* differ considerably from those he had defended in *Being and Nothingness*. While I believe that due attention to certain salient elements of Sartre's position in *Being and Nothingness* (such as his concepts of facticity, coefficient of adversity, and the Look of the Other; his distinction between freedom of choice and freedom of obtaining; and his idea of radical conversion) reveals far more continuity between the works than is commonly supposed, it cannot be denied that Sartre's thought undergoes an evolution from *Being and Nothingness* to *Saint Genet*. Happily, most of the changes can be fairly characterized as advances.

For example, one obvious limitation of *Being and Nothingness* is that it contains very little about childhood, or, more specifically, about the influence of childhood experiences on later adult decisions. And this omission distorts Sartre's treatment of freedom and of responsibility in that book. The doctrines of *Being and Nothingness* all seem to assume that everyone is a mature, fully autonomous, and cognitively well-equipped adult. Sartre's discussion of Genet obviously does not suffer from this defect, and the result is a more balanced and realistic description of freedom.

Or again, while Sartre in *Being and Nothingness* seems to share the view, common at the time he was writing, that homosexuality is a vice, in *Saint Genet* his hero is a gay man, and the entire book has as one of its themes opposition to the oppression of homosexuals.[2]

On the other hand, this is not to suggest that Sartre's existential psychoanalysis of Genet is beyond criticism. For example, whereas Genet seems to have subscribed to the theory that homosexuality is innate,[3] Sartre accepts psychoanalytical explanations for

---

[1] Sartre, interviewed by Simone de Beauvoir in her "Conversations with Jean-Paul Sartre," in her *Adieux: A Farewell to Sartre*, trans. Patrick O'Brian (New York: Pantheon, 1984), 354–55.

[2] It is worth pointing out, in this connection, that Sartre gave his very last interview to a gay newspaper, *Le Gai Pied* ("Jean-Paul Sartre et les homosexuals" [April 1980, pp. 1, 11–14]), in which he offered the observation that fascism and Stalinism had both committed horrible crimes against homosexuals.

[3] Loren Ringer, "The Imaginary Homosexual: Sartre's Interpretive Grid in *Saint Genet*," *Sartre Studies International* 6, no. 2 (2000): 29.

homosexuality that have since been thoroughly discredited. (See, for example, SG, 91.) A more fundamental criticism is that Sartre's principles of explanation are extremely broad, giving him lots of leeway in fitting the facts into his preferred interpretive grid.

Still, it can't be denied that Genet himself accepted Sartre's analysis of his life, for the most part, and was obviously powerfully affected by it. He commented that Sartre's book

> filled me with a kind of disgust because I saw myself stripped naked— by someone other than myself. I strip myself in all my works, but at the same time I disguise myself with words, with attitudes, with certain choices, by means of a certain magic. I manage not to get too damaged. But I was stripped by Sartre unceremoniously. My first impulse was to burn the book. . . . It took me some time to get over my reading of [it]. I was almost unable to continue writing. . . . Sartre's book created a void which made for a kind of psychological deterioration. . . . I remained in that awful state for six years. . . .[4]

Understanding that Overcomes Difference

Sartre's apparent success in understanding Genet raises important questions of great interest about issues of interpretation, objectivity, and truth. Many contemporary "postmodern" thinkers deny that we have access to objective truth. They claim that we cannot know how things "really" are in themselves, in part because we are finite, contingent beings, who are thoroughly conditioned by our history, culture, gender, race, ethnicity, socioeconomic status, personal life experiences, and so forth. We therefore, so this argument goes, cannot help but view the objects in question through a partial and distorted lens. Accordingly, it might be argued that Sartre, whose comfortable childhood could not have differed more radically from that of Genet, and who was neither a criminal nor a homosexual, could not possibly be in a position to understand Genet. To this way of thinking, it might well be supposed that Sartre's account of Genet will tell us much more about Sartre— about his interests and obsessions, his theories and concepts, his way of seeing the world—than it ever could about Genet.

---

[4] Genet, interviewed in *Playboy* (April 1974), 51–52, as quoted in *A Preface to Sartre*, Dominick LaCapra (Ithaca, NY: Cornell University Press, 1978), 179.

Sartre offers a powerful reply to this objection (though he does so in the context of making a general, theoretical point—he is not responding defensively to his own critics):

> It is claimed that the novelist depicts himself in his characters and the critic in his criticism. If Blanchot writes about Mallarmé, we are told that he reveals much more about himself than about the author he is examining. . . . See what [this] leads to: Blanchot has seen, in Mallarmé, only Blanchot; very well: then you see, in Blanchot, only yourself. In that case, how can you know whether Blanchot is talking about Mallarmé or about himself? That is the vicious circle of all skepticism. (SG, 605)

While Sartre does not deny that "the critic is a historical creature," he does deny that this entails any kind of "idealistic subjectivism" that would debar us from knowing "transhistorical truths." Sartre offers, as an example of such a truth, "Descartes wrote the *Discourse on Method*," about which he comments: "that is true for all ages. This truth . . . is transhistorical, for it does not depend on the economic, social, or religious evolution of mankind. It will be as true in a hundred years as it is today."

To be sure, not all truths are of this sort, and Sartre concedes that when it comes to the issue of the *significance* of a work of literature, it may be that the best a critic can do is identify its meaning "*for our age*." But Sartre immediately points out that this significance, while not transhistorical, "is objective. In short, we must return to very simple and very vulgar verities: in a *good* critical work, we will find a good deal of information about the author who is being criticized. . . . Man is an object for man; the value of objectivity must be restored in order to dispose of the subjectivist banalities that always try to beg the question" (SG, 605–6).[5]

Still, while Sartre's formal refutation of postmodern subjectivism is logically compelling, and his example of an objective,

---

[5] Sartre even offers an interesting and plausible explanation for the popularity of such "subjectivist banalities": "I am reminded of the bourgeois salons where the hostess knows how to avoid quarrels because she has the art of reducing objective value judgments (that play is *bad*, that political operation is *blameworthy*) to purely subjective opinions (I *don't like* that play, etc.). If it is taken for granted that you are merely depicting yourself in condemning police repression of a miners' strike, you will not be disturbing anyone" (SG, 606).

transhistorical truth that is utterly accessible to us in spite of our condition as thoroughly contingent beings is unassailable, this still does not explain precisely how it is that historically and culturally conditioned critics can discover objective truths about the literary works (and their authors) that they study.

Sartre's answer rests, in part, on a distinction between conjecture and confirmation. He concedes that the critic's peculiar "passions, sensibility and turn of mind" will "incline him to make one conjecture rather than another." But Sartre nonetheless maintains that it is the writer being studied who will confirm or disconfirm the critic's conjecture. "The conjecture, whether true or false, helps to reveal. If it is true, it is confirmed by the evidence; if false, it indicates other paths."

To grasp Sartre's point, it might be helpful to recall his example of the crag from *Being and Nothingness*. In order for a crag to manifest itself as climbable, or movable, or interesting to paint, someone—a subjectivity, a consciousness—must approach it (that is, focus on it, inquire into it, make a conjecture about it) in a certain way. The climbability of the crag cannot emerge by means of a project of attempting to remove it or to paint it. But once one tries to climb it, the crag itself will have a good deal to say about its climbability. To try to climb a crag, a project of my own choosing, flowing from my distinctive and perhaps idiosyncratic temperament, passions, and interests, is to cause the crag to reveal something about itself. Thus, I learn about the crag. Subjectivity *reveals* objectivity. Similarly, while different critics, because of their different interests, passions, biases, and so forth, might approach a given author in different ways, leading to the formulation of different hypotheses about the author, it is still possible to test those hypotheses against the evidence of the author and his or her works.

On the other hand, it must be granted that the critic might ignore or distort the evidence, so as to make the writer under study conform to the critic's preferred theory. But the mere fact that this can happen, and that we can sometimes recognize it when it does, "is precisely proof that [the critic] can also shed light on [the writer's] objective reality." After all, as Sartre's initial argument on this subject makes clear, the doctrine that all readings are subjectivist misreadings cannot be advanced as a truth claim without refuting itself.

Moreover, on Sartre's view the fact that it is possible to understand a person quite unlike oneself poses no great mystery. The reason is that, for all our differences, we share a universal human *condition*. He explains that by "condition" he refers to

> all the *limitations* which . . . define man's fundamental situation in the universe. His historical situations are variable: man may be born a slave in a pagan society, or may be a feudal baron, or a proletarian. What never vary are the necessities of being in the world, of having to labour and to die there. These limitations are neither subjective nor objective, or rather there is both a subjective and an objective aspect of them. Objective, because we meet with them everywhere and they are everywhere recognizable: and subjective because they are *lived* and are nothing if man does not live them—if, that is to say, he does not freely determine himself and his existence in relation to them. And, diverse though man's projects may be, at least none of them is wholly foreign to me, since every human project presents itself as an attempt either to surpass these limitations, or to widen them, or else to deny or to accommodate oneself to them. Consequently every project, however individual it may be, is of universal value. *Every project, even that of a Chinese, an Indian or an African, can be understood by a European.* To say it can be understood, means that the European of 1945, though his situation is different, must deal with his own limitations in the same way, and so he may re-conceive in himself the project of the Chinese, of the Indian or the African. *In every project there is universality, in the sense that every project is comprehensible to every man. . . . There is always some way of understanding an idiot, a child, a primitive man or a foreigner if one has sufficient information.* (EH, 46–47, emphasis added, translation modified)

Here Sartre affirms the insight, much emphasized by Husserl, that there is an "eidetic" dimension of human experience. The idea is that, while the particular details of my experience may differ from yours, those different details typically instantiate the same (or, at least, very similar) generic structures of experience. For example, if you are a great athlete, and I am not, I might still be able to understand your experience of losing in a championship competition, since I, too, have experienced disappointment. In general, our condition and experiences have enough in common that we can understand one another to a large degree, provided, of course, that we approach our human interactions with adequate sympathy, intellectual rigor, and imagination—and, as Sartre reminds us, provided we are able to obtain enough information. That is why we are able to understand works of literature set in distant times and places. And that is why Sartre is able to understand Genet.

7

Critique of Dialectical Reason

Whereas in *Saint Genet* Sartre makes a heroic attempt to understand a single human life, in the *Critique of Dialectical Reason*, which ranks, with *Being and Nothingness*, as one of his two major philosophical works, he turns his attention to the social sphere. Instead of focusing on the dyadic and triadic relationships of *Being and Nothingness* and *No Exit*, however, Sartre's *Critique* addresses the relations among members of large-scale collaborative organizations. Similarly, in the moral sphere the *Critique* is not so much concerned with issues of personal authenticity and salvation, which had occupied Sartre in his earlier works, as with broad problems of social injustice. These two interests intersect, since, as it turns out, social injustice can only be eradicated or significantly ameliorated through coordinated group activity. And the issue of a concentrated social struggle against injustice raises, in turn, the means/end problem, and especially the question of the moral justification of violence—themes which Sartre had earlier explored in *The Devil and the Good Lord*.

The *Critique* appeared in 1960. It is a massive work, even longer and more complex than *Being and Nothingness*, and vastly more obscure. This obscurity can be explained, in part, by the fact that Sartre wrote it in a rush, and under the influence of corydrane, an amphetamine mixed with aspirin, which he consumed in enormous quantities in an effort to accelerate the writing process. But Sartre, while not denying these causes, or, for that matter, the legitimacy of the criticism that the *Critique* is difficult to read, nonetheless insists that "the basic reason why each sentence is so long, and bristles with parentheses, inverted commas, 'in so far as', etc., is that each sentence represents one whole dialectical movement" (WL, 117). (I will discuss the idea of a "dialectical movement" in due course.)

The boundaries of the book are somewhat indeterminate. The original French version, but not the English translation, includes a lengthy 1957 essay that had originally been written as a self-contained piece, not part of a larger project. This essay has been published as a separate book in English, under the title *Search for a Method*. Moreover, in Sartre's preface he announces that the *Critique* as published is unfinished, and that it requires a second volume, to be published subsequently, for its completion. He eventually abandoned this project unfinished, but the parts he had completed were published, posthumously, as *Critique of Dialectical Reason*, volume 2.

Marxism

One of the forces driving the book is Sartre's engagement with Marxism, which had been steadily increasing throughout the 1950s. The *Critique* is his attempt to reconcile Marxism with his earlier philosophy. In *Search for a Method* Sartre displays uncharacteristic modesty in setting the terms for this reconciliation. He claims that Marxism is the philosophy of our time, and that existentialism is a mere "ideology," a "parasitical system living on the margin of Knowledge, which at first it opposed but into which today it seeks to be integrated" (SFM, 8).

This modesty reaches its high point at the conclusion of *Search for a Method*. Whereas many great philosophers of the past have implied (or, in some cases, explicitly stated!) that their own philosophical system represents the pinnacle of human thought, the never-to-be-superseded summit toward which all previous intellectual efforts have been unknowingly heading, Sartre, in radical contrast, projects a future state in which his own philosophy will be rendered obsolete:

> From the day that Marxist thought will have taken on the human dimension (that is, the existential project) as the foundation of anthropological Knowledge, existentialism will no longer have any reason for being. Absorbed, surpassed and conserved by the totaliz-

ing movement of philosophy, it will cease to be a particular inquiry and will become the foundation of all inquiry. The comments which we have made in the course of the present essay are directed—within the modest limit of our capabilities—toward hastening the moment of that dissolution. (SFM, 181)

Nor is this modesty to be explained merely in terms of a shifting alliance on Sartre's part from existentialism to Marxism. For he prophesies that Marxism, too, will eventually be superseded: "As soon as there will exist *for everyone* a margin of *real* freedom beyond the production of life, Marxism will have lived out its span; a philosophy of freedom will take its place. But we have no means, no intellectual instrument, no concrete experience which allows us to conceive of this freedom or of this philosophy" (SFM, 34).

Dialectic

Sartre displays this newfound sensitivity to historical change with increasing frequency in his post–*Being and Nothingness* works, and it often leads him to speak, as he does here, of ideas and stages that are helpful now, but which should eventually be abandoned as no longer necessary (and, perhaps, as harmful in the long run) once they have achieved their purpose. For example, we find such a move in his 1948 essay, *Black Orpheus*, which is noteworthy as one of his many engagements with racism:

> Negritude appears like the upbeat [unaccented beat] of a dialectical progression: the theoretical and practical affirmation of white supremacy is the thesis; the position of negritude as an antithetical value is the moment of negativity. But this negative moment is not sufficient in itself, and these black men who use it know this perfectly well; they know that it aims at preparing the synthesis or realization of the human being in a raceless society. Thus, negritude is *for* destroying itself; it is a "crossing to" and not an "arrival at," a means and not an end. (BO, 327)

Here Sartre provides an excellent example of "dialectic," a concept he borrows from the Marxist tradition (which had, in turn, adopted it from Hegel). Dialectic has to do with advancement by means of the collision of contradictory forces or ideas. In the intellectual world it might mean a method of arriving at the truth by resolving a conflict between opposing ideas, not by rejecting one in favor of the other, or even by finding some sort of compromise between them, but rather by incorporating both of them in a new synthesis.

In Marxism, the processes of history are also said to be dialectical. History results from the clashing of opposed forces—especially economic or material forces (hence the term "dialectical materialism"). Sartre's negritude example illustrates a historical dialectical movement. He is saying that one historical force, the denigration of blacks by white racists, provokes another in the form of a response by blacks—they make a special point of noticing and celebrating the cultural achievements of blacks. This is "negritude." But the negritude movement is not (and is not intended to be) an end in itself. Rather, it is used as a tool for destroying both itself and white supremacy, and for bringing about a new synthesis incorporating the positive aspect of both (that is, the appreciation of cultural achievements), but without the (ultimately) irrelevant and morally objectionable fascination with racial distinctions.

(Notice, incidentally, how this example prefigures Sartre's analysis of the morality of violence. Just as racial pride is intrinsically arbitrary, irrational, and harmful, but nonetheless perhaps defensible in the short term as a necessary tool in the fight against an even greater evil [in this case a much more virulent form of racism], so might violence, which is obviously intrinsically bad, be defensible on the same grounds. We will take up this issue below.)

Sartre contrasts dialectical reasoning with analytical reasoning. The latter proceeds by breaking complex phenomena down into their constituent parts; while the former, as we have seen, involves grasping the parts in their relations with each other and to the whole. Moreover, while analytical reason tends to be static (its results are often understood to be timelessly valid), dialectical reason is dynamic. It focuses on the transformative properties of the parts in relation to each other and to the whole. Finally, while analytical reason reveals distinctions and separations (*this* is not *that*; we must choose; it is a matter of "either/or"), dialectical reason reveals the ways in which seeming oppositions are overcome and preserved in new syntheses (it is, in a sense, a matter of "both/and").

Interestingly, while Sartre's purpose in the *Critique* is to clarify, defend, and make use of dialectical reason, he does not merely condemn or reject analytical reason. Rather, he offers a dialectical appreciation of it. According to Sartre, by breaking society down into its parts, namely, individual persons, analytical reason had, during an earlier historical period, helped to liberate individuals from some oppressive social structures. (For example, while Sartre himself does not emphasize this example, analytical reason, on his analysis, gave rise to the concept of human rights.) But precisely because of its commitment to atomization, analytical reason is a poor instrument for the understanding of class, and thus, of the issues of class interest and struggle (and class oppression and exploitation) that are central to Marxism.

Finally, whereas analytical reasoning proceeds by studying a phenomenon from without, dialectical reasoning requires active participation in the events that one is trying to understand. Sartre's endorsement of dialectical thinking thus fits in well with his general rejection of the model of philosophizing—perhaps the historically dominant one—which sees it as a passive, contemplative, and spectatorial endeavor. For Sartre embraces, instead, the existentialist model of philosophizing, which considers the quest for understanding to be part of a person's active, full-blooded engagement with the world. And, of course, Sartre's adoption of dialectical thinking harmonizes with his more recent enthusiasm for Marxism—especially Marx's famous idea that the point of philosophy is not merely to understand the world, but (also) to change it.

Practico-Inert and Counter-Finality

In part because of the increasing influence of Marxism on Sartre's thinking, in the *Critique* he devotes much more attention to the social and historical dimension of human experience than he had in his early works. He sets for himself the task of attempting to explain how it is that history, while the product of the actions of free beings, conditions and limits future human choices. We make history; and then it makes us. Our freedom becomes alienated.

In explaining this, Sartre introduces two new concepts: "practico-inert" and "counter-finality." The former term refers to the tendency of human creations, or even of natural objects that human beings have worked on and altered, to restrict our freedom in the future. We freely create (or modify) things, systems, organizations, conventions, and so forth; and then, ironically, the meanings that we have thereby created tend to harden, and to resist our future attempts to alter them (or to escape from them) through further acts of freedom. I am free, in the face of a crag in its natural state, to see it as something to be cleared away, or to be climbed, or to be painted, and so forth. But if the crag has already been worked on to facilitate climbing (stairs have been carved into it, and handrails and a standing platform have been erected on it), it becomes much more difficult to envision alternative ways of apprehending the crag, or to undertake radically different kinds of projects with respect to it. One of its possible meanings, lent to it as a result of free human practice, has now become "inert," that is, stable and resistant to change.

So my freedom can escape from me, become encrusted in things, and then come back to restrict my freedom. Sartre's concept of "counter-finality" refers to a particularly radical way in which it can do so. A "counter-finality," according to Sartre, is the "contradiction . . . which develops within an ensemble, in so far as it opposes the process which produces it . . ." (CDR, 193). He gives the example of the deforestation of China's mountainsides and hillsides by Chinese peasants. They had undertaken this action so as to increase the amount of land on which they might farm. The result, instead, was massive flooding and the erosion of the land they already had (CDR, 162). Other examples are readily available. The automobile, which may initially have been intended to serve us as a time-saving transportation tool, instead leads to traffic jams, highway carnage, air pollution, and global warming. Such counter-finalities demonstrate that we can become estranged from our own freedom. This links Sartre's concept of counter-finality to Marx's idea of alienation. But whereas Marx had argued that workers typically find that their labor estranges them from their human characteristics (such as creativity and deep sympathy for others), Sartre's focus is specifically on alienation from freedom. And that is something that all of us must confront.

Accordingly, in the *Critique* Sartre devotes a great deal of attention to traditions, institutions, ideologies, and economic, technological, and familial structures and arrangements—any kind of complex human creation that can condition human freedom. Each of these entities facilitates some choices and stands as an obstacle to others. This sets up a dialectical relation between persons and their environment (and their history), whereby agents "interiorize" the latter (they are not acted on by it in the manner of mechanistic causality, but rather through the mediation of interpretation and understanding); and persons' projects, in turn, are "exteriorized"—they modify the world, becoming part of the practico-inert.

The Progressive-Regressive Method

This relates to another of Sartre's new conceptual tools, his "progressive-regressive" method. The regressive part deals with all of the aspects of a person's history and environment to which she must respond. It seeks to discover the social and historical context and background against with or within which the person acts. The progressive part, in turn, deals with the person's aims and goals. It refers to the ways in which the individual freely and creatively responds to these givens, which in turn involves understanding the ways in which she interprets them in the light of her project. For, "the individual is conditioned by the social environment and . . . he turns back upon it to condition it in turn; it is this—and nothing else—which makes his reality" (SFM, 71). Sartre tries to show the coherence of all of this, including the unity of the person's project. Thus, the regressive-progressive method is dialectical in that it synthesizes opposites: past and future, inside and outside, freedom and conditioning.

Here is one of Sartre's examples. I am studying with a friend. Suddenly he gets up and walks to the window. I immediately comprehend his purpose in doing so—he is going to open the window. This is the progressive moment. But then, regressively, I recognize that the room is hot. But that doesn't mean that the heat *caused* my friend's action. After all, I had not opened the window. We might both have continued to work, either not noticing in a clear and specific way that the room was hot, or else choosing to put up with the heat.

This idea that people are to be understood both as situated and as free agents pursuing freely chosen projects within their situation is a constant in Sartre's intellectual career. Despite his greater emphasis in his later works on the ways in which freedom is conditioned by circumstances, Sartre continues to maintain that *conditioned* freedom is, nonetheless, *freedom*, and that no circumstances, no matter how oppressive they might be, relieve the person confronting them of the responsibility to respond to them. Accordingly, he asserts, in *Search for a Method*, that "man can be enslaved only if he is free" (SFM, 180), thus reaffirming his notorious claim from *Being and Nothingness* that even slaves retain their ontological freedom.

His basic point here is that we must not

> confuse the alienated man with a thing or alienation with the physical laws governing external conditions. We affirm the specificity of the human act, which cuts across the social milieu while still holding on to its determinations, and which transforms the world on the basis of given conditions. For us, man is characterized above all by his going beyond a situation, and by what he succeeds in making of what he has made. (SFM, 91)

Criticisms of Marxism

As one might suspect from this brief sketch, Sartre's attitude toward Marxism, despite his deferential rhetoric, is far from uncritical. Sartre complains that contemporary Marxism, especially as exemplified by the French Communist Party of his time, has become a hardened, "ossified," "petrified," dogma, which needs to be reinvigorated by existentialism. And even classical Marxism, at least as it is usually interpreted, is a deterministic philosophy, and it therefore lacks the dimension of subjectivity and freedom that is so central to all of Sartre's thinking. Sartre proposes in the *Critique* to take seriously the Marxist insistence on the weight and force of history, without going so far as to endorse historical determinism. His project, then, is to synthesize Marxist insights on class and other large group structures (the collective subject) with his own discoveries regarding individual freedom and responsibility.

Similarly, while Sartre endorses the Marxist idea of complete, totalizing, explanation, he utterly rejects Marxism's claim to be a science. Human actions, on his view, must be studied phenomenologically, rather than in the manner of the physical sciences. The latter method would threaten to deny or to swallow up human freedom and subjectivity. Indeed, it is partly on this basis that Sartre criticizes Marxism's treatment of socioeconomic classes as independent things, rather than as creations of human beings.

The fact that Sartre embraces some aspects of Marxism while rejecting others raises the question of whether or to what extent his later writings should be regarded as contributions to Marxist thought. As we have seen, at the time of the *Critique* Sartre intended them to be taken in this way. But he subsequently expresses second thoughts. In a 1975 interview, Sartre announces that he no longer considers the *Critique* to be a Marxist work. He also claims to have made a mistake in declaring existentialism to be a mere enclave of Marxism, since his idea of freedom makes his thought ultimately a separate philosophy. Finally, he declares that he no longer considers himself to be a Marxist and would prefer, if asked to choose between them, the label "existentialist."[1] Similarly, in "Self-Portrait at Seventy," when asked whether he prefers to be called "existentialist" or "Marxist," he replies, "if a label is absolutely necessary, I would like 'existentialist' better" (L/S, 60). He also comments that we are "witnessing the end of Marxism."[2] On the other hand, in an interview conducted at about the same time, he declares that "the essential aspects of Marxism are still valid," but adds that "another way of thinking is necessary. We must develop a way of thinking which takes Marxism into account in order to go beyond it, to reject it and take it up again, to absorb it. That is the condition for arriving at a true socialism" (L/S, 60–61). Perhaps this inconsistency is merely verbal (or even merely apparent), and this general question of whether or not Sartre's late works should be considered Marxist more verbal than substantive. For it seems that when Sartre announces his allegiance with Marxism he generally has in mind the philosophy of Marx himself (and only some aspects at that, and then, only as interpreted by Sartre!), but when he announces that he is not a Marxist he is primarily thinking of the dogmatic, sclerotic version of some contemporary French Marxists, most notably those in the French Communist Party. Moreover, since Sartre is an independent thinker, whose thought sometimes converges with, and sometimes diverges from, Marxism (however that is to be understood), the question of whether or not Sartre is a Marxist boils down to the

---

[1] Sartre, "An Interview with Jean-Paul Sartre," in *The Philosophy of Jean-Paul Sartre*, ed. Paul Arthur Schilpp (La Salle, IL: Open Court, 1981), 20, 22.

[2] Sartre, "An Interview with Jean-Paul Sartre," in *The Philosophy of Jean-Paul Sartre*, 20.

question of whether we are more impressed by the similarities than by the dissimilarities. Fortunately, we can bypass the question simply by evaluating Sartre's thought on its own terms.

In any case, Sartre's insistence on freedom underlies his rejection of the idea, held by many Marxists, that a certain historical outcome is inevitable. Rather, he declares:

> I cannot count upon men whom I do not know, I cannot base my confidence upon human goodness or upon man's interest in the good of society, seeing that man is free and that there is no human nature which I can take as foundational. I do not know whither the Russian revolution will lead. . . . I cannot affirm that [it] will lead to the triumph of the proletariat: I must confine myself to what I can see. Nor can I be sure that my comrades-in-arms will take up my work after my death and carry it to the maximum perfection, seeing that those men are free agents and will freely decide, to-morrow, what man is then to be. To-morrow, after my death, some men may decide to establish Fascism, and the others may be so cowardly or so slack as to let them do so. If so, Fascism will then be the truth of man, and so much the worse for us. In reality, things will be such as men have decided they shall be. (EH, 40)

On this point Sartre remains consistent throughout his intellectual career: no external circumstances can, by themselves, motivate any human action whatsoever. No state of the world can produce class consciousness or motivate revolution. Human freedom is incompatible with historical inevitability.

Two Kinds of Freedom

But the sort of freedom that precludes historical inevitability is not the only kind of freedom that Sartre recognizes. Rather, without in any way renouncing this ontological freedom (the "freedom of choice" with which *Being and Nothingness* had been exhaustively concerned), in the *Critique* and in his other post–*Being and Nothingness* works Sartre increasingly devotes his attention to practical freedom (or, in the language of *Being and Nothingness*, "freedom of obtaining"). This is evident, for example, in the famous passage, noted above, in which he refers to "a margin of *real* freedom beyond the production of life," and laments the fact that we are so far from living in a world in which everyone enjoys such freedom that we cannot even conceive of what such a world would be like (SFM, 34). Similar passages abound in his later writings. He tells us that "freedom—not metaphysical but practical freedom— is conditioned by proteins. Life will be human on the day that everyone can eat his fill and every man can work at a job under suitable working conditions."[3] Or again, he declares that freedom "is a word that lends itself to numerous interpretations. In the West it is taken to mean abstract freedom. But to me it means a more concrete freedom—the right to have more than one pair of shoes and to eat when one is hungry."[4]

This does not mean, of course, that the two freedoms are unrelated to each other. Recall in this connection, from our discussion of freedom in the *Being and Nothingness* chapter, that in Sartre's later works he insists that "if man is not originally free, but determined once and for all, we cannot even conceive what his liberation might be," that "if man were not free, it would not be worth moving a finger for him," that "only a freedom can be oppressed," and that "if we pretend that man is not free, the very idea of oppression loses all meaning," since "a stone does not oppress, [and] one does not oppress a stone."

These passages help to clarify the ethical connection between *Being and Nothingness* and Sartre's later social and political writings, such as the *Critique of Dialectical Reason*.[5] The political

---

[3] Sartre, speaking in an interview with Jacques-Alain Miller, in his "Sartre 1960: Entretian avec Jean-Paul Sartre," excerpt quoted in *The Writings of Jean-Paul Sartre,* vol. 1: *A Bibliographical Life,* Michel Contat and Michel Rybalka, trans. Richard C. McCleary (Evanston, IL: Northwestern University Press, 1974), 387.

[4] Sartre, "The Writer Should Refuse to Let Himself Be Turned into an Institution," in *The Writings of Jean-Paul Sartre,* vol. 1, 453.

[5] In an interview in Max Charlesworth, *The Existentialists and Jean-Paul Sartre* (London: George Prior, 1976), Sartre responds as follows to an interviewer who asks whether, in embracing Marxism, he had come to reject existentialism: "I still accept it. I wrote *Critique of Dialectical Reason* to show to what extent I am modifying certain notions in *Being and Nothingness,* and to what extent I stand by the whole of that book. I still uphold the realism of *Being and Nothingness* and its theory of consciousness. . . . I still retain absolutely this conception of consciousness" (106–7). And in "An Interview with Jean-Paul Sartre," Leo Fretz, trans. George Berger, in *Jean-Paul Sartre: Contemporary Approaches to His Philosophy,* ed. Hugh J. Silverman and Frederick A. Elliston (Pittsburgh: Duquesne University Press, 1980), 225, he remarks: "BN is a general point of

oppression and economic deprivation described and denounced in the later writings is revealed by the analysis of the former work to be unacceptable not merely because it results in pain and the thwarting of desires, but also, and much more seriously, because it stands in the way of the full unfurling of freedom. Sartre's main point in the ethical and political sphere is that we should oppose whatever interferes (at the practical level) with the carrying out of freely chosen (at the ontological level) projects. Thus, in response to a question from Simone de Beauvoir as to how he defines "what you call Good and what you call Evil," Sartre replies, "Essentially, the Good is that which is useful to human freedom, that which allows it to give their full value to objects it has realized. Evil is that which is harmful to human freedom."[6]

Scarcity and Violence

And the chief obstacle to human freedom, according to Sartre, is material scarcity, understood as the lack of resources necessary to meet one's basic needs. No one would freely choose to exhaust his or her life in a desperate struggle for bare survival. As Sartre puts it, "It is not likely that the worker would have chosen to do *this* work under *these* conditions and within *this* length of time for *these* wages, had it not been forced upon him" (MR, 237). So the content of the lives of many workers counts as powerful *evidence* of their (practical) unfreedom, that is, of their lack of other meaningful options.

Moreover, a life spent in perpetual pursuit of the bare essentials of organic existence, such as food, drink, clothing, shelter from the elements, and so forth, leaves little time or energy available for the carrying out of other freely chosen projects. And such ceaseless struggle also tends to lead to an atrophying of one's distinctively human faculties (such as intellect, imagination, moral sense, creativity, aesthetic sense, and so forth), which further has the effect

---

view, a fundamental point of view. And CDR is a point of view that on the contrary is social and concrete. The one is abstract, studies general truths, and the other is not so concerned with that and places itself upon the plane of the concrete."

[6] Sartre, speaking to Simone de Beauvoir, in her "Conversations with Jean-Paul Sartre," in her *Adieux*, trans. Patrick O'Brian (New York: Pantheon, 1984), 439.

of disabling one from freely pursuing projects rooted in them (such as creating and appreciating art, pursuing close personal relationships, engaging with others in critical discussion and in political action, pursuing knowledge, and so forth). Rather, the condition of material scarcity tends to reduce us to an animal level, one in which we become exclusively concerned with our basic needs. On this point Sartre quotes his *Les Temps modernes* colleague, Claude Lanzmann, who offers an example:

> A working woman who earns 25,000 francs a month and contracts chronic eczema by handling Dop shampoo eight hours a day is wholly reduced to her work, her fatigue, her wages and the material impossibilities that these wages assign her: the impossibility of eating properly, of buying shoes, of sending her child to the country, and of satisfying her most modest wishes. Oppression does not reach the oppressed in a particular sector of their life; it constitutes this life in its totality. They are not people plus needs: they are completely reducible to their needs.[7]

According to Sartre, the relevance of this to the problem of violence is direct. For on his view it is precisely because the current social order generates scarcity (and the recognition of scarcity) that it is also characterized by violence. This is not to say, of course, that everything takes place directly *by* violence. Rather, Sartre's claim is that everything takes place *in an atmosphere* of violence, which is to say an atmosphere of "interiorized" material scarcity (CDR, 153). As Sartre puts it,

> Violence is not necessarily an action. . . . Nor is it a feature of Nature or a hidden potentiality. It is the constant non-humanity of human conduct as interiorized scarcity; it is, in short, what makes people see each other as the Other and as the principle of Evil. Thus the idea that the economy of scarcity is violence does not mean that there must be massacres, imprisonment or any visible use of force, or even any present project of using it. It merely means that the relations of production are established and pursued in a climate of fear and mutual mistrust by individuals who are always ready to believe that the Other is an anti-human member of an alien species. . . . This means that

---

[7] In *Les Temps modernes,* nos. 112–113 (1955): 1647; as quoted in CDR, 232.

scarcity, as the negation of man in man by matter, is a principle of dialectical intelligibility. (CDR, 148–49)

In order to understand Sartre's point it is necessary to add that scarcity is no longer imposed on us by nature. There is enough to go around, and there are no technological barriers to an equitable distribution of the world's resources. The problem, then, is that we persist in social patterns left over from the interiorization of past physical scarcity. The rich continue to hoard the goods of the world, and the poor continue to die because of it. This results, naturally enough, in a social environment pervaded by violence.

Totalization

And this violence tends to be preserved, in dialectical fashion, as events unfold, and to become encrusted in our institutions and practices. Sartre adopts the concept of "totalization" in an attempt to make this point. Totalization is the bringing together of seemingly distinct or even unrelated actions and events so that they form a synthetic whole. The idea is that any given moment of history in some sense contains within it and sums up the entire historical sequence leading up to it. A particular boxing match, Sartre's example from the second volume of the *Critique*, makes sense only in the light of other boxing matches, and the history of boxing, which it summarizes. The match "incarnates" this history, and, indeed, all conflict. Boxing also only makes sense against a background of scarcity. One is unlikely to choose an occupation requiring him to be hit repeatedly in the head, neck, and upper body by powerful athletes if other reasonable options are available. Little wonder, then, that boxers almost never arise from the ranks of the rich. Boxing is therefore exploitive. It involves profiting from, and/or enjoying as entertainment, violence that people inflict on one another because their unfortunate circumstances, which are themselves attributable to unjust social arrangements, fail to afford them any viable alternatives. And all involved in it—spectators, boxing writers, promoters, managers, referees, gamblers, and so forth—are, given Sartre's understanding of the nature of responsibility, complicit in this exploitation, and, indeed, in the carnage itself.[8]

---

[8] A chess game is another example of totalization. At any given point in the

Series and Group

But Sartre's assertion that our social structures are pervaded by violence need not be taken as referring to acts of violence as obvious as those involved in a boxing match. To be sure, there is no shortage of cases in which individuals are literally destroyed by overt acts of violence. Sartre's point, however, is that seemingly nonviolent forms of interaction are, within the context of interiorized scarcity, also characterized by violence. By way of illustration, let's consider two distinct types of social organizations that Sartre identifies, noting particularly the roles that scarcity and violence play in their foundation and structure.

First, we have the form of social organization that Sartre calls a "series." A series is a somewhat unstructured and uncoordinated social collective. It is a collection of people who each have the same individual purpose, but who do not share a common purpose. Sartre gives the example of a line of people waiting to board a bus (CDR, 256–69). What is interesting about such a series is that it is an organization even though none of its members has any special interest in any of the other members. In fact, because of the *scarcity* of seats on the bus, each may wish that the others were not there. Thus, each member is, to each of the others, superfluous (at best) or an obstacle (at worst). However, since each one knows that he or she fills this role for each of the others, and that each member has the same goal as each other member of the series (to secure for himself or herself a seat on the bus), each may be willing to cooperate with the others, at least in such a minimal way as to wait peacefully in line and to board the bus in turn, in a nonviolent, orderly manner. And yet it is clear, according to Sartre, that they undertake this cooperative activity solely for the purpose of avoiding a fight. Thus, violence serves as the basis for the forming of the series.

The other basic kind of social organization that Sartre discusses is a "group." A group is a collection of people who, unlike those

---

game, the arrangement of the pieces inscribes the history of moves made earlier in the game. The positioning of the pieces also illustrates the concept of practico-inert. The players move the pieces freely, but then, once they have been moved, their positioning takes on a meaning. This positioning is the given, or the facticity, on the basis of which future moves will be made. Depending on the skill level of the players, many of these moves, though freely undertaken, may be highly predictable.

in a series, *do* share a collective purpose. Thus, in a group, the individual members actively band together in a common cause. They self-consciously adopt each other's goals as their own, and engage each other in a complex coordination of efforts to achieve the ends that they mutually desire, as is the case with a soccer team or a revolutionary political organization. Clearly, a group can actually get things *done*. Indeed, Sartre argues in the *Critique* that it is primarily groups, rather than individuals, that make history.[9] But a series, on the other hand, is impotent in the face of any serious challenge. (Accordingly, Sartre remarks that "*it is seriality* which must be overcome in order to achieve even the smallest common result" [CDR, 687].)

Sartre's distinction between series and group underlies one of his major criticisms of the French Communist Party, which had often claimed that the working class is a collectivity that can be counted on to act collaboratively to oppose or support certain political actions or policies—a claim that is tantamount to the assertion that the working class is, in Sartre's parlance, a group. For Sartre, by contrast, class-being is an instance, on a vast scale, of mere seriality, the only kind of interpersonal organization that can be thrust on individuals simply by virtue of their sharing in common certain objective circumstances. But groups, according to Sartre, can only be formed as the result of the free choice of individuals to band together—a choice that can be *motivated* by external economic and political factors, but not *caused* by them. (And, as we will discuss below, Sartre also makes the point that workers, having freely consented to form a group, also remain free to withdraw that consent, with the result that the group can devolve back into seriality.) This issue stands as an instance of Sartre's criticism of (orthodox) Marxism for its insufficient appreciation of human freedom.

---

[9] Consider, for example, the American civil rights movement of the 1960s. Its spectacular successes required the courageous, coordinated efforts of thousands of persons, most of whom have been forgotten by history, having received no recognition for their contribution. It is simply easier to give credit to a small number of leaders. As a result, we tend to overestimate the effectiveness of individuals, such as Martin Luther King, Jr. (whose magnificent efforts would have come to nothing had he not worked effectively in concert with others), and to underestimate the importance of collective action. (It is noteworthy that Sartre's emphasis on groups in the *Critique* represents an evolution in his thinking away from the individualism of *Being and Nothingness*.)

What has this to do with violence? For one thing, under conditions of scarcity the group is (often) formed only as a result of an external threat of violence. Thus, the origin of the group can be traced to the discovery that we face a choice of either working together in common cause or else dying by fighting each other.

But groups are also connected with violence, according to Sartre, in that the constant threat of violence is the only guarantee against the dangerous tendency of all groups to dissolve into seriality.

Groups break down into series in many ways and for many reasons. For example, the immediate threat that had led to the group's formation might be temporarily removed, leading to a diminution of passion and commitment on the part of group members. Or the group's structure may evolve in a hierarchical direction, leading to resentment on the part of those left in subordinate positions. Or group members may gradually lose sight of their common goals, eventually reaching a point at which they are remaining together merely through inertia and tradition. This condition, which Sartre calls "sclerosis," prefigures the group's dissolution. Or sectarian conflicts may rip the group apart, with different interpretations of the group's mission leading to the creation of warring factions.

The Ethics of Violence

To avoid this danger of dissolution, then, individuals freely give their pledge to the group, and agree to an arrangement whereby that pledge is to be enforced by violence. Thus,

> we fraternize because we have made the same pledge, because everyone has limited his freedom by the other; and the limit of this fraternity (which also determines its intensity) is everyone's right of violence over the other, that is to say, precisely the common, reciprocal limit of our freedoms. . . . This violence, born in opposition to the dissolution of the group, creates a new reality, the act of treason; and this act defines itself precisely as that which transforms fraternity (as positive violence) into Terror (negative violence). (CDR, 440)

The ultimate purpose of the group is to eliminate the very scarcity that makes its own violent existence necessary. It may turn out, however, that this can only be accomplished through violent revolutionary struggle. In that case, part of the justification of the use of violence in political struggle, according to Sartre, is that such activity does not introduce violence into what would otherwise have been a peaceful society. The reason is that violence is already present everywhere. Sartre's position is similar in this regard to that of his colleague Maurice Merleau-Ponty, who argues that "we do not have a choice between purity and violence but between different kinds of violence. . . . To abstain from violence toward the violent is to become their accomplice."[10]

Sartre makes a similar point in his play, *Dirty Hands*, when one of his characters remarks:

> How you cling to your purity, young man! How afraid you are to soil your hands! All right, stay pure! What good will it do?. . . . Purity is an idea for a yogi or a monk. You intellectuals and bourgeois anarchists use it as a pretext for doing nothing. To do nothing, to remain motionless, arms at your sides, wearing kid gloves. Well, I have dirty hands. Right up to the elbows. I've plunged them in filth and blood. But what do you hope? Do you think you can govern innocently? (DH, 223–24)

It must be emphasized, once again, that the violence that Sartre here associates with governing is necessary only to the extent that we live in a world of interiorized material scarcity. If that scarcity can be eliminated, there would, according to Sartre, no longer be a need for violence at any level of social interaction. But can it be eliminated? And, if so, will violent revolutionary activity be required to bring it about? And if *that* is so, would it be sufficient to render such violence morally justified?

While Sartre has wavered a bit in answering these questions, he has consistently rejected the ethics of principled nonviolence. His position rests on three fundamental points. The first is that the doctrine that violence is absolutely wrong—under any circumstances and for any reason—would only make sense if nonviolence were the single most important value. Otherwise, there is nothing to prevent the possibility that the value of nonviolence might come into conflict with other values of even greater importance, to

---

[10] Merleau-Ponty, *Humanism and Terror*, trans. John O'Neill (Boston: Beacon Press, 1969), 109.

which it might rightly be asked to yield. Examples from U.S. history would include the use of violence in the struggles to abolish slavery and to establish labor unions.

Secondly, in order for it to make sense to claim that we must always be nonviolent we would have to assume that it is always *possible* to be nonviolent. After all, it cannot reasonably be maintained that we ought to do what it is in fact impossible for us to do, for, as Kant memorably put it, "'ought' implies 'can.'" But Sartre, as we have seen, denies that nonviolence is one of our genuine possibilities at present. He argues that to refrain from using violence against the violence that is going on all around us is not at all the same thing as to choose nonviolence (or to be nonviolent). It is, rather, to choose one kind of violence (that of the status quo, which one passive tolerates) over another kind (that required by active resistance).

Finally, Sartre's "existentialist" understanding of responsibility entails that we are as responsible for our omissions as for our actions, and thus that there is no morally significant distinction to be drawn between what we actively do and what we merely allow to happen. Sartre makes this point clearly in discussing "The Responsibility of the Writer":

> If . . . a writer has chosen to be silent on one aspect of the world, we have the right to ask him: why have you spoken of this rather than that? And since you speak in order to make a change, since there is no other way you can speak, why do you want to change this rather than that? Why do you want to alter the way in which postage stamps are made rather than the way in which Jews are treated in an antisemitic country? And the other way around. He must therefore always answer the following questions: What do you want to change? Why this rather than that?[11]

This claim that we are responsible for our omissions (or "silences") entails that choosing to refuse to engage in violent conduct personally is by no means equivalent to choosing "nonviolence." And

---

[11] Sartre, "The Responsibility of the Writer," trans. Betty Askwith, in *The Creative Vision: Modern European Writers on their Art*, ed. Haskell M. Block and Herman Salinger (New York: Grove Press, 1960), 170. He says much the same thing in WIL (especially on p. 39) and in ILTM.

if this point is granted, the result is that the choice of means is shown to involve complexities sufficient to render the simple distinction between violence and nonviolence of minimal usefulness as a guide. Sadly, the realities of the world at the present time are such as rarely to allow the luxury of the choice of pure means.

While Sartre makes a powerful case, I think his defense of violence is open to at least three objections. First, as Sartre presents his case he often seems to assume that only two options are open to us: violent resistance to oppression or passive acquiescence in it. But nonviolence need not be equated with acceptance or passivity. After all, we have learned from Thoreau, Gandhi, and King that nonviolent action can still be *action*. Indeed, it can be highly *effective* action.

Secondly, Sartre tends to proceed as if questions concerning the effectiveness of nonviolent or violent actions in different circumstances in struggles against various forms of oppression were not substantially empirical in character. But surely one has to try to learn from history what works and what doesn't, and in what circumstances. Moreover, given the intrinsic badness of violence, it would be wrong merely to *assume* that only violence can be effective. To the contrary, it is the advocate of violence who should, in every case, bear the heavy burden of proving that violence is necessary.[12] But Sartre often ignores such considerations, and instead issues sweeping, unqualified, statements along the lines of "it is only in violence that the oppressed can attain their human status."[13]

---

[12] Note that this is not the same thing as maintaining that violence is absolutely impermissible, a doctrine rejected even by such apostles of nonviolence as Gandhi and Thoreau. Thoreau defended John Brown's use of violence in the struggle against slavery in his famous "Plea for Captain John Brown"; and Gandhi often emphasized that his insistence on nonviolence was based on his assessment of the specific conditions in India in his time. Moreover, in his essay "The Doctrine of the Sword," Gandhi wrote: "I do believe that where there is only a choice between cowardice and violence, I would advise violence. Thus, when my eldest son asked me what he should have done, had he been present when I was almost fatally assaulted in 1908, whether he should have run away and seen me killed or whether he should have used his physical force which he could and wanted to use, and defended me, I told him that it was his duty to defend me even by using violence" (in *Nonviolent Resistance* [New York: Schocken Books, 1961], 132).

[13] Sartre, quoted in *The Force of Circumstances*, Simone de Beauvoir, trans. Richard Howard (New York: G.P. Putnam's Sons, 1965), 591.

Finally, there is some justice, I think, in Albert Camus's complaint that Sartre tends to treat violence as an abstraction, and avoids facing up adequately to the full horror of it. The contrast with Camus on this point is instructive. Camus, while denying that he preaches nonviolence, and while conceding that it would be "utopian" to say that "we must do away with all violence," nonetheless adds: "I think we should set a limit to violence, restrict it to certain quarters when it is inevitable, [and] muffle its terrifying effects by preventing it from going to the limit of its fury. I loathe comfortable violence."[14] In Sartre's justifications of violence, by contrast, he rarely shows interest in setting limits or restrictions on it; and while he certainly acknowledges that violence is often an evil, he rarely musters Camus's passion in condemning it.

But I would not suggest that this shortcoming shows Sartre to be some kind of monster. Rather, I think the explanation lies in the fact that Sartre's focus is deliberately partial. He takes the side of the oppressed and exploited, perhaps reasoning that those who are more fortunately situated can fend for themselves. Moreover, he does not apologize for this one-sided focus, but rather argues that it is, morally speaking, the proper one for any well-situated writer and intellectual to adopt. But it leads to certain consequences with regard to one's orientation toward violence.

To see why this is so, let's consider a real historical example, but with a hypothetical, indeed counterfactual, twist at the end. In April 1984 Nicaragua brought a complaint against the United States to the World Court. Nicaragua charged the U.S. with aggression and international terrorism, claiming that the U.S. had mined its harbors, attacked its territory, and funded, trained, and directed a band of terrorists (the "Contras"), who carried on a campaign of rape, torture, and murder, primarily directed against "soft targets" (e.g. schools, hospitals, agricultural collectives, and so forth). Though the U.S. was at the time subject to the jurisdiction of the World Court, President Ronald Reagan nonetheless announced later that month that the U.S. would not recognize any

---

[14] Camus, "Première réponse," in *Actuelles I: Chroniques, 1944–1948* (Paris: Gallimard, 1950), 184, trans. Ronald E. Santoni in his *Sartre on Violence: Curiously Ambivalent* (University Park, PA: The Pennsylvania State University Press, 2003), 107.

of its decisions. This was illegal. There were lawful means by which a nation under the jurisdiction of the court could remove itself from such jurisdiction, but the U.S. had not made use of any of these. Nor was it possible, of course, to pull out in the middle of a case that one was likely to lose. The U.S. then did lose. The World Court ordered the U.S. to cease and desist and to pay reparations. This order was contemptuously ignored. (Incidentally, none of this was reported in the newspaper I read daily, the *Chicago Tribune*.) Nicaragua then took the matter to the United Nations Security Council, submitting a resolution calling on all member nations to obey international law. The U.S. vetoed it. Nicaragua, continuing to pursue lawful, nonviolent means, then brought two similarly worded resolutions before the General Assembly of the U.N. Both passed overwhelmingly, in one case with only three "no" votes (the U.S., Israel, and El Salvador), and in the other case with only two dissenting votes (the U.S. and Israel). (Once again, this just isn't news, according to the *Tribune*.) At this point Nicaragua essentially let the matter drop.[15]

But now let's consider the counterfactual. Let's suppose that Nicaragua (or, perhaps, an independent, nongovernmental group of Nicaraguans) had engaged in a campaign of terror directed against Americans in an attempt to pressure the U.S. government to stop its own campaign of aggression. Would such a campaign have been morally justified? Perhaps the answer depends on lots of specifics: To what extent was the terror directed at individuals responsible for the campaign of terror in Nicaragua? And to what extent was it directed against innocent parties (children, for example)? What was the scale of violence? What were the prospects that it would succeed in its objective? This would be an important inquiry, and I would not suggest that it would in principle be wrong for Americans (including American writers and philoso-

---

[15] See, for example, "Nicaragua v. United States of America," http://www .everything2.com/index.pl?node_id=1176442 (accessed Mar. 9, 2008); "Military and Paramilitary Activities in and Against Nicaragua (Nicaragua v. United States of America)," http://www.icj.org/docket/ index.php?p1= 3&p2=3&k=66&PHPSESSID=05fad554ae9feecbf32e8fcea282db53&case=70 &code=nus&p3=4 (accessed Mar. 9, 2008); and "Summary of Judgment of 27 June 1986," http://www.icj.org/docket/index.php?sum=367&code=nus&p1= 3&p2=3&case=70&k=66&p3=5 (accessed Mar. 9, 2008).

phers) to contribute to it. But surely the primary responsibility of any American intellectual, of whatever sort, in such a case would be to call attention to, and to attempt to stop, the American outrages that had precipitated such a campaign of terror. And surely this would be so even if one took the position that these hypothetical Nicaraguans were not morally justified in conducting a campaign of terror, but should rather have pursued Gandhian methods. In any case, I'm quite confident that this would be Sartre's position, and I think it explains why his objections to the violence and terrorism carried out by the colonized and exploited tends to be so muted. Indeed, I think it also explains why he sometimes lapses, if that's the right word for it, into an attitude of enthusiasm for such violence. If that is indeed the explanation, then, while his position may not be defensible, at least it clears him of the charge of being a moral monster (and I'll leave it to others to defend Ronald Reagan and the editors of the *Chicago Tribune* from that charge).

Indeed, it seems to me that the Reagan/*Chicago Tribune*-style barbarism pervades mainstream American political culture. As an illustration of this claim, consider Colin Powell's answer when he was asked, in the aftermath of the Gulf War of 1991, how many Iraqis the U.S. military had killed. "Frankly," Powell responded, "that's a number that doesn't interest me very much."[16] Now recall that, according to the official line, the enemy of the U.S. in that war was the administration of Saddam Hussein, and not the Iraqi people. And yet Powell's morally obtuse statement of callous indifference to the large-scale maiming and killing of innocent civilians has elicited little commentary (and absolutely none in "mainstream" circles, to my knowledge). One can imagine a political and cultural climate in which the public expression of such sentiments would damage a person's reputation and career, just as Senator Trent Lott's statements regretting that an arch-segregationist had not been elected president hurt his. But we're obviously not there yet—not even close.[17]

---

[16] Colin Powell, quoted in "One Tear," Deda Divine. http://www.awakenedwoman.com/tear.htm (accessed Mar. 9, 2008).

[17] Similar comments apply to Madeleine Albright's snappy "we think it's worth it" statement, issued in response to the observation that the U.S.-backed U.N. sanctions against Iraq had killed 500,000 Iraqi children (quoted in "The Reasons

To the contrary, in the corporate media, for example, the Powell doctrine reigns supreme. Fox News Channel's Brit Hume, in explaining why he and his fellow journalists paid no attention to the issue of civilian deaths resulting from U.S. attacks in Afghanistan, gave as his reason that "civilian casualties are historically, by definition, a part of war, really."[18] Mara Liasson from National Public Radio agrees. Civilian casualties are not news because, as she puts it, "Look, war is about killing people. Civilian casualties are unavoidable."[19] Michael Barone of *U.S. News & World Report* is also keen to join this bandwagon: "Civilian casualties are not, as Mara says, news. The fact is that they accompany wars."[20]

But how plausible is this explanation for the refusal to cover civilian casualties in Afghanistan (or Iraq)? "If journalists shouldn't cover civilian deaths because they are a normal part of war, does that principle apply to all war coverage? Dropping bombs is also standard procedure in a war; will Fox stop reporting airstrikes?"[21] For that matter, American deaths are also a normal part of wars in which the U.S. is engaged, but we all know that this fact does not undermine the newsworthiness of American casualties. No, the much more parsimonious explanation for the fact that Afghani and Iraqi civilian deaths are not news is that in the culture of the corporate media the lives of such "others" just don't count for much. Similarly, violence done by "us" isn't really "violence," which explains why Bill Clinton, in responding to the Columbine School massacre in Littleton, Colorado, was able to say, with a straight face, that "we must teach our children to solve their problems with words rather than guns."[22] At that very moment he was bombing both Serbia and Iraq.

---

for Hate," Joel Beinin, http://www.mediamonitors.net/joelbeinin1.html (accessed Mar. 9, 2008). (In fairness, it should be noted that Albright's comment did receive a small amount of mainstream media attention, perhaps in part because it was uttered on the popular television show, *60 Minutes*.)

[18] Britt Hume, quoted in "Fox: Civilian Casualties Not News," Fairness & Accuracy in Reporting, http://www.fair.org/index.php?page+1668 (accessed Mar. 9, 2008).

[19] Mara Liasson, quoted in "Fox: Civilian Casualties Not News," Fairness & Accuracy in Reporting,

[20] Michael Barone, quoted in "Fox: Civilian Casualties Not News," Fairness & Accuracy in Reporting.

[21] Fairness & Accuracy in Reporting, "Fox: Civilian Casualties Not News."

[22] Bill Clinton, quoted in "Young White Men," Paul Kivel, http://www.immotionmagazine.com/pkivel3.html (accessed on Mar. 9, 2008).

What the examples I've been discussing seem to suggest is that we live in a culture in which compassion and concern for the victims of violence is manifested only when those victims are "us," with outrage at the perpetrators of violence being reserved exclusively for those perpetrators who are "other." To overcome this, what is needed, perhaps, is a combination of Camus's loathing of violence with Sartre's recognition of the identity of, and concern for, its most frequent victims. We must also rediscover the elementary Sartrean point that our primary responsibility is for what we ourselves do (or allow to happen). That is why, to return to our hypothetical example, Americans should be more concerned to oppose American atrocities (actions for which they bear some degree of responsibility, and with regard to which their voices of protest may conceivably carry some influence) than the hypothetical Nicaraguan atrocities (with regard to which both their responsibility and possible influence are much lesser) provoked by them.

Little wonder, then, that Sartre expresses more outrage at the practice of torture carried out by his country and its allies in waging the Algerian war than he does at acts of violence perpetrated by the Algerian resistance. Moreover, in addition to pointing out the barbarity of the practice of torture, and (frequently) the hypocrisy of those who administer it, in "A Victory" Sartre offers an argument with empirical elements: many people refuse to talk under torture, and others, even if they know nothing, will say anything in a desperate and pathetic effort to make the pain stop. As a result, torture is an ineffective and unreliable method of obtaining information. As Sartre puts it, torture "costs human lives and does not save any" (CN, 73). Given the current use of torture by the U.S. and its allies in conducting the so-called "War on Terror," it is disappointing that so few contemporary Americans have been willing to follow Sartre's example by raising their voices in opposition to this practice.

Inauthenticity

One possible reason why some of them do not is that they want to blend in with the crowd, not stand out from it. In the *Critique* Sartre illustrates this sort of inauthenticity with the example of a person who buys records, not because of personal taste or interest, but rather because the records are popular: "if he listens to the radio every

Saturday and if he can afford to buy every week's No. 1 record, he will end up with the record collection of the Other, that is to say, the collection of no one. . . . Ultimately, the record collection which is no one's becomes indistinguishable from everyone's collection—though without ceasing to be no one's" (CDR, 650–51).

This record collector's conduct is unfortunate in several respects. He is wasting his time and money on records that he does not find intrinsically interesting, and his life is, at least in this regard, inauthentic—he is not living his own life, but rather that of the public in general, that is, of no one in particular. To this general critique, familiar from Sartre's earlier writings and from those of many other existentialist writers, going all the way back to Kierkegaard, Sartre adds the point that the record collector perhaps suffers from a confused understanding of social life. In buying the same records that others do, he may think he is joining a group, in Sartre's technical sense, with all of the benefits that inclusion in such a collective would bring, when in fact he has merely become part of a series.

Propaganda

A more politically significant example of seriality is that of individuals listening to the same radio broadcast, reading the same newspaper, or buying the same product. Members of a series are easily manipulated because they are disconnected from one another. Sartre argues that states take advantage of this and attempt to manipulate their citizens through constant propaganda. In addition to its goal of simply getting a particular message across, such propaganda bombardment has the larger aim of diminishing the critical thinking skills of the citizens and of inducing in them a passive attitude congruent with uncritical patriotic obedience to authority. Even those who manage to see through the propaganda find, owing to their isolation from like-minded others, that there is nothing they can do about it. Sartre thus paints a vivid and disturbing picture of radio listeners and TV watchers, each "consuming" their mediated messages in the privacy of their own home, seething with impotent range at the propaganda to which they are constantly subjected.

Another important aim of this propaganda offensive is to foster a diminished sense of, and respect for, truth. It is very hard work to convince a public that values truth, and is discerning in its quest for it, that a thousand lies are in fact true. But a public that is indifferent to or contemptuous of truth is much more easily persuaded. It is easy to convince them, "with calm, careful reason," that, for example, "the violence of the 'haves' [is] always . . . 'in the defense of peace,'" and that the "self-defense counter-violence of the 'have-nots' [is] terroristic."[23] On the other hand, there is a public dimension to truth that leads Sartre in the *Critique* to say that truth is "disalienating." To believe based on evidence, rather than on private fantasy, is an invitation to reciprocity—a free act addressing itself to the freedom of another. Knowledge of the object is *our* good, not mine privately. And such objective knowledge holds the key to the resistance to propaganda.

One propaganda technique is noteworthy in that it explicitly appeals to the idea of objective truth. This is the technique of attempting to foster a systematic confusion among objective truth (that is, the drawing of conclusions that accurately reflect how things are, based on a logically responsible assessment of the relevant evidence), neutrality (the refusal to draw any conclusions, or to take any sides, at all), and centrism (the a priori conviction, in defiance of the evidence, that the truth must lie roughly in the middle of some narrow spectrum of "respectable" opinion). Sartre, in a conversation with some American students, explains the point of this confusion: "In your country, all your teachers tell you to think carefully and try to be objective. . . . They want you to keep looking at a situation from *all sides*, as they say. That's so you say, 'On the one hand, this; on the other, that.' That's so you *do* nothing."[24]

Priorities

But what *should* we do? Whereas the early Sartre stresses personal authenticity (the avoidance of bad faith, the rejection of the desire to be God, the celebration of freedom and of projects rooted in

---

[23] Sartre, speaking to American students, as quoted in *Jean-Paul Sartre: Hated Conscience of His Century*, John Gerassi (Chicago: University of Chicago Press, 1989), 6.

[24] Sartre, as quoted in *Jean-Paul Sartre: Hated Conscience of His Century*, John Gerassi, 6.

freedom, and so forth), the later Sartre, without renouncing that
in the slightest, puts more emphasis on the social dimension, and
on the circumstances in which we must act. To put it more suc-
cinctly, while the early Sartre focuses on the need to make good
choices within our situation, the later Sartre, without taking that
back, stresses the need to bring about better situations—situations
that will present us with much better options from which to
choose than we enjoy at present. For example, consider this comment on anti-Semitism:

> Since [the anti-Semite], like all men, exists as a free agent within a sit-
> uation, it is his situation that must be modified from top to bottom.
> In short, if we can change the perspective of choice, then the choice
> itself will change. Thus we do not attack freedom, but bring it about
> that freedom decides on other bases, and in terms of other structures.
> (ASJ, 148)

How are we to explain this change in focus? Partly it is simply a
matter of developing an improved sense of priorities as a result of
life experiences. Sartre was, by temperament and training, a
philosopher, and thus it is understandable that he would initially
be attracted to fundamental philosophical issues, in all of their
lofty abstractness. But eventually he came to realize that "alienation, exploitation of man by man, under-nourishment, [rele-
gate] to the background metaphysical evil which is a luxury.
Hunger is an evil: period" (LBSM, 61). Moreover, he came to
realize the full horror of material scarcity, and of all that comes
with it—endless war, poverty, racism, colonialism, and every
other kind of oppression, exploitation, and injustice. These are
the primary obstacles to the achievement of everything that is
good in life, including authenticity, meaningful practical freedom, warm, honest, and unselfish relations with others, and creativity. For Sartre, this realization should make the order of our
priorities clear: "First all men must be able to become men by the
improvement of their conditions of existence, so that a universal
morality can be created. . . . What matters first is the liberation
of man" (LBSM, 62).

Sartre's political radicalism is fueled by his insistence that we are
free. This freedom entails that existing social institutions and
arrangements are our free creations, and are in no sense necessitated or made inevitable by our nature. Our freedom and lack of

ready-made nature mean that we are not stuck with them. We are free to evaluate them, and, if the evaluation is negative (as it is for Sartre), we are free to change them. And that is what we should do.

Suggestions for Further Reading

The writings that I have stressed in this book are far from the only works of Sartre's that are well worth reading. So I will begin this list of suggestions for further reading with a brief description of some of his other works that are especially interesting. This is followed by a short list of recommended writings *on* Sartre.

By Sartre

"The Wall" is the first short story that Sartre published as an adult. It appeared in 1937, and has taken on the status of a classic, having been reprinted in countless literary anthologies, and made into a movie in 1967. It is a tense, suspenseful, atmospheric account of how a prisoner of war spends what he believes will be his final night prior to his execution. Written in response to the Spanish Civil War, the story is one of the most politically charged of Sartre's early writings. The fact that several key events in the story happen by sheer chance evidences Sartre's interest in contingency and the idea of absurdity. Highly uncharacteristically for Sartre, crucial to the plot is a twist ending of the sort that is more typical of the works of O. Henry. It is available in *The Wall and Other Stories*, trans. Lloyd Alexander (New York: New Directions, 1975).

"The Childhood of a Leader" was published in 1939 in Sartre's first and only volume of short stories. It tells the story of an insecure man who seeks a sense of self-identity and the respect of others by attempting to "be" a fascist and anti-Semite. The story anticipates, in the context of an entertaining story, several themes that Sartre more famously develops in later works: the discussion of bad faith in *Being and Nothingness*, the analysis of anti-Semitism in *Anti-Semite and Jew*, and the psychological critique of the fascist mentality in several of Sartre's later political writings. It is included in *The Wall and Other Stories*.

"**François Mauriac and Freedom,**" also appearing in 1939, is, with the possible exception of lengthy, general works, such as *What is Literature?*, the most famous of Sartre's many works of literary criticism. While Sartre has never shied away from polemics, this piece is uncharacteristically severe in its intense attack on a fellow writer, Sartre's older contemporary, the conservative Catholic novelist, François Mauriac. It set off an intense literary debate in France at the time over the question of the fairness and merits of Sartre's criticism. Sartre faulted Mauriac for treating his characters as pawns, as mere instruments for the communication of their creator's vision, rather than as free beings. The essay contains the memorable, oft-quoted, line: "God is not an artist. Neither is Monsieur Mauriac." The most important general idea developed in this essay, now a critical commonplace, is that the formal aspects of fictional writing, no less than their explicit content, can entail and imply a metaphysical and ethical world view. It is available in *Literary and Philosophical Essays*, trans. Annette Michelson (New York: Collier Books, 1962).

In 1943 Sartre's first published play, *The Flies*, appeared. It is a political drama on the nature of freedom, using characters drawn from classical Greek tragedies. Sartre chose this device in part to disguise from the censors (the play was written and first performed under Nazi occupation) the contemporary relevance of his message. It is available in *No Exit and Three Other Plays* (New York: Vintage, 1955).

"**The Republic of Silence**" is a terse, but extremely eloquent, essay of 1944. It contains the much misunderstood, and seemingly paradoxical, assertion that "we were never more free than under the German occupation." Ontologically, the French were neither more nor less free than they had been previously and were again subsequently. Practically, they were clearly much less free. So what could Sartre have meant? It appears that his claim is psychological—the awareness of freedom is dramatically heightened when one's daily choices have life-or-death consequences. The piece has frequently been translated, quoted, and anthologized. It is available in *The Republic of Silence*, ed. A. J. Liebling (Phoenix: Simon Publications, 2003).

"**A More Precise Characterization of Existentialism,**" another essay of 1944, is noteworthy as Sartre's first attempt to defend "existentialism" (the term was then new and fashionable) against criticisms, mainly emanating from the French Marxists. It is available in *The Writings of Jean-Paul Sartre,* vol. 2: *Selected Prose,* ed. Michel Contat and Michel Rybalka, trans. Richard McCleary (Evanston: Northwestern University Press, 1974).

Roads to Freedom is Sartre's only novel aside from *Nausea.* It is a lengthy work, published in three volumes, though Sartre eventually abandoned the project, leaving the novel unfinished. In 1945 the first two volumes, entitled *The Age of Reason* and *The Reprieve,* appeared. *Troubled Sleep* followed in 1949. (Excerpts from the projected fourth, and concluding, volume, were published in *Les Temps modernes* later that year.) While *Roads to Freedom* is, in my judgment, on every level much less successful than *Nausea,* it is not without interest. The theme of the novel, as its title suggests, is freedom. As Paris moves toward its liberation from Nazi occupation, the central characters also move, although in most cases less successfully, toward their own liberation. Sartre's growing interest in the social and political dimensions of freedom, complementing his already well-developed concern for freedom on the ontological and psychological levels, is apparent here. The trilogy is available (New York: Bantam, 1968) in translations by Eric Sutton (for *The Age of Reason* and *The Reprieve*) and Gerard Hopkins (for *Troubled Sleep*).

"Cartesian Freedom," an essay of 1945, makes clear Sartre's indebtedness to Descartes in his concept of freedom. Sartre's discussion of Descartes's distinction between freedom and power is also very helpful in showing that the standard criticism of Sartre's view of freedom as "extreme" is based on a conflation of two distinct senses of "freedom." The essay is included in *Literary and Philosophical Essays.*

"Existentialism is a Humanism" is Sartre's most famous lecture, originally presented in 1946, and since widely translated and anthologized. In it Sartre presents a simplified, and in some respects misleading, version of his philosophy, which he also defends against criticisms and misunderstandings. It is available as *Existentialism & Humanism,* trans. Philip Mairet (London: Methuen, 1973).

Sartre's play, **The Respectful Prostitute,** appeared in 1946. It was subsequently filmed, released as an audio recording, and later adapted as a musical. It addresses the issue of racism in the United States—an example of Sartre's intense interest, rare among philosophers at that point in history, in race and racism. The play was a success in the U.S., despite problems with censors in many cities. It was also performed in the Soviet Union and in Cuba. It is included in *No Exit and Three Other Plays.*

In the book *Anti-Semite and Jew,* which appeared in 1946, Sartre further develops his ideas on racism. He argues that anti-Semitism is a species of inauthenticity. The book is available in a translation by George J. Becker (New York: Schocken Books, 1965).

"Materialism and Revolution," an essay of 1946, is a polemic against orthodox Marxist thinking of the period. It is useful in showing some of the ways in which Sartre's thought was turning toward social, political, and historical questions. He distinguishes between two senses of freedom here, claiming that only a being that is ontologically free can be oppressed (that is, made practically unfree). The essay is included in *Literary and Philosophical Essays.*

Published in 1947, *Baudelaire* is Sartre's first book-length biography, and his first lengthy essay in the existential psycho-analysis of one person. It is interesting primarily for the light it sheds on the development of Sartre's method of existential psy-choanalysis, which he would employ more successfully in later works on Genet and Flaubert. *Baudelaire* is available in a transla-tion by Martin Turnell (New York: New Directions, 1950).

"What Is Literature?," originally published in 1947 as a series of articles, is Sartre's most extensive discussion of his ideas on com-mitted literature and literary aesthetics. Sartre argues that every lit-erary work must necessarily, whether intentionally or not, present an implicit philosophy—a general view of what is good, and true, and important. Since this is so, writers should recognize it, and take full responsibility for the picture of the world that they pres-ent to their readers. They should consciously consider whether they are using their influence as writers to promote a better world, or whether they are instead, perhaps unwittingly, helping to per-petuate oppression, and acting as an obstacle to the creation of a fairer and more just social order. (They do not, on Sartre's view, have the option of true neutrality, since a posture of neutrality has the effect of helping the status quo). Thus, "what I ask of [the writer]," says Sartre, "is that he should not ignore reality and the fundamental problems which are before us: world hunger, the atomic menace, man's alienation."

"What Is Literature?" also contains one of Sartre's first attempts to show what authentic interpersonal relationships are like (as opposed to the Hellish ones described in *Being and Nothingness*). His model is the author-reader relation, wherein authors must rely on the freedom and generosity of their readers in interpreting and making sense of (and, indeed, in bringing to life) their works, just as readers, in order to understand a text, must appeal to the freedom of the author in understanding his or her work as the product of free, creative decisions. Freedom, authenticity, reciprocity, generosity, and trust are notions that are central to authentic human relationships. We must respect the freedom of others, try to prevent others from oppressing them, help them to overcome their oppression, and aid them in realizing their goals. All of this, according to Sartre, is implied by the relation between authors and readers.

Moreover, one of our fundamental duties to others is that of honesty and intellectual scrupulousness: to disclose the world, to perceive it accurately and to report on it and discuss it sincerely with others. The writer/reader relation exemplifies this clearly. Our duty to disclose the world is especially strong for Sartre, given his ontology. (Recall his argument that being is undifferentiated, and becomes a world only as we freely carve it up, and thus articulate it.) This, in turn, implies an especially strong duty on the part of artists and writers. As they carve up the world, they suggest to us ways of constituting it. This should be done responsibly, with sensitivity to the (often implicit) moral, political, and ethical content of one's work. Furthermore, the work should engage readers in such a way as not to trample on their freedom to respond. (This point goes to the heart of Sartre's critique of Mauriac, discussed above). "What Is Literature?" is available in *"What Is Literature?" and Other Essays* (Cambridge, MA: Harvard University Press, 1988).

Sartre's play ***Dirty Hands*** appeared in 1948. It was an enormous hit, and was made into a movie in 1951. It is a political play, and deals in part with the question of political violence. It is included in *No Exit and Three Other Plays*.

Though written in 1948 as a screenplay, ***In the Mesh*** was never filmed. However, it has several times been adapted for the stage. It takes up the issue of political repression in the context of the Cold War. It is available in a translation by Mervyn Savill (London: Andrew Dakers, 1954).

"Black Orpheus," an essay of 1948, is noteworthy for its discussions both of race and of poetry. It is included in *"What Is Literature?" and Other Essays.*

"Consciousness of Self and Knowledge of Self," a 1948 lecture, is addressed to philosophers rather than to the general public (and, perhaps for that reason, is much more accurate in its interpretation of Sartre's thought and more careful in its argumentation than is the much better-known *Existentialism Is a Humanism*). It offers a concise treatment of some of the main theses of *Being and Nothingness.* The published lecture includes a transcript of the discussion following the lecture. It is available in *Readings in Existential Phenomenology,* ed. Nathaniel M. Lawrence and D. J. O'Connor (Englewood Cliffs, NJ: Prentice-Hall, 1967).

"Colonialism is a System," an essay of 1956, exemplifies Sartre's opposition to colonialism and his support, which many in France regarded as treasonous, for the Algerians in their struggle to gain independence from France. It is available in *Colonialism and Neocolonialism,* trans. Azzedine Haddour, Steve Brewer, and Terry McWilliams (New York: Routledge, 2001).

The Condemned of Altona, a 1959 play, deals with torture. It was successful with critics and audiences, and ran throughout the 1959-1960 theatrical season, with a revival in 1965. It was made into a movie in 1963. It illustrates the concept of seriality from the *Critique of Dialectical Reason.* It is available in a translation by Sylvia and George Leeson (New York: Vintage, 1961).

The Words, Sartre's autobiography of 1963, confines itself almost entirely to his childhood. It is a beautifully written work, one of the few by Sartre to be almost unanimously admired. Shortly after its publication Sartre was awarded the Nobel Prize for literature (which he declined). Sartre explains in *The Words* that he has abandoned his thirty-year neurosis, in which he had regarded literature as sacred, a path to salvation (this is highly relevant to *Nausea*). He now prefers action, even if it is merely the action of an intellectual. The book is available in a translation by Bernard Frechtman (Greenwich, CT: Fawcett Crest, 1966).

On Genocide, an essay of 1967, is a product of Sartre's work as president of the International War Crimes Tribunal organized by Bertrand Russell. The essay is one of Sartre's many efforts in opposition to the Vietnam War. It is available in an uncredited translation (Boston: Beacon Press, 1968).

The Family Idiot, Sartre's biography of Flaubert (another exercise in existential psychoanalysis), is his longest, and perhaps most demanding, work. One critic called it a "verbal Himalaya." The first two volumes were published in 1971, with a third appearing the following year. A projected fourth volume was abandoned, unfinished. Sartre makes full use here of the progressive-regressive method he had developed in the *Critique*. The work takes up many themes from all phases of Sartre's career. It deals extensively with the imaginary, the subject of Sartre's earliest philosophical work, makes use of many categories from Sartre's early ontology, and continues his work on Marxist and psychoanalytic themes. It is available in a five-volume translation by Carol Cosman (Chicago: University of Chicago Press, 1981, 1987, 1989, 1991, and 1994).

The War Diaries of Jean-Paul Sartre, written in 1939-1940, was published posthumously in 1983. These notes document Sartre's initial development of some of the ideas that would appear in *Being and Nothingness*. They are available in a translation by Quintin Hoare (New York: Pantheon, 1984).

Written in the late 1940s and posthumously published in 1983, *Notebooks for an Ethics* contains some of the fruits of Sartre's abortive project, promised at the end of *Being and Nothingness,* to work out an ethics. To show how different the tone of this work is from that of its predecessor, compare Sartre's analysis of love in *Being and Nothingness* with this brief description of authentic love from the *Notebooks*: "Here is an original structure of authentic love . . . to unveil the Other's being-within-the-world . . . ; to *rejoice* in it without appropriating it; to give it safety in terms of my freedom, and to surpass it only in the direction of the Other's ends" (NFE, 508). The book is available in a translation by David Pellauer (Chicago: University of Chicago Press, 1992).

Written in 1948 and posthumously published in 1989, *Truth and Existence* deals with epistemology, the nature of truth, and the ethics of belief. It further clarifies Sartre's discussion of "the faith of bad faith" in *Being and Nothingness*. It is available in a translation by Adrian van den Hoven (Chicago: University of Chicago Press, 1992).

Hope Now is Sartre's last major work, and perhaps his most controversial. It is a collaborative work, carried out through conversations with a much younger interlocutor, Benny Lévy. Since Sartre seems in these interviews to retract many of his most famous ideas, and to endorse others that he had previously rejected, and to do so, in many cases, only when under pressure from his younger colleague to do so, many question whether Sartre's contribution to this work accurately represents his views at the time. (The fact that he was old, blind, weak, and dying during the conversations has given rise to the suspicion that he may simply have been too weak to resist the younger and more assertive Lévy.) These conversations were initially published in March 1980, just a month prior to Sartre's death. The book is available in a translation by Adrian van den Hoven (Chicago: University of Chicago Press, 1996).

About Sartre

Turning now to writings *on* Sartre, good general introductions to his work include *Sartre: A Philosophic Study* by Anthony Manser (New York: Oxford University Press, 1967); *Sartre* by Arthur C. Danto (London: Fontana, 1979); *Sartre* by Hazel E. Barnes (Philadelphia: J.B. Lippincott, 1973); *How to Read Sartre* by Robert Bernasconi (New York: Norton, 2007); and *Sartre Today*, ed. Adrian van den Hoven and Andrew Leak (New York: Berghahn Books, 2005). Manser's book, despite its overall philosophical orientation (as indicated by its subtitle), includes ample treatment of Sartre's novels and plays. Barnes, the translator of *Being and Nothingness* (and, in my judgment, the finest English-language Sartre scholar), provides balanced coverage of Sartre's philosophy and literature. Danto's clear, sympathetic discussion, which focuses primarily on *Being and Nothingness* and *Nausea*, is a rare example of an extensive engagement with Sartre's work by a major philosopher from the analytic tradition. Bernasconi's concise book introduces Sartre's work by commenting briefly on ten important passages from his writings, drawn from all stages of his career. *Sartre Today* is a collection of new essays, by a variety of scholars, addressed to many different aspects of his work. The volume celebrates the one hundredth anniversary of Sartre's birth. Similarly comprehensive is the journal *Sartre Studies International*, which is published twice annually.

The best biography of Sartre is *Sartre: A Life* by Annie Cohen-Solal, trans. Anna Cancogni (New York: Pantheon, 1987). *Jean-Paul Sartre: Hated Conscience of His Century* by John Gerassi

(Chicago: University of Chicago Press, 1989) is a much briefer, and more personal, insider's account. It is especially interesting in connection with Sartre's political views and activities.

The following four book-length commentaries provide excellent help to anyone attempting to work through some of Sartre's most difficult books: *A Commentary on Jean-Paul Sartre's "Being and Nothingness"* by Joseph S. Catalano (Chicago: University of Chicago Press, 1980); the same author's *A Commentary on Jean-Paul Sartre's Critique of Dialectical Reason, Volume 1* (Chicago: University of Chicago Press, 1986); *Sartre's Second Critique* by Ronald Aronson (Chicago: University of Chicago Press, 1987) (on the second, posthumously published, volume of the *Critique of Dialectical Reason*); and *Sartre & Flaubert* by Hazel E. Barnes (Chicago: University of Chicago Press, 1981) (on *The Family Idiot*).

The best book on Sartre's literature, in my judgment, is *Humanistic Existentialism* by Hazel E. Barnes (Lincoln: Bison Books, 1959). This book also contains insightful analyses of the literary works of Sartre's colleagues, Simone de Beauvoir and Albert Camus.

Many of the most interesting works on Sartre are addressed to his views on ethics. The reason, I suspect, is that, while almost all of Sartre's writings are saturated with an intense ethical concern, he was never able to work out his thinking on ethics to his own satisfaction, and thus never published a substantial work on this subject during his lifetime. As a result, his numerous, though scattered, remarks on the subject have left the field open to conflicting interpretations; and commentators who have attempted to reconstruct his ethical theory have therefore had to be somewhat creative. Some of the most noteworthy efforts are *The Foundation and Structure of Sartrean Ethics* by Thomas C. Anderson (Lawrence: The Regents Press of Kansas, 1979); the same author's *Sartre's Two Ethics* (Chicago: Open Court, 1993); *An Existentialist Ethics* by Hazel E. Barnes (New York: Vintage, 1971); *Sartre's Ethics of Authenticity* by Linda A. Bell (Tuscaloosa: University of Alabama Press, 1989); *Freedom as a Value: A Critique of the Ethical Theory of Jean-Paul Sartre* by David Detmer (La Salle, IL: Open Court, 1988); *Sartre's Ethics of Engagement* by T Storm Heter (New York: Continuum, 2006); *Sartre and the Problem of Morality* by Francis Jeanson, trans. Robert V. Stone

(Bloomington: Indiana University Press, 1980); *Good Faith and Other Essays: Perspectives on a Sartrean Ethics* by Joseph S. Catalano (Lanham, MD: Rowman & Littlefield, 1996); and *Bad Faith, Good Faith, and Authenticity in Sartre's Early Philosophy* by Ronald E. Santoni (Philadelphia: Temple University Press, 1995). Anderson's first book, *The Foundation and Structure of Sartrean Ethics,* offers an interpretation of Sartre's work as expressing a single, coherent, ethical theory. But in *Sartre's Two Ethics* he argues, based largely on Sartre's unpublished works, that Sartre's thought had changed significantly over time, and that he had actually developed two different ethical theories, and a sketch of a third. Barnes's book, *An Existentialist Ethics,* is an attempt not so much to interpret Sartre's ethics as to develop the author's own approach, though this approach is inspired by, and adopts as its starting point, Sartre's philosophy. Bell's *Sartre's Ethics of Authenticity* and Detmer's *Freedom as a Value,* as their titles indicate, differ in their emphases, with Bell holding authenticity to be the central concept in Sartre's ethics and Detmer assigning that role to freedom. Detmer also offers an interpretation reconciling Sartre's many apparently conflicting statements about freedom. Heter's main contribution in *Sartre's Ethics of Engagement* is to make a convincing case that even Sartre's seemingly most individualistic ethical notions imply the need for a strong social and political engagement. Jeanson's book, *Sartre and the Problem of Morality,* which was originally published in France in 1947 (and thus does not consider Sartre's later works), holds the distinction of having been enthusiastically endorsed by Sartre himself. Catalano's *Good Faith and Other Essays* and Santoni's *Bad Faith, Good Faith, and Authenticity in Sartre's Early Philosophy* are perhaps a bit more narrowly focused than are the other works listed here. They each examine, in painstaking detail, the difficult issues surrounding Sartre's analyses of bad faith and of authenticity. Finally, readers of French may want to consult *Fondements pour une morale* by André Gorz (Paris: Galilée, 1977). It is an interesting attempt, by a close friend of Sartre's, to write the ethical sequel to *Being and Nothingness* that Sartre himself failed to produce.

With regard to Sartre's politics, I recommend five books: *Sartre Against Stalinism* by Ian H. Birchall (New York: Berghahn Books, 2004); *Sartre and Marxist Existentialism* by Thomas R. Flynn (Chicago: University of Chicago Press, 1986); the same author's *Sartre, Foucault, and Historical Reason, Volume One: Toward an Existentialist Theory of History* (Chicago: University of Chicago Press, 1997); *Sartre's Political Theory* by William L. McBride (Bloomington: Indiana University Press, 1991); and *The Radical Project: Sartrean Investigations* by Bill Martin (Lanham, MD: Rowman and Littlefield, 2001). In *Sartre Against Stalinism* Birchall thoroughly examines the political activities that Sartre engaged in, and the many political stands he took, over the years. McBride's *Sartre's Political Theory* and the two books by Flynn are more theoretically oriented, focusing on Sartre's social and political writings. (The second Flynn book, *Sartre, Foucault, and Historical Reason*, vol. 1, incidentally, is almost exclusively on Sartre. The discussion of Foucault is mostly left for a second volume that appeared subsequently). Finally, Martin's *The Radical Project* is not so much a thorough analysis of Sartre's political philosophy as an attempt to apply Sartrean insights to contemporary political issues (thus illustrating the continuing relevance of Sartre's thought).

On Sartre's aesthetics, two of the best books are *Sartre and the Artist* by George Bauer (Chicago: University of Chicago Press, 1969); and *An Existentialist Aesthetic: The Theories of Sartre and Merleau-Ponty* by Eugene F. Kaelin (Madison: University of Wisconsin Press, 1962).

Sartre's philosophy of the body is explored from an analytic perspective in *The Bodily Nature of Consciousness: Sartre and Contemporary Philosophy of Mind* by Kathleen V. Wider (Ithaca, NY: Cornell University Press, 1997). *Sartre and the Sacred*, by Thomas M. King (Chicago: University of Chicago Press, 1974), demonstrates that, in spite of his atheism, Sartre's thought can be profitably approached from the standpoint of theological concepts and themes. Similarly, while Sartre's record with regard to gender-based oppression is not nearly as impressive as is his achievement in connection with racist, colonialist, or economic oppression, *Feminist Interpretations of Jean-Paul Sartre* ed. Julien S. Murphy (University Park, PA: Pennsylvania State University Press, 1999), nonetheless makes the case that he has something positive to contribute to feminist thought. The best book on Sartre's critique of racism is *Bad Faith and Antiblack Racism* by Lewis R. Gordon (Atlantic Highlands, NJ: Humanities Press, 1995.) Finally, the most comprehensive and informative discussion of Sartre and the issue of violence is *Sartre on Violence: Curiously Ambivalent* by Ronald E. Santoni (University Park, PA: Pennsylvania State University Press, 2003).

Index

absence, 67–71, 80
absurdity, 52–53, 55–57, 217
aesthetics, 58–60, 220, 227
Albright, Madeleine, 209
Algerian War, 2, 5, 10–12, 211, 222
analytical reason, 190–91
Anderson, Thomas C., 225–26
anguish, 27–29, 37, 70–75, 82, 107, 122, 129
Aquinas, Thomas, 130
Aristotle, 58, 146, 168
Aron, Raymond, 17
Aronson, Ronald, 225
art, 58–60
atheism, 8–10, 18, 57, 129, 138, 156–57, 162–66, 227
authenticity, 60, 76, 88–89, 138–41, 171, 213–14, 221, 223, 226

Bachelard, Gaston 47, 99
bad faith, 27–29, 75–89, 96, 109–10, 124, 131, 134–35, 137–140, 147–49, 151, 156–57, 165, 176, 213, 217, 223, 226
Barnes, Hazel E., 88, 97, 224–26
Barone, Michael, 210
Baudelaire, Charles, 173, 220
Bauer, George, 227
Beauvoir, Simone de, 9–10, 12–13, 17, 198, 225

being-for-itself, 64–65, 87, 89, 92, 97–98, 101–4, 110–12, 114, 119, 128, 130, 138–39, 154
being-in-itself, 64–68, 89, 92, 97, 103–4, 111–12, 115, 119, 128–30, 154
being-in-itself-for-itself, 104–6, 109, 111, 128–30
Bell, Linda A., 225–26
Bernasconi, Robert, 224
Birchall, Ian H., 226–27
Blanchot, Maurice, 182
body, 25, 36, 96–103, 227
boxing, 38, 200
Brentano, Franz, 30
Brown, John, 206

Camus, Albert, 57, 207, 211, 225
Castro, Fidel, 14
Catalano, Joseph S., 225–26
Chomsky, Noam, 4, 11
Clinton, Bill, 210
coefficient of adversity, 47, 99, 113–15, 119–20, 133, 180
Cohen-Solal, Annie, 224
committed writing, 60–61, 220
concrete relations with others, 103–10, 134–38, 149–53, 156–57, 161, 171, 214, 221
consciousness, 31–50, 64–65, 67, 69–71, 74, 76, 78, 80, 89,

94, 98, 101, 103–04, 124–25,
129, 149, 197
as embodied, 25, 36, 96–103,
110–11
as nonegological, 20–29
positional/nonpositional
distinction, 22–23, 26, 28,
48, 82–83,
124, 147
thetic/nonthetic distinction,
22–23, 26, 28, 48, 82–83,
124, 147
prereflective/reflective distinction,
21–23, 26, 28, 36–37, 44,
58–59, 71, 82–85, 93–94, 96,
149–50, 175
contingency, 52–53, 58–60,
100–101, 129, 131, 217
counter-finality, 191–92
crime, 176–78
cynicism, 86

Danto, Arthur C., 224
death, 153–57
Descartes, René, 21–22, 32–33, 36,
55, 89, 97, 182, 219
destruction, 66–67, 71
determinism, 18, 32, 37–38, 48, 66,
72, 74, 123–24, 126, 174,
179, 194
Detmer, David, 225
Dewey, John, 4
dialectic, 137, 188–93, 199–200
dialectical materialism, 190
Dostoyevsky, Fyodor, 8–9
Duchamp, Marcel, 10

ego
empirical, 23–29, 58–59, 74
transcendental, 18–29
eidetic dimension of human
experience, 184–85
emotion, 34–45
ethics, 29, 44, 76, 86–87, 89, 110,
134–41, 164–69, 198, 214,
221, 223, 225–26
evidence, 84–85

existential psychoanalysis, 111,
122–35, 171, 174–78, 220,
223

facticity, 78–82, 88, 113–24, 127,
147, 174, 178–81, 201
Fadayev, Alexander, 5
feminism, 227
Flaubert, Gustave, 173, 220, 223,
225
Flynn, Thomas R., 226–27
Foucault, Michel, 75, 227
freedom, 27–28, 44, 47–49, 58, 60,
66–71, 74–75, 100–108,
110–36, 140–41, 150,
155–57, 164, 169–70, 174,
177–81, 191–99, 201–3,
214–15, 218–21, 226
noetic, 69–70
ontological, 122, 194
ontological/practical distinction,
115–17, 121, 180, 196–98,
218–20
practical, 13, 189, 214
Freud, Sigmund, 76, 124
Freudianism, 3, 18, 26–27, 123–24,
129

Gandhi, Mohandas, 206, 209
Gaulle, Charles de, 11
Genet, Jean, 171, 173–85, 220
Gerassi, John, 42, 224–25
God, 129–31
Gordon, Lewis R., 227
Gorz, André, 226
group, 187, 194, 201–3, 212

hate, 108–10
Hegel, G. W. F., 10, 189
Heidegger, Martin, 10
Henry, O., 217
Heter, T Storm, 225–26
Hippocrates, 18
homosexuality, 81–82, 173, 175,
178–81
human condition, 184
Hume, Brit, 210

Hussein, Saddam, 209
Husserl, Edmund, 10, 16–17,
  19–20, 28–30, 34–35, 46,
  49–51, 54–55, 92, 184

idealism, 34
imagination, 46–50, 53, 71, 223
inauthenticity, 211–12, 220
indifference, 108–9
intentionality, 29–50, 53–54, 64,
  68–70, 94, 125
interrogation, 65–66
intuition, 89–92

James, William, 36
Janet, Pierre-Marie, 27–28
Jeanson, Francis, 11, 225–26

Kaelin, Eugene F., 227
Kafka, Franz, 51
Kant, Immanuel, 18, 167, 205
Kierkegaard, Søren, 10, 130, 212
King, Martin Luther, 202, 206
King, Thomas M., 227
knowledge, 89–92

language, 54
Lanzmann, Claude, 199
Lefebvre, Henri, 5
Lévy, Benny, 141, 223–24
Liasson, Mara, 210
look, the, 25, 94–96, 103–4, 107,
  109, 149–50, 175, 180
Lott, Trent, 209
love, 106–7, 223

Mallarmé, Stephané, 173, 182
Manser, Anthony, 224
Maoism, 12
Marcel, Gabriel, 5
Martin, Bill, 227
Marx, Karl, 10, 191–92, 195
Marxism, 3, 5, 13, 116, 174,
  188–91, 194–97, 202,
  219–20, 223
masochism, 107
Matisse, Henri, 10

Mauriac, François, 218, 221
McBride, William L., 227
Merleau-Ponty, Maurice, 97, 204
mind-body problem, 97–99

Nietzsche, Friedrich, 10, 162
nihilation, 65–71, 74, 78, 104, 110,
  112
North American Sartre Society,
  5–6

objective truth, 181–83, 213
objectivity, 182–83
others, 25, 92–98, 101–3, 110–11,
  199, 212
  concrete relations with, 103–10,
    134–38, 149–53, 156–57,
    161, 171, 214, 221

Pauling, Linus, 4
phenomenological reduction, 54–55
phenomenology, 16–51, 63–64, 68,
  70, 73–74, 94, 146, 194
Picasso, Pablo, 10
play, 134–37, 139
politics, 161–62, 214–15, 226–27
Pollock, Jackson, 10
Powell, Colin, 209–10
practico-inert, 191–93, 201
problem of evil, 162
problem of other minds, 95
progressive-regressive method,
  193–94, 223
project, 24, 45, 49, 53, 55–56, 70,
  78, 80, 99–102, 104,
  108–11, 113–14, 118–20,
  122, 124–29, 131–36, 140,
  150, 171, 175–77, 183–84,
  188, 193, 198–99
  of being God, 128–29, 131,
    134–41, 164, 213
  of taking freedom as the highest
    value, 135–41, 164, 171,
    177, 213–14
propaganda, 212–13
psychoanalysis, 26, 123–24, 129,
  174, 177, 180–81, 223

existential, 111, 122–35, 171,
174–78, 220, 223

racism, 2–3, 15, 86, 189, 214,
219–20, 222, 227
radical conversion, 29, 110, 132–33,
136–40, 163–65, 180
Reagan, Ronald, 207–9
realism, 29–35, 49–50, 53–54, 60,
197
reason, 86–87
reflection, impure/pure (or
purifying) distinction, 28–29,
44, 134, 136, 139–40
reflection, accessory/nonaccessory
distinction, 28–29, 44, 134,
136, 139–40
responsibility, 44, 74–75, 87–88,
129, 140–41, 156–57,
164–65, 179–80, 193–94,
200, 205, 220–21
Rorty, Richard, 4
Russell, Bertrand, 4, 11–12, 222

sadism, 108
Santoni, Ronald E., 226–28
Sartre, Jean-Paul
bombing of home and office of, 5,
12
censorship of, 4–5
courage of, 11–13
fame of, 1–7, 11
political activities of, 2–5, 10–13,
225, 227
as prolific writer, 1
reputation of, 4–15
success of, 1–7, 9, 11
versatility of, 1, 4, 6
writings of
Age of Reason, The, 219
Anti-Semite and Jew, 2–3, 86,
217, 220
Baudelaire, 220
Being and Nothingness, 1, 7, 16,
19, 23, 25, 29, 33, 37,
46–47, 63–141, 145–47, 149,
152, 154, 161, 163–64, 169,

171, 174–76, 180, 183, 187,
196–98, 202, 217, 221–26
"Black Orpheus," 2, 189, 222
"Cartesian Freedom," 219
"Childhood of a Leader, The," 2,
86, 217
"Colonialism is a System," 222
Condemned of Altona, The, 222
"Consciousness of Self and
Knowledge of Self," 222
Critique of Dialectical Reason, 1,
7, 16, 171, 187–215,
222–23, 225
Critique of Dialectical Reason,
volume 2, 188, 200, 225
Devil and the Good Lord, The, 15,
159–71, 187
Dirty Hands, 5, 204, 221
Emotions, The, 35–45, 140
"Existentialism is a Humanism,"
7–9, 166–67, 169, 219,
222
Family Idiot, The, 2, 223, 225
Flies, The, 63, 218
"François Mauriac and Freedom,"
218
Genocide, On, 222
Hope Now, 223–24
Imaginary, The, 46–50
Imagination, 46
In the Mesh, 221
"Intentionality," 29–35, 45, 55
"Itinerary of a Thought, The," 33,
179
"Materialism and Revolution,"
220
"More Precise Characterization of
Existentialism, A," 218–19
Nausea, 2, 15, 47, 50–61, 219,
222, 224
No Exit, 5, 15, 143–57, 159, 161,
171, 187
Notebooks for an Ethics, 2, 116–17,
136–39, 164, 169, 223
"Purposes of Writing, The," 145
Reprieve, The, 63, 219
"Republic of Silence, The," 218

Respectful Prostitute, The, 2, 219–20
Roads to Freedom, 219
Saint Genet, 2, 16, 173–85, 187
Search for a Method, 188
"Self-Portrait at Seventy," 16, 61, 195
Situations, 16
Transcendence of the Ego, The, 19–29, 44, 58, 123, 140, 149
Troubled Sleep, 219
Truth and Existence, 87–88, 223
"Victory, A," 211
"Wall, The," 2, 44, 217
War Diaries of Jean-Paul Sartre, The, 9, 223
"What is Literature?" 54, 58, 60, 218, 220–21
Words, The, 222
Sartre Studies International, 6, 224
scarcity, 198–201, 203–4, 214
series, 201–3, 212, 222
sexual desire, 108
shame, 37, 92, 94–96
shyness, 102–3

situation, 70, 74, 101, 117–21, 193–94, 214
skepticism, 32, 90–91, 182
Stalin, Joseph, 5, 13

Temps modernes, Les, 2–3, 5, 11, 14
Thomas Aquinas, 130
Thoreau. Henry David, 206
torture, 12, 15, 211, 222
totalization, 188–89, 194, 200–201
transcendental ego, 18–29
transphenomenality, 52–54, 58–60
truth, 84–87

unconscious, 18, 26–27, 76, 124

Vietnam War, 2, 12, 222
violence, 15, 159, 164, 166, 169–71, 187, 190, 198–201, 203–11, 221, 227–28
Voltaire, 11

Wider, Kathleen V., 227
Wittgenstein, Ludwig, 10